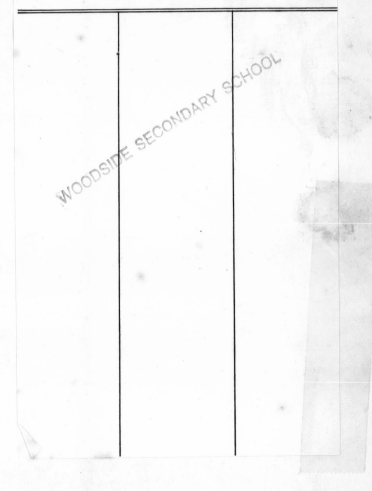

ESSAYS IN ANTIQUITY

PETER GREEN

Essays in Antiquity

John Murray

FIFTY ALBEMARLE STREET

LONDON

Made and printed in Great Britain by
William Clowes and Sons, Limited,
London and Beccles

For Flora and Stavros Papastavrou

duodecimo amicitiae anno

Contents

Acknowledgments

I am grateful to Mr Peter Quennell and Mr Alan Hodge, Joint Editors of *History Today*, for permission to reprint 'Hodge on Helicon', *Imperial Caesar, Two Gentlemen of Rome*, and the larger part of *Roman Satire and Roman Society*. I must also thank two successive Editors of the *Times Literary Supplement*, Mr Alan Pryce-Jones and Mr Arthur Crook, for permission to use 'Homeric Patterns', 'Odysseus Translated', and much of the material that has gone into *Clio Perennis* and *The Garden and the Porch*. Indeed, the benign influence of Printing House Square can be discerned in most of these essays: like those unscrupulous builders who, in the emergency of the Persian Wars, used old statuary as rubble to fill the walls of the Acropolis, I have not hesitated to work into a fresh context material which originally appeared as part of a *T.L.S.* article or review. *The Humanities Today*, in a modified form, was originally delivered as a lecture under the auspices of the Classical Association; *Venus Clerke Ovyde* is based on a B.B.C. Third Programme script; *Some Versions of Aeschylus* has been developed from a lecture given at Morley College.

I must thank the following authors and publishers for permission to use copyright material: Mr Louis MacNeice and Faber & Faber Ltd. for passages from *Autumn Journal* and Mr MacNeice's translation of the *Agamemnon*; Messrs Routledge & Kegan Paul for extracts from the late Sir John L. Myres' *Homer and His Critics*; Mrs W. B. Yeats and Macmillan & Co. Ltd. for Yeats's poem 'The Scholars' from *Collected Poems of W. B. Yeats*; Professor W. K. C. Guthrie, Master of Downing College, Cambridge, and Methuen & Co. Ltd. for an extract from *In the Beginning*; Professor Richmond Lattimore and the University of Michigan

Press for a passage from Professor Lattimore's translation of Hesiod; Mr Kimon Friar, and Secker & Warburg Ltd., for a dozen lines from Mr Friar's translation of the late Nikos Kazantzakis' *The Odyssey: A Modern Sequel*; Professor Geoffrey Barraclough and Basil Blackwell Ltd. for matter from *History in a Changing World*; Mr T. S. Eliot and Faber & Faber Ltd., for passages from *East Coker, Murder in the Cathedral*, and the essay 'Euripides and Professor Murray'; Mr Erich Auerbach and the Princeton University Press for an extract from *Mimesis*; Professor M. L. Clarke and Cohen & West Ltd. for an extract from *The Roman Mind*; my friends Mr G. S. Fraser, Mr Iain Fletcher and Mr Ian Scott-Kilvert, for permission to use their translations of Ovid, originally broadcast on the Third Programme; Professor Gilbert Highet, and the Delegates of the Oxford University Press, for several passages from *Juvenal the Satirist*; Professor Eduard Fraenkel, and the Delegates of the Oxford University Press, for an extract from *Horace*; Mr Robert Conquest and Macmillan & Co. Ltd. for two stanzas from 'The Classical Poets'; the Trustees of the estate of the late George Orwell, and Secker & Warburg Ltd., for a passage from 'Politics and the English Language', in *Shooting an Elephant*; Mr J. B. Leishman and Bruno Cassirer Ltd. for a passage from *On Translating Horace*; the Trustees of the late Professor Gilbert Murray's estate, and Allen & Unwin Ltd., for two extracts from Professor Murray's translation of the *Agamemnon*; the Society of Authors, and Jonathan Cape Ltd., for three passages from A. E. Housman's *Fragment of a Greek Tragedy*; and Mrs Frances Cornford and the Delegates of the Oxford University Press for part of the Introduction to the late Francis Cornford's translation of Plato's *Republic*.

I

The Humanities Today

Everybody remotely concerned with that ancient industry, the teaching of the classics, is agreed that something has gone very wrong with it somewhere: but no two voices seem to be making the same complaint. You can find those who place the blame squarely on the scientists' shoulders, and others who claim that the humanities can only be revivified by applying a more scientific technique to them. Some say that abolishing compulsory Latin will deal the tradition a death-blow; others retort that this is the only way of preserving the classics as a serious subject. There are those whose formula for success is less emphasis on grammar, and an equal number convinced that slackening the linguistic standard any further will destroy what little scholarship remains. One faction want to shut the door and bolt themselves inside while the tide of new disciplines surges up past the windows; another group are all for letting the waters pour in, and seeing who floats. But they are all agreed that *something* is amiss. Why, when Dr Rieu's *Iliad* and *Odyssey* sell a million copies, do scholars and teachers speak despondently about the decline of the classics, the triumph of science and barbarism? Most important of all, is there any real congruity of aim between a 'classical education' as commonly understood, and the serious study of the ancient world in all its aspects?

There seems little doubt, indeed, that a singularly wide discrepancy exists between what a classical education could or should be, and what it actually is. Few intelligent people would deny

I

the value of studying the many branches of Greek and Roman civilization and culture: their literature, their philosophy, their scientific theories and political thought, their great achievements in law and government, their tragic historical failures, their acute awareness of the individual in a corporate society. Few would claim, however, that the present system is remotely adequate for the purpose—even allowing for the sporadic, rather pathetic attempts made by more enlightened teachers to 'brighten up the curriculum'. This curriculum bears a singular resemblance to the Court of Chancery in *Bleak House*: an anomaly which has been suffered for years in the sacred name of Tradition. Mr Louis MacNeice describes the phenomenon with pithy brevity. Not everyone, as he remarks, had had

> The privilege of learning a language
>   That is incontrovertibly dead
> And of carting a toy-box of hall-marked marmoreal phrases
>   Around in his head.
> We wrote compositions in Greek which they said was a lesson
>   In logic and good for the brain;
> We marched, counter-marched to the field-marshal's
>   blue-pencil baton,
>   We dressed by the right and we wrote out the sentence again.
> We learnt that a gentleman never misplaces his accents,
>   That nobody knows how to speak, much less how to write
> English who has not hob-nobbed with the great-
>   grandparents of English,
>   That the boy on the Modern side is merely a parasite
> But the classical student is bred to the purple, his training in
>   syntax
>   Is also a training in thought
> And even in morals; if called to the bar or the barracks
>   He always will do what he ought.

This passage attacks, with wit and cogency, some of the more obvious oddities and anomalies in the teaching of the classics—the sclerotic over-emphasis on formal linguistics, the passion for traditional *clichés*, and, above all, the curious tendency to correlate the humanities with social and moral superiority: classics as a badge of ascension in the class-structure.

It also reminds one of those familiar complaints made in after-life by literary notabilities of the present century—that they never got a chance to find out anything about classical authors or the ancient world in its wider context till they had long left school; or, worse, that the senseless curriculum put them off classics for life. Sir Osbert Sitwell, who describes himself in *Who's Who* as having been educated 'in the holidays from Eton', epitomizes this attitude. Mr Cyril Connolly is highly suspicious of the methods used to teach ancient, as opposed to modern, languages: if he could learn French and German at school with comparative ease (he justifiably enquires) why should the situation be so radically different with Greek and Latin? A distinguished American scholar put the case against the grammarians in a nutshell when he remarked that it was as if 'years of study of the violin were to get the pupil no further than the first two positions of the left hand'. If the most the average boy can do when he leaves school is to stumble through a few dog-eared pages of the

> *De Bello Gallico*
> Bound in blue calico

(without understanding its political background) or construe one of Ovid's more jejune pseudo-erotic elegies, which a public school education had hardly equipped him to appreciate in any case—then why *should* he shed any tears at the demise of the classical tradition?

The peculiarities of the humanities as an educational discipline are so familiar that we tend to take them for granted, rather like the British coinage system. In order to track down their *raisons d'être* we have to look surprisingly far back into the past. Indeed, the most remarkable single aspect of the entire curriculum is its incredible rigidity: the passionate, almost hieratic conservatism with which it adheres to old precepts long after the historical conditions which produced them have passed away.

The obsession with grammatical and syntactical minutiae, together with those parrot-like exercises normally used to illustrate every paradigm and declension, can be traced back in a direct unbroken line to the Hellenistic pedants of Alexandria. Obviously it is essential that any language—particularly a complex dead language—should be learnt with great thoroughness and accuracy; but it is hard to believe that so peculiarly inefficient and wasteful a system survived so long on its practical merits. There is a ritual air about it almost comparable to the hallowed archaisms of the Authorized Version.

This method of education grew and flourished in a society which set a high value on rhetoric and linguistics—and which, for several excellent historical reasons, was quite justified in doing so. As always, the formal system long outlasted its own cause. It was corrupt and obsolete before the fall of the Julio–Claudian dynasty, and came in for some withering criticism from authors such as Petronius, who had a taste for picaresque life and the living vernacular speech of Italy. It survived indomitably through the monkish Dark Ages and the pseudo-pagan Renaissance. It was calculated to appeal to a powerful scribal minority, for whom linguistics still had a strong tinge of exclusive magic, and the very fact of literacy alone symbolized knowledge, authority, power. Nothing multiplies pedantry and gibberish so fast as an intellectually strait-jacketed private guild, with an absolute monopoly over learning, and an ingrained contempt for the natural sciences.

Besides, theological authoritarianism is contagious: it was only a short step from proclaiming the absolute veracity of Holy Writ in spiritual matters to the canonization of Aristotle, Quintilian, Plato and the rest as far as secular knowledge was concerned. The mediaeval cosmology represented the universe as a ladder or chain of Being, a fixed and hierarchic world-order in which everyone and everything from God to a cabbage knew their precise, unchanging position. The habit of unquestioned authority and the notion of a static natural order are hard convictions to shake; and their psychological effects may have survived longer than most people suspect.

Every mediaeval schoolman, moreover, from Aquinas to John of Salisbury, had to face one great perennial problem: how to integrate a body of potentially dangerous pagan literature and

4

philosophy into Christian dogma? It was not possible, even it if had been desirable, to reject the classical heritage *in toto*: even the most bigoted Early Father was forced to realize that. One Pope might burn the works of Sappho and Menander so effectively that the texts failed to survive; but Sappho was by then a minority author, and Menander the property not of the stage but the study. (After all, it took a European upheaval to destroy the literature of Manichaeism.) The dangerous thinkers were already far too widely disseminated; the only course was to allegorize them, expurgate them, and wrench their texts into conformity with religious requirements by every sophistry which keen brain and devotional heart could devise in combination. A condition was thus generated in which the vague but insistent connection between classical learning and Christian morality was laid down.

This process of circle-squaring involved a basic misinterpretation of the ancient world; and though time has erased the more obvious follies inherent in the moral attitude which the process implied, a strong emotional legacy still remains. The revulsion against Aristotle became so strong after the Reformation and the advent of Newtonian physics—he was identified with Catholic scholasticism in its narrowest form—that today, presumably as good Protestants, we never read him at all till we reach University level, and not always then. Plato, on the other hand, with his legacy of Gnosticism, has always been fairly easily adapted to the imprecise requirements of Christian mysticism. He remains perennially popular as sixth-form reading: for his prose style, scholars often tell us, as if in reassurance.

A third remarkable instance of conservatism is afforded by the continuing primacy of textual criticism in classical studies. This scholarly technique retains a *cachet* entirely out of proportion to its intrinsic value: it is after all, as Professor Highet pointed out when discussing Housman, little more than a glorified form of intellectual proof-reading. Again, there is an obvious historical reason for this. Before the advent of printing, much of a scholar's duty lay in purging his MSS of scribal errors and preserving a pure text for posterity: with the violence and uncertainty of life in those times an author was, on the whole, lucky to survive at all. After the Renaissance, with the flood of new texts which Poggio and others discovered, there was ample scope for textual critics to continue their work, though never again would they have such unique responsibilities. But, as in other fields, what had begun out of physical necessity was prolonged and exalted by tradition and emotional inclination. The mentality which at one level relishes syntactical exercises and rhetorical tropes will, at another, take naturally to the delights of an *apparatus criticus*. Professor Highet, again, tells the illuminating story of one sixth-form master who announced to his class: 'Boys, this term you are to have the privilege of studying the *Oedipus Coloneus* of Sophocles—a veritable treasure-house of grammatical peculiarities.'

There were, of course, signal exceptions to this generic attitude of mind. Erasmus and Milton both strove to shift the predominant interest from mastery of language to mastery of knowledge. Jowett and Arnold in the nineteenth century made valiant efforts to open up the study of the ancient world on a broad front, and relate it to the moral here-and-now of Victorian England. When Gladstone was at Oxford, we are told by Sir John Myres,

> on the side of Classics . . . it was no question of special periods and set books, or of limited aspects for the evidence of ancient life. It was the Graeco-Roman world in all its fullness, with the whole of its literature and all its antiquities which the Renaissance or recent endeavour had recovered. . . . The only limits to the quest were the will and endurance of the student, the wisdom of his advisers, and the contents of the Bodleian Library.

But such happy eras were few and far between; from Colet's day on a rigid and alarming conservatism invaded every aspect of the classical tradition.

Instances are plentiful, and may be found assembled in such a work as Professor M. L. Clarke's *Classical Education in Britain*. Historians, even in Renaissance times, were not read for their subject matter, but 'partly for their styles and partly as a source of moral tales and examples'. On the other hand, verse composition flourished: in 1597 one ingenious usher published a book showing how the same sentiment could be expressed no less than four hundred and fifty ways in a single elegiac couplet. Despite constant sniping (John Clarke described it as 'a Diversion a Degree above Fidling') this odd mental exercise survived, and still survives. So conservative were university scholars in the sixteenth century that—pleasant paradox—they even banded themselves together under the name of 'Trojans' to ban the introduction of Greek. Archaeology was always stigmatized as 'unsound', but moral and religious fashions tended to infiltrate the study of the ancient texts in a somewhat hair-raising fashion: Chapman hunted allegory through the epic verses of Homer, while in 1830 a Professor of Moral Philosophy at Oxford treated Plato's *Republic* as 'a kind of prophecy of the Catholic Church'. The schools, with their vast reams of parrot-repetition and stubbornly obsolete methods, were even worse than the Universities: Lily's Grammar was still in use at Eton till the eighteen-sixties.

Now this basic conservatism of method and outlook has survived, in its essentials, to the present day, despite all the revolutionary activities of heterodox scholars, and the leavening enthusiasm of well-educated public figures. The nineteenth century merely shifted some of its moral emphasis from pure religiosity to a puritan social ethic. Boys were still flogged for making a mistake in grammar or prosody, and the classics were still (for all Sir James Frazer's fertility rituals) a gentleman's moral hall-mark rather than an objective study of a vital phase in European culture.

Except in highly technical aspects of the subject, criticism of an aesthetic or evaluative kind was—not surprisingly—seldom to be found in the writings of professional scholars; it was left, scornfully, to 'amateurs' such as Matthew Arnold. When scholars did condescend to dabble in this messy pond, the results were normally disastrous. Housman, to his credit, recognized this. 'When it comes to literary criticism', he wrote, 'heap up in one scale all the literary criticism that the whole nation of professed scholars ever wrote, and drop in the other the thin green volume of Matthew Arnold's *Lectures on Translating Homer* . . . and the first scale, as Milton says, will straight fly up and kick the beam.' This tradition of superiority in attitude combined with incompetence in performance has persisted almost unchallenged to the present day. Here the conservatism operates in a slightly different fashion: most so-called literary criticism of classical authors is a long-delayed emotional hang-over from Pater and John Addington Symonds. One distinguished scholar, in fact, writing on (of all authors) Sappho, restricted his judgments in this field to quoting three pages of Symonds *in extenso*: and that was only three years ago.

History for a great while fared very little better. It has long been a truism among modern historians that their colleagues of the ancient world are not quite as other men; and the cause is probably to be sought in the ossified morality which prejudged every notable figure of antiquity, such as Pericles or Augustus, and made the facts square, willy-nilly, with their preconceptions. In this field, happily, enlightenment has come earlier and spread wider than in other more deeply entrenched branches of the humanities: historians such as Syme, Momigliano, and Rostovtseff can more than hold their own with any mediaeval scholar or modern political theorist.

The result of such a generally ossified discipline was inevitable and obvious. Where previously the humanities had been attracting the cream of the nation's brains, they began increasingly to draw the *dilettanti* who had a talent for linguistics and gentlemanly pastiche, and no particular interest in thinking discriminatively for themselves. The subject had lost touch with its broad human roots and become mere antiquarianism; it had even lost its social appeal. A large number of classicists today might be classified as romantic escapists, impelled to burrow for warmth into the womb of a pre-industrial, non-atomic, unmechanized antiquity.

Till the recent long overdue (and hardly radical) revisions in the Cambridge Classical Tripos, it was possible—*experto credite*—to get a First in Part I without exercising one's mind at all; nothing was required except a good memory and a capacity for elegant translation. The paper on ancient history and kindred subjects was a farce, and so regarded by examiners as well as examined. What it meant, in fact, was that the candidate had to read a certain number of prescribed texts: whether he understood them, or formed any critical opinions about them, was totally irrelevant. This state of affairs came about in a typically haphazard fashion. It was not till 1822 that a Classical Tripos was established in Cambridge at all; and then it was initially a voluntary examination for mathematical candidates, and modelled almost entirely on the University Scholarships and Chancellor's Medals. This meant that it consisted of nothing but passages for translation. Moreover, as Professor Clarke rightly points out, the Cambridge examining tradition, being mathematical, demanded an order; and translation was easier to assess in this way than any other kind of question. In other words, the study of the ancient world was being quite casually butchered to facilitate the production of an Order of Merit; and so it has continued almost to the present day. Yet even in 1850 there had been furious protests against the system; 'it was alleged', reports Professor Clarke, 'that the Tripos demanded merely linguistic skill and that it was possible to obtain high honours without acquiring any real knowledge of antiquity'. *Plus ça change.*

There is often too great a distinction drawn between classical studies at school and University level. It often seems to be assumed that the only alternatives are specialist research and sixth-form generalities: this is simply not true. The bulk of classical undergraduates do not proceed to classical fellowships, and their curriculum is, by and large, simply an extension of the one they endured at school. In many cases a scholar first begins to *think* about the ancient world when he finds himself pitched into a research studentship. It is true that any progress that may come tends to begin in the Universities and filter outwards slowly; but the whole nexus of the humanities is linked by a common grounding and shared assumptions. Progressive scholars, alas, are seldom those who set examination papers; they merely set an example, which takes an unconscionably long time to penetrate. But the Universities as a whole are responsible, ultimately, for the development of the subject. However enlightened teachers may be—and some are very enlightened indeed—they have to conform to an externally imposed examination system; and that system is the product of University examiners, who, in their turn, are influenced by the tradition of academic research:

ipse,
Ipse rotam adstringit sufflamine mulio consul.

Housman's brilliant emendation in that line of Juvenal could not have been achieved without a deep knowledge of, and affection for Latin literature. Yet he maintained, what countless scholarly predecessors had held, that the academic mind was contaminated by aesthetic opinions, and should disregard literature *qua* literature altogether. Scholarship should be an end in itself—'that minute and accurate study of the classical tongues', as Housman put it, 'which affords Latin professors their only real excuse for existing'. According to this creed there was nothing to choose between a fragment of Sappho and the most banal Hellenistic epigrammatist: both offered equal grist to the scholar's textual mill. 'If you prefer Aeschylus to Manilius', Housman wrote to his colleague Arthur Platt, 'you are no true scholar; you must be deeply tainted with literature, as indeed I always suspected that you were.'

Creative writers have not been slow to fasten on this aesthetic and moral indifference, which they have satirized with some relish. Browning's Grammarian, George Eliot's Mr Casaubon—examples quickly spring to mind. There is an obvious piquancy in the contrast between the full-blooded protagonists of Greek and Roman life and those who undertake to interpret their motives for posterity. Yeats's lines are not easily forgotten:

> Bald heads forgetful of their sins,
> Old, learned, respectable bald heads
> Edit and annotate the lines
> That young men, tossing on their beds,
> Rhymed out in love's despair
> To flatter beauty's ignorant ear.

All shuffle there; all cough in ink;
All wear the carpet with their shoes;
All think what other people think;
All know the man their neighbour knows.
Lord, what would they say
Did their Catullus walk that way?

This casts doubts on the proper qualifications of scholars in more than one sense. They reject literary evaluation themselves; and all too often they are ill-equipped by nature and upbringing to judge with authority on matters of psychological or emotional importance. There is always a tendency in mankind to dismiss as irrelevant what they cannot understand: we should not wonder, then, that classical literature is largely a matter of textual *cruces* and *Quellenforschung*; nor that ancient history concerns itself so enthusiastically with abstract trends and the dry joys of epigraphy.

As Housman quite rightly observed, no one in his right senses would go to the average classical scholar for a judgment on literature; but he left unresolved the paradox of how, in that case, any scholar dared to meddle with a text, which requires aesthetic discrimination of the first order. As though to underline this dilemma, he devoted some time in his *Introductory Lecture* of 1892 to mocking Bentley's ludicrous edition of *Paradise Lost*—the classic instance of textual criticism at its cranky extreme, without the benefit either of common sense or common taste. And yet Bentley was the greatest textual critic in Europe! Housman's point was that a scholar should stick to his last; he apparently failed to see that the example he chose cast doubts on the scholar's abilities even in his own limited field. By no means all textual critics are also lucky enough to be poets, and thus possess a kind of built-in sensibility over and above their academic training.

It would be fair, I think, to say that the traditional order of grouping by which special subjects are designated for Part II of the Cambridge Classical Tripos gives an accurate estimate of the official repute in which they are held. Group A, rather misleadingly called 'Literature', concentrates on the techniques of textual criticism; over and above this the luckless student draws Epic,

Comedy, Tragedy, or Lyric, according to what year he happens to sit his papers. Group B deals with ancient philosophy, Group C with ancient history, Group D with archaeology and epigraphy, Group E with comparative philology, that latter-day darling of Max Müller and the Sanskrit enthusiasts. To judge from Cambridge classics at undergraduate level (or from that revealing publication edited by Mr Maurice Platnauer and entitled *Fifty Years of Classical Studies*) it would be hard to guess that a tremendous and revolutionary change has been going on over a long period in the upper echelons of the humanities: perhaps the most radical change of approach since the Renaissance.

There are two main aspects of this revolution, one good, one bad. It will be convenient to deal with the bad side first. One characteristic of professional classical scholars has always been (and to a great extent remains) a disinclination to admit alien disciplines or new techniques to their ancient mysteries. Classics were, apparently, to be preserved inviolate, as a subject, from the march of time. The result, paradoxically enough, has been a strenuous attempt during the last thirty years or so to convert them from an Arts subject—from the humanities, in fact—into an exact science.

What led to this change? There was, first, the uneasy awareness that rival faculties, particularly those to do with the natural sciences, were forging ahead uncommonly fast. Most classicists were, by 1930 or thereabouts, feeling the need to defend their choice of subject; and one way to do this was by putting it on the same methodological footing as, say, physics. The movement began in Germany and America, and gradually spread to this country, where it soon swamped the initial, unformulated objection that the classics were a subject for gentlemen, and no gentleman worked like a professional. It was a case of *aut disce aut discede*: too many would-be dons were chasing too few lectureships, and with such a spirit of cut-throat competition in the air the display of thesismanship became really astonishing. Classical research took on a progressively more abstruse and Alexandrian tone, and was less and less bound up with large questions of history, culture and morality.

This attitude had its effect, at several removes, on the schools: they were called upon once more to coach examination candidates in a *crambe repetita* of grammar, translation, and linguistics, with scant regard for the underlying realities of classical culture. Many prospective scholars or exhibitioners, sensing instinctively that classics were withering as a discipline at their inner heart, turned elsewhere for enlightenment.

Perhaps I exaggerate scholarly conservatism a little; but here is the Regius Professor of Greek at Oxford, writing in August 1950:

> 'To my fellow-professionals I perhaps owe some defence of the use which I have made in several places of recent anthropological and psychological observations and theories. In a world of specialists, such borrowings from unfamiliar disciplines are, I know, generally received by the learned with apprehension and often with active distaste . . .'

That is part of Professor Dodd's preface to *The Greeks and the Irrational*; and it only hints at the ingrown, Alexandrian suspiciousness which is supported—amusingly enough—by the current passion for specialization.

Greek literary studies today may with some justification be compared with a large, thriving, yet still half-unexplored colony. Look at the map. Here are the state highways, confidently marked in red, establishing communications from one boundary to the other: Homer, Aeschylus, Thucydides, Demosthenes, Plato. These roads, and the towns they serve—Homeric Society, the House of Atreus, Solon's Reforms, the Peloponnesian War, the struggle with Macedonia, the Theory of Ideas—we know and travel over regularly. Then there are the minor roads and less-frequented villages: Theocritus, Apollonius Rhodius, Polybius; Hellenistic culture, Alexandrian epic, Greco-Roman historiography. Finally there is the bush, where tenderfoots never venture at all, but where you may find the old professional diggers staking out their claims: Lycophron, Aeneas Tacticus, Diodorus Siculus, Cercidas, Parthenius, and never-dry watering-holes labelled 'Unedited Papyri', 'Scholia', or 'Fragments'. Development, we hear, is going on; but the reports from upcountry are generally in code, and for restricted circulation only.

This is a curious and not wholly beneficial state of affairs. The classical student's reading list is limited—necessarily limited, perhaps—to certain major authors of proven literary excellence; and he is seldom actively encouraged to forage for himself among minor eccentrics, deadbeat pamphleteers, or the lunatic fringe of Alexandrian pseudo-science. This at once distorts his overall picture of Greek civilization and literature alike. Skimming off the cream makes for indigestion; if there is one thing the Greeks have perennially suffered from, it is the deadening myth of perfection. A wider exploration reassuringly dissolves this illusion. In the first place, it makes us well aware that the corpus of Greek literature which has survived represents only a small fraction of the whole. In the second, it rubs in beyond doubt that the majority of writers in the ancient world, like the majority of writers anywhere else, at any period, were second-rate hacks with third-hand styles and the instincts of popular journalists. They also suffered from professional rhetoricians, sedulously aped their poetic betters, were garrulous, gullible, and addicted to excruciatingly unfunny stories. Professional academics tend to reserve them for specialist research and sweep them behind the curtain when lecture-time comes round.

If the classics have survived at all in a vital sense, it is a minority we have to thank, many of them not professional scholars at all, and the rest tarred with brush of academic odium—Frazer, Cornford, Jane Harrison, P. N. Ure, even Gilbert Murray. They made mistakes; they held some fantastic and not-so-fantastic theories; but they were the first systematically to destroy the scholastic myth about the ancient world, and approach their subject without irrational genuflections. They aimed to explore the Greek and Roman civilizations historically, in their immediate context; and this necessitated the jettisoning of two thousand years of slowly accreted myth—the whole sterile grammarian's folly erected by the rhetoricians, the legend of literary perfection and philosophical highmindedness, the rational sweetness and light so beloved of

Lowes Dickinson, the Glory that was Greece and the Grandeur that was Rome.

Without measuring the emotional opposition such an act would provoke—the ancient world had long provided an almost religious matrix of symbolism for Christians and aesthetes alike, for the Gibbons as well as the Pascals—they ripped all the dusty ivy off the tower of classical learning. And what emerged? Why, the 'beastlye devyces of the heathen', the realization that these people were no more symbolic or talismanic *per se* than anyone else. 'Why', asks Professor Dodds (very reasonably, but anticipating contradiction),'why should we attribute to the ancient Greeks an immunity from 'primitive' modes of thought which we do not find in any society open to our direct observation?'

'Legions of seminall *Ideas*,' wrote Sir Thomas Browne, 'lye in their second Chaos and *Orcus* of *Hipocrates*; till putting on the habits of their forms they show themselves upon the stage of the world.' Anyone who has studied modern trends in classical studies will at once recognize the validity of this pronouncement, and perhaps be tempted to read a veiled irony into its tone. Then he will turn to his bookshelf, where Professor Onians' *Origins of European Thought* rubs shoulders with Professor Dodds' *The Greeks and the Irrational*, and clear a place beside Professor Popper's *The Open Society and its Enemies* for Professor Havelock's *The Liberal Temper in Greek Politics*. Having done this, he may legitimately sit down and ask himself how it comes about that the view of the 'Greek miracle' presented in these works has only been fully formulated today.

Most of the evidence, of course, was always there. The additional material discovered by the archaeologist or in the rubbish-heaps of the Fayyum has done less than is often supposed to alter the general picture. Can it be that the change is not in the Greeks, but in ourselves? Professor W. K. C. Guthrie writes:

> . . . Every age tends to bring into prominence those features of the past which chime in best with its own ideas and preoccupations. The heydey of classical studies was also a time of general optimism . . . Since the classics played so large a part in [the Arnold-Jowett

educational system] . . . there was a natural tendency to look upon the Greeks and Romans as embodying the ancient counterparts of our own ideals . . . Today we are not so confident. Much has happened to make us more doubtful about the rightness of our ways and the nature of the goal which lies ahead of us. . . . The ruling concept of Victorian science was biological evolution, and in philosophy one still saw the creation of bold and all-embracing metaphysical systems. The characteristic science of our own age is the introspective one of analytical psychology, and in philosophy we have seen the dethronement of metaphysics in favour of linguistic analysis. . . . We look at our own habits of thought and speech rather than at the external world about us. So in historical study, whereas every age is liable to project its own mind unconsciously into the past, it has been left for us to look consciously and anxiously for analogies to our present situation.

The implications of this statement can be extended into wider fields. On the simplest level, our ideas about the Greeks have been affected by the new scientific disciplines of psychology (which has, *inter alia,* made it impossible for us ever to look at a myth again in quite the same way), anthropology, and Marxist or near-Marxist economics. But these are only the conscious formulations of deeply-felt emotional instincts; they are symptom rather than cause. When Professor Dodds edited Euripides' *Bacchae* with one eye on the abnormal psychology of Maenadism, he was doing something more than utilize a handy elucidatory technique. The enormous paradox about devoting a book to the Greeks' irrational qualities—their superstitions and powerful primitive traits—is that they were not *characteristically* irrational. Similar traits can be found in equally civilized communities today; they are ubiquitous and ineradicable. Why, then, place such strong emphasis on a subsidiary phenomenon?

It seems clear enough that Professor Dodds, like P. N. Ure before him in the economic field, like Professor Popper and Professor Havelock in that of political theory, was reacting strongly against the nineteenth-century classical myth—the myth of benevolent Periclean paternalism, of authoritarian Platonic ideals (their delicate flavour of aristocratic homosexuality offset with imagined Christian premonitions): the Golden Age refurbished for a scholarly caste betrayed by the Industrial Revolution. The curious viability of this myth is revealed by the fact that it was pressed equally into the service of Jowett's Christianity and Swinburne's militant atheism. The former, aided by a long line of circle-squarers from the Early Fathers onwards, whose piety was only equalled by their ingenious logic, assimilated Aristotelian metaphysics and Virgil's Imperial propaganda. The latter, in reaction against puritan restraints, made a sophisticated plunge for aesthetic hedonism and Aristophanic bawdry. Both managed to find what they needed in the immense panorama spread out before them.

This nineteenth-century myth and the assumptions—moral, religious, political—which sustained it have been to a great extent invalidated for the modern mind. In the political field, parallels have been only too easily discovered between ideological dictatorships and the projected utopias of Plato and Aristotle. With this distrust of ideologies—*docet experientia*—has come a violent rejection of the ideal as such, a wholesale jettisoning of metaphysical systems in what might be described as the Vienna cleanup. The vast advances of science, and the gradual spread of scientific habits of thought, have set up strong, though often unformulated resistances against aprioristic ethics or philosophies, and shifted our focus of interest in the study of a civilization. The modern thinker, whose instinct is for the historical continuum rather than the static concept, has little patience with mystic rhapsodizing about that highly local and temporary phenomenon the city-state. Furthermore, the social climate in which he has grown up will not give him a natural sympathy with the kind of exclusive aristocratic *ethos* that refuses to consider slaves as human beings.

The results of these developments have been such as we might expect. Pericles' stock has fallen catastrophically. We forget his inspired building programme and famous ideals ('ideals' has become a dirty word in our contemporary vocabulary) and remember more his ruinous imperialism, his all-too-familiar

17

assumption of justifiable aggression. Yet the idol who has fallen with the most spectacular crash is without doubt Plato: his 'closed society' ethics and perfectionist assumptions have provoked the most furious attacks, and in the process a large number of forgotten men are suddenly finding themselves thrust into the limelight of approval—Democritus, Epicurus, Antiphon, Gorgias (rhetoric is back), Protagoras, Thrasymachus. Diels's *Fragmente der Vorsokratiker* and all the latest papyrus fragments are ransacked for liberal, scientific, anti-authoritarian sentiments. The totalitarian bias can work both ways now; it is equally easy— and equally anachronistic—to damn Plato as a Communist or a Fascist.

Obviously these developments have their dangers; but orthodox scholars are perhaps a little over-apt, in a negative and reactionary way, to damn them out of hand, and later to borrow their most objectionable features as bricks to reinforce the academic edifice. (Turning humane studies into a pseudo-science is only the most obvious instance.) Perhaps, too, such scholars resent the fact that here are the messy, yeasty spores which alone keep their subject alive—if not always progressive. It is a sad but undeniable truth that the most stimulating work of preservation has always been achieved, not so much by professional scholars as by the literary amateurs they so despise, from Sir Thomas Browne to Benjamin Bickley Rogers, from Philemon Holland and North to the translators of the Penguin Classics. Perhaps most galling to the academic mind, the really great discoveries have been made by amateurs as well, generally in the teeth of professional incredulity and ridicule: Champollion, Schliemann, and Michael Ventris were all engaged professionally in affairs remote from the classics. There seems to be a moral of a kind here.

Some of these criticisms were made, and made well, by Professor Trevor-Roper in his recent Inaugural Lecture; and it is a sign of the changing times that such a protest could be voiced from a Regius Chair:

'The study of the classics is now described [by its external critics] as "too narrow". I do not believe that a study which was wide enough to educate Gladstone and Derby and Asquith and Curzon is too narrow for us. What has happened is not that the subject has lost its value but that a humane subject has been treated as an exact science: professional classical scholars have assumed that they are teaching only other professional classical scholars; consequently they have killed the classics.'

It is perfectly true (as Mr Hugh Lloyd-Jones pointed out afterwards in a letter to *The Times*) that this is only one side of the matter. A minority of future scholars and potential translators must obviously pass through a long, rigorous discipline: no less is required of every candidate for a learned profession. What finally reaches the lay reader must be filtered through the sieve of scholarly research first; truth must be honoured above popular success.

> 'This [Mr Lloyd-Jones wrote] is not always easy for us. The period we study is remote: much of the material has perished; the texts that survive are in difficult languages, and are often imperfectly preserved. It follows that studies designed to attain the truth cannot always be made palatable to the general reader. But it by no means follows that the general reader will not profit, perhaps at several removes, by the results of this kind of detailed work.'

There is room, in fact, for several types of scholar and historian in the field of classical studies; and they would do better to help each other rather than indulge in petty mutual denigration, with angry cries of 'Pedant' and 'Popularizer'.

Meanwhile scientists, anthropologists, psychologists, and members of other collateral professions look on in bewildered amazement and a certain degree of pique: any offer of collaboration is stiffly rejected. They can at least console themselves with the reflection that classicists are not over-prone to share secrets even inside the family. But here too prejudice is slowly being broken down. It is no coincidence, I think, that at two recent Cambridge Inaugural Lectures—those by the Laurence Professor of Ancient Philosophy and the Kennedy Professor of Latin—a plea was made for greater collaboration between technically distinct faculties, for a more flexible, all-embracing discipline. Professor Brink, for example, constructed a scarifyingly probable argument between three rival critics (one of them a recognizable parody of Dr I. A. Richards) to prove—as if it needed proving outside the academic world—'that the division of labour which confines to separate compartments criticism textual, stylistic, and literary, is not always a salutary one.'

We should not under-estimate the strength of this new wind blowing through the Groves of Academe: it represents a change of attitude more radical than might appear at first sight. The character of the traditional classical scholar has remained constant for so long that it is hard to believe it capable of change. Here is Montaigne:

> 'This fellow, all dirty, with running nose and eyes, whom you see coming out of his study after midnight, do you think he is seeking among his books how to make himself a better, happier, and wiser man? No such news. He is going to teach posterity the metre of Plautus's verses and the true spelling of a Latin word, or die in the attempt.'

I must, I fear, confess that portrait to be a speaking likeness of at least one Cambridge contemporary of mine.

Such scholars, our latter-day Edward Casaubons, have their uses. It is seldom pointed out that nine-tenths of their research, at a conservative estimate, consists of mechanical fact-grubbing which could be done by any filing-clerk with an orderly mind and a head for languages. But sensible filing-clerks have better things to do; and true scholars owe a debt of gratitude to the Casaubons for the material they assemble. Without much patient spade-work nothing could ever be built. It is only when, tired of acting as academic hodmen, they attempt to build for themselves that their inadequacy manifests itself.

It is a direct result of such academic myopia that the humanities are everywhere fighting a rearguard action, on extremely bad ground. There is some difficulty in countering the charge that classical studies are 'dead' when that is patently how the majority of their professional exponents wish them to remain: safe, dead, mummified, unreal. If the numbers reading classics at Oxford, Cambridge, London, and other universities remains fairly constant, that is, in the main, because the subject is regarded as a soft option; and indeed, with any kind of secondary school grounding in the more advanced rudiments, a soft option it is. But the vast majority of schoolchildren, even in these enlightened days of State grants, do not proceed to a university. It is in *their* interests that the unwieldy and atavistic classical curriculum, designed for monks and leisured gentlemen who would learn comparatively little else, is being ruthlessly pushed off the school timetable. Teachers are by no means primarily to blame for this. They are compelled to work from the books they have, and satisfy the obsolete whims of stubborn examiners; so yearly the pupil is dragged through a thorny grammatical hedge, sweating at the Cabbalistic mystique of deponent verbs and the ablative absolute, only to abandon the whole vexed discipline with a sigh of relief just when it might be of some ultimate use. His attitude is one of boredom, disgust, and incomprehension.

It is not hard to see why, from his or any point of view. He is not—with a few fortunate and enlightened exceptions— being taught about two civilizations which provided the impetus in almost every field for the enduring pattern of European thought and society. He is not being taught, except in the most superficial way, to appreciate or discuss some of the most powerful and seminal literature in the world. He is not arguing over the knotty human truths of political science or historical method; he hears nothing of Ionian biological speculation, Roman law, or the principles of architecture. He is not even learning—the great Greek gift to the world—to think independently and sceptically. Far from it; what he absorbs over and above his syllabus is a set of stylized attitudes. The humanities are, through several historical accidents, the only curriculum which *could* provide a first-rate general education, in the widest and highest sense of that ambivalent word: they offer us a cross-section of an entire civilization, and enough ancient writers with a sense of the transcendental human verities to equip any student to live by both the Delphic mottoes—*Nothing too much*; *Know Yourself*.

Pedantry, over-specialization, and ossified tradition have,

between them, killed the schoolboy's sense of ancient reality, the knowledge that these were men, who lived, thought and suffered. He knows that the word *xenos* in Greek means both 'host' and 'guest'; it never occurs to him that this whim of vocabulary could tell him something about Greek society, and very seldom to his instructor to enlighten him on the point. What he studies, in fact, has no essential *meaning* for him. And why should it? What does it offer but the *disiecta membra* of a discipline that properly belonged to the rhetoricians' schools, and was outmoded even then? It is the mere mouthing of a traditional shibboleth.

Again one runs up against that astonishing, unshakable conservatism. Under modern conditions it is patently obvious that the function of a classical education has to be radically modified; and what happens? Nothing. The hapless child is sent stumbling through the initial stages of a curriculum that once would have monopolized his green years—only now he must (very properly) learn biology, physics, modern languages, advanced mathematics, and heaven knows what besides. The classical curriculum remains unchanged, and its victims merely escape a quarter of the way through it, there being no time for more. If the child has sensibility, he will know that Caesar wrote dull prose and Ovid second-rate poetry, and wonder what all the fuss was about. If he is indifferent to learning, he will simply regard the whole episode as due to the inscrutable malignity of the adult world. And well he may; for the excuses made for the retention of the old syllabus are so feeble that one suspects them of being merely a cloak for an emotional hankering after time-hallowed ritual. The most fantastic theory of all is that the classics (as taught) equip a student with a discriminative mind, capable of forming independent judgments; they are far more likely to harden his mental arteries with post-Arnoldian moral propaganda and the indefatigable peddling of polite *idées reçues*.

Apathy, indifference, resentment, a dying tradition, an obsolete gesture—and yet, and yet, outside on the bookstalls Penguin Classics are selling like hot cakes; Aristophanes, at the time of writing, is packing audiences in at a West End theatre (and if

London patronizes the *Lysistrata* for its bawdy, so, make no mistake about it, did Athens); Homer on the Third Programme sends audience research figures soaring; Thucydides and Herodotus are as sharply relevant to contemporary political problems as to their own. What is there to explain this exquisite paradox— that at a time when the humanities, as part of the educational curriculum, are struggling for sheer survival, more people than ever before in recorded history are reading—and enjoying— classical authors purged (as Professor Trevor-Roper puts it) of otiose learning, re-animated by lay interest?

For once, I suspect, public instinct has formulated a just judgment. Readers and listeners have recognized that those ancient authors whom scholars honour so highly—and others whom perhaps they do not honour enough—lie at the very heart of the European tradition. We carry their beliefs and discoveries in our very bloodstream; any pretensions to humanity we possess are drawn, in the first instance, from this source. There is a half-formulated awareness in the air that they, and they alone, present us with a civilization we can understand, complete and finished, from its raw inception through its highest achievements to its final decline and fall. Here, in all its splendour and complexity, is the whole ancestral pattern of our thought, our symbolism, our assumptions.

Those who turn to the classics today are not concerned with educating themselves as gentlemen, or perpetuating a scribal myth, or celebrating yet another grammarian's obsequies. They need the Greek awareness of transcendental values, the strong, muscular Roman sense of order. Today, more than ever before, it is imperative, they know, to hold fast by those values of scepticism, tolerance, clear-sightedness, and liberal behaviour which they bequeathed to Europe. They no longer need the dead myth of perfection, the glory and the grandeur: enough for them to recognize that the great human failings are perennial, as Thucydides saw so clearly, and that changing values may topple idols even from the securest niche. They have come to see that the mystic qualities which a study of the Latin tongue is supposed to impart are largely illusory; and that it is better—if we must lose something—to know *what* these people felt and said and believed than to slave, ineffectually, at mastering the complex tongue in which they said it.

Such, I imagine, is the inchoate feeling animating many of those who today make a sharp distinction between a classical *education*, as currently conceived, and a genuine interest in the classics, uncontaminated with mediaeval and Renaissance flummery, free from nineteenth-century social, religious, and cultural infiltrations —the 'classics, cricket, and Christianity' complex. I must confess that my own sympathies are, with very few reservations, on the side of the public. I believe that the whole cultural and philosophical legacy of Greece and Rome is one of our vital and precious possessions; but I see it slipping beyond our reach through pedantry, fear, selfishness, intellectual snobbery, sterile traditionalism, and sheer pigheadedness. I have seen too many scholars and lecturers whose major concern is jockeying upwards in their Faculty, playing the game of academic politics, and who therefore avoid anything smacking of the heterodox: what is new is automatically dangerous, and 'sound' is the highest word of praise. I know too many teachers who pass on by rote the *clichés* they learnt in boredom; who have ceased seriously to believe in their subject except as a reminder of the 'good old days' when Cicero's *De Finibus* and *De Officiis* were known as Tully's Ends and Offices; who seem hardly to realize that they have the inestimable privilege—and responsibility—of studying some of the greatest leaders and thinkers who ever lent dignity to the name of Man.

There are, as I have attempted to show, some signs that the breach is in the process of being healed. The dangers of academic obscurantism and over-specialization are now so patent that every new professor seems obliged to inveigh against them *ex cathedra*. Scholars are far readier than they were even a few years ago to produce work designed for an intelligent lay audience. The dreaded sneer of 'vulgarizer' sounds much less often than it did: television and Pelican Books between them have drawn *that* sting. It is beginning to penetrate the minds of even the most diehard traditionalists that communication need not be a compromise with standards of scholarship; that large sales do not automatically mean superficial writing, and comprehensibility is not an academic crime. Nor is there any danger of the real scholar being elbowed aside by the shallow synthetist: only a specialist, in the last resort, can produce a book on his own subject which is both authoritative and intelligible. (The gift is not possessed by all specialists, either; many a one who has attempted a general study with condescending panache has discovered, in somewhat chastened mood, that the thing is harder than he thought. The apparatus of scholarship—quotations in foreign languages, footnotes, bibliographical references and academic polemic, familiarity with out-of-the-way learned periodicals—is a wonderful camouflage for muddled thinking or plain paucity of ideas.)

But the books *are* being written—Dodds' *The Greeks and the Irrational*, Syme's *Roman Revolution*, Onians's *Origins of European Thought*, Gilbert Highet's great treatise on *The Classical Tradition*, which ranges freely over the whole field of European literature, and his hardly less stimulating *Poets in a Landscape*. Translations are reaching a higher standard of accuracy—and sensibility towards the original—than ever before. The great new disciplines of anthropology and psychology continue to fertilize our re-exploration of antiquity: the convulsions that have shaken Europe in the last thirty years send us back with a new understanding to Thucydides' Corcyra or the Rome analysed by Polybius and Tacitus. In this day and age the classics are more alive than they have been since the Renaissance; and, paradoxically, the scholars whose livelihood depends on classical studies have been the last to see it. That (as I believe) enough of them have seen it now, before things have arrived at a completely hopeless pass, is due in no small measure to the amateurs—who had no professional axe to grind, who were animated only by love of their subject, and by that measure clearer-sighted; for whom these dead bones were always clothed in living flesh, who could say with Juvenal:

Quicquid agunt homines, votum, timor, ira, voluptas,
Gaudia, discursus, nostri est farrago libelli.

2

A Triptych for Calliope

I. HOMERIC PATTERNS

'That song', Telemachus remarks to his mother near the beginning of the *Odyssey*, 'ever is sweetest which most newly assails men's ears'; and the same might be said with regard to Homeric criticism. The historical survey conducted in *Homer and his Critics*[1] offers a melancholy, if illuminating, testament to the human mind's infinite capacity for self-delusion, special pleading, and the framing of false analogies. It also demonstrates, as perhaps nothing else could, the frightful gap—still not by any means entirely bridged—between the aesthetic and the academic approach to a classical text. Nor, indeed, is this curious dichotomy absent within the scholars' walled city itself. Professor Momigliano, in a recent contribution to the *Rivista Storica Italiana*, has reminded us of the nineteenth-century split between historians and philologists; and it is only in comparatively recent times that textual critics have grudgingly admitted that archaeology might be a more exact discipline than they had supposed. When we contemplate the more grandiose lunacies of the Homeric Question it is essential to bear in mind that they were largely generated by obsessional scholars who had studied one aspect of their subject to the exclusion of all others.

We should not forget, either, that academic research is frequently motivated by considerations—conscious or unconscious —that have very little to do with the matter in hand, being the product either of the researcher's personal *credo* and unspoken assumptions, or of the immediate historical context in which he lives. As the late Sir John Myres has reminded us, 'it is we, and

[1] John L. Myres. Edited by Dorothea Gray (Routledge & Kegan Paul).

our tools and methods, that change, not the genius of Homer nor the perennial humanity of the poems'. There can be no doubt that the fresh perspectives on Homeric society, opened up first by Schliemann and later developed by the anthropologists, profoundly shocked those conservative scholars who had identified the Homeric with the later, Hellenic, genius. At all costs—so the unspoken assumption ran—Homer's dignity must be preserved from contamination by the barbarian primitivism of Mycenae. So it was that, when Helbig, foiled in his attempts to find archaeological confirmation for an 'Ionian Homer', turned somewhat desperately to the Southern Italian tombs of the seventh and sixth centuries B.C., so great a scholar as Wilamowitz welcomed his conclusions with open arms. Mycenae and all its works could be written off as 'pre-Homeric'.

Scarcely less odd—but very revealing—is the entrenched prejudice which almost all classical literary critics revealed against admitting that the *Iliad* and the *Odyssey* were the product of a primarily oral method and technique of composition. Now this fact has been staringly obvious to any student of comparative literature for at least a century; yet it was not till Milman Parry (whose shining name has acquired extra lustre from the peculiar dimness of Homerology when he entered upon it) that the academic world nerved itself to swallow such a disagreeable pill. When Professor Wade-Gery referred to Parry as the Darwin of Homeric studies he did not, one suspects, intend his remark as an unqualified compliment. The emotional prejudice against the oral theory has been well expressed both by Professor Dodds, who remarked that this was not the aesthetic school's notion of how great poetry was produced, and, most recently, by Mr Cedric H. Whitman in his *Homer and the Heroic Tradition*. 'Few Homerists', Mr Whitman writes, 'have actually heard oral poets at work, and it is only human, perhaps, that men of a literate society tend to regard illiteracy in anyone, whatever the compensations, as an emblem of semibarbarism'. Today, when the new fields opened up by Parry and the Chadwicks have been further explored and illuminated by Sir Maurice Bowra, there is no longer any arguing with the oral theory; but the legacy of prejudice remains. And that, in essence, sums up the history of the Homeric Question: a stubborn tussle between emotionally charged, but largely illusory, *idées reçues*, and the physical facts that could not, by the most subtle casuistry, be made to square with them.

Temperament, no less than intellectual conviction (which too often is little more than emotional bias rationalized into a logical form) has throughout dictated what positions the various protagonists in the battle took up: whether they believed Homer to be one poet, or two, or an agglomeration of the collective tribal memory; whether they placed him in Ionia, Thessaly, or Attica; whether they plumped for oral composition or a literary tradition; whether they found patterns or discrepancies in the two epics; whether they believed Achilles was a historical chieftain or a solar myth; whether Troy for them existed under Hissarlik or in the realm of faëry. It is no accident that the defenders of a single Homer and unity in the *Iliad* and *Odyssey* have almost always been either literary critics who were not professional scholars, or scholars with strong literary interests outside their special field; nor that linguists in the Alexandrian tradition should demonstrate a marked distaste for actually visiting the Troad and studying problems of topography. Each possessed a private *a priori* vision of Homeric truth, and instinctively selected the evidential field best suited for their purposes. Reasonable justification was never hard to find.

When, for example, Friedrich August Wolf published his epoch-making *Prolegomena ad Homerum* in 1795, stating (to summarize briefly) that Homer was not Homer but a congeries of folk-ballad and folk-literature on which the compilers and editors had been at work, he rested his case on two main contentions: first, that alphabetical writing did not exist at the time of the poems' composition; and second, that the oral composition of a work on such a scale was utterly impossible. The first contention has since been disproved, and was never more than a dangerous *argumentum ex silentio*; the second could only be proposed and accepted—even in Wolf's day—by a closed society of scholars who resolutely shut their eyes and ears to the outer world. There was no need to go hunting among the peasants of Yugoslavia or the Kara-Kirghiz tribesmen: a visit to Eton would have been quite enough. As Myres tells us, boys at the older public schools were frequently required to learn by heart, within two or three years, not only the whole of Homer, but the *Aeneid* as well. In any case, that remarkable traveller Robert Wood—to whom Myres pays well-deserved tribute—had already, in 1767, propounded both the oral theory and the topographical actualities underlying Homer's Troy. His *Essay on the Original Genius and Writings of Homer* was based, not on aesthetic or allegorical speculation, but observant travel through the Aegean, where he heard balladmongers and poets at their trade, and could correlate Homeric geography with demonstrable fact.

Yet it was Wolf who found a ready audience: the explosive charge with which he fragmentated Homer into a patchwork of rhapsodes' scraps touched off a whole series of further academic bombs during the succeeding decades. Zoëga's striking phrase about the collective Homer—*essi popoli Greci erano quell'Omero* 'those people of Greece *were* that Homer of theirs'—became a symbol of the general attitude. Karl Lachmann divided the *Iliad* into eighteen 'lays' (*Kleinlieder*), and propounded the notion, as insidious as it was fallacious, that internal discrepancies of fact precluded single authorship: not, apparently, realizing that the creative mind of an oral poet worked rather differently from a German professor's, and that in any case there are more glaring inconsistencies to be found in the pages of *Pendennis* or *Don Quixote* than anything Homer can show us. Grote, to his credit, realized that this theory made no account of the obvious overall design in the *Iliad,* at least; but even he would admit no more than an original nucleus, a kind of *Ur-Iliad*, round which later accretions were supposed to have accumulated. And of course, there was the much-debated recension of the poems by Pisistratus or Solon at Athens, in the sixth century: this, carefully handled, could be and was used to explain almost any oddity in the textual transmission. Myres sums up the situation at this point admirably:

The assumption of a sixth-century recension of the poems was supplemented by the theory of an original poem or poems of relatively high literary merit, expanded and interpolated by clumsy and spiritless patchwork. The question how the collective result had acquired its admitted vigour and charm remained, not only quite unanswered, but almost unasked.

At this point the Homeric corpus—and indeed, Homer himself, single or multiple—bore an uncommon resemblance to Patroclus' body on the battlefield, tugged this way and that by angry and irreconcilable factions, with each clinging to a leg or an arm, and refusing to let go. Lack of co-operation, coupled with sheer ignorance of rival and collateral disciplines (or unwillingness to accept their findings simply because they *were* rival) form the most prominent and curious feature of the whole protracted debate. Aesthetic critics accused the analysts of niggling pedantry, while analysts wrote off aesthetes as subjective dilettanti. If conservative scholars could no longer indulge in the kind of moral allegorizing that Chapman had made his own (and which found its final apotheosis—together with much good historical sense—in the Homeric writings of Gladstone) at least they now had comparative mythology to play with: backed by the philology of Max Müller they could cheerfully interpret the whole Trojan war as 'astronomy tinged with emotion'. Against this profoundly antihistorical trend the steadily accumulating evidence of the archaeologists could at first make little headway; and the opposition fought to the last ditch in an effort to prevent Homer receding into the slough of an all too physical barbarian antiquity. Jebb at one point even attempted to prove that Tiryns was Byzantine on the strength of a Byzantine church discovered over the site.

All this meant that progress was far slower than the rate of discovery warranted, and that errors persisted uncorrected from one generation to the next. There was no one to convince Lachmann of his folly in arguing from the Eddas or the *Niebelungenot* (where in any case his conclusions have proved somewhat shaky) to Homer's *Iliad*; no one to make the analysts in general ask themselves just why the Epic Cycle as a whole passed into oblivion, while Homer survived the centuries; no one who could persuade the more extreme Unitarians to apply more rigid historical or linguistic criteria to their arguments for Homer one and indivisible. By the turn of the century it should have been apparent that the total sum of the evidence on which so many diametrically opposed theories rested was not, *per se*, self-contradictory. Discrepancies need not imply multiplicity of authorship; a single author could have gathered together the most diverse traditional material for his own purposes; a historical background for the events of the poems did not preclude the exercise of poetic imagination in shaping them; and logical inconsistencies did not automatically signify a hopelessly corrupt text which could be cured only by that substitute for intelligent thought, wholesale excision. Yet no such general enlightenment took place. The quarrel raged happily and pointlessly on: despite a very considerable degree of *rapprochement* achieved during the last thirty years or so, it is by no means dead yet.

What really forced both sides to take fresh stock of their positions was the unanswerable case for oral composition presented by Milman Parry. Miss Dorothea Gray, who has edited and completed Myres' posthumous work with scrupulous devotion, summarizes the consequences of Parry's findings. Dating by archaistic elements is ruled out: with a long tradition of oral epic behind him, Homer could compose a mosaic passage that borrowed from many sources and periods; and (a blow to slavish adherents of *Quellenforschung*) identical lines in two different poems could well have been borrowed independently from a common stockpot. Metrically variant epithets were employed, irrespective of provenance, to suit the particular requirements of a hexameter; and, on the principle of 'epic economy', were restricted to one position, and one only, in the line. Thus, in Miss Gray's words, 'analytic arguments from internal inconsistencies lose most of their relevance', while 'unitarian arguments from elaborate cross-referencing become even more suspect than they were'. As a result the more extreme outposts on both sides have been tacitly abandoned. Linguists are more disposed to admit the unique qualities of the *Iliad*, which distinguish it from such works as the *Mahabarata* or *Beowulf* in terms of creative achievement; and literary critics are more ready to make concessions over inconsistent points of detail. Though there have been exceptions (Professor Page's *The Homeric Odyssey* being the most notable) the general trend of recent Homeric scholarship has been towards a modified Unitarianism, which is prepared to absorb the lessons of archaeologists, historians, and literary critics alike.

The paradoxical result of this truce—at any rate during the past two or three years—has been a slight but distinct tendency to go whoring after the old gods once more: perhaps the feeling that this generation of Homerologists is above falling into the pits which its predecessors dug for themselves has lulled all concerned into a comfortable sense of false security. Professor Page, taking the nineteenth-century German analyst Kirchhoff as his mentor, has given many of the hoarier Separatist bogies a new airing; and on the other side of the fence Mr Whitman, following a tortuous trail blazed by Schadewaldt, Hampe, Snell, Notopoulos, and Myres himself, has elaborated a thesis which should give his opponents ammunition and to spare for some time to come. Briefly, he claims that there is an organic resemblance between the structure of the *Iliad* and the patterns to be found in Geometric art. This is the central motif of his book, and he argues it with great verve and ingenuity: encouraged, no doubt, by Professor Webster's *From Mycenae to Homer,* which recently flung Linear B and a good deal more besides into the scales to support precisely the same theory.

Now it is perfectly true, as Mr Whitman says, that any Unitarian must depend very largely on demonstrating some recognizable pattern or design in the Homeric poems as evidence of single authorship. It is also true that Mr Whitman's analysis produces considerable evidence for a large, overall balance of design between the earlier and the later books, for essential unity of imagery and symbolism (his treatment of fire as a metaphorical and demonstrative link throughout the *Iliad* is particularly enlightening and persuasive), for technical articulation of dramatic

effect, and for calculated consistency of characterization. Further—
and here he has scholars such as Nilsson and Dodds on his side—
he lays bare with some cogency the *Iliad*'s continual double
motivation, divine and human: every mortal action has its parallel,
sub specie aeternitatis, on Olympus. 'It is the intuitive levels of
imagery and divine machinery in the *Iliad*,' he writes, 'which
reveal its soundness as the work of a single mind.' And again, with
deep insight: 'Though the gods may surpass men in essential
power and being, they are barred by their own deathlessness from
the dignity of tragedy, or the greatness of self-mastery'. They
form, in effect, a perfect fugal counterbalance to the human
tragedy being played out below them.

If Mr Whitman had been content with exercising his undoubted
gift for literary criticism, all might have been well. In an age when
most classical scholars still look back, as far as aesthetics go, to
Pater or John Addington Symonds, Mr Whitman has at least
taken the trouble to bring himself up to date. But this has led him
into dangers of a different sort: at times he views Homer through
the essentially modern polarized lenses of the New Criticism,
American style. To begin with, he is determined to find the
necessary quota of imagistic complexity in his text, or die in the
attempt. Hence casuistic statements such as this: Homer's language, Mr Whitman declares, 'if it lacks metaphor in the modern
sense, is nevertheless a tremendous imagistic texture, and metaphoric in the sense that all language is, in a way, metaphoric'.
Armed with Susanne Langer's *Philosophy in a New Key*—a curious
weapon for a Homerologist—he extends the term 'symbol' till it
includes any word that has a 'presentational' over and above a
'grammatical' impact; so we are not surprised to learn a little later
that Homer's whole world is 'a metaphor, an enormously
articulated symbolism of the heroic life'.

This leads Mr Whitman into deeper waters still. He may pay
lip-service to Milman Parry and the oral tradition; but he is
armed with a technique developed entirely by and for a study
of self-conscious and literary texts. Now the second main plank
in modern critical method, after symbolic analysis, is the study of

formal design: and this is often developed in terms of a different art, most often graphic or musical. It is no coincidence that Mr Whitman draws parallels between Homer's supposed methods of composition and Mozart's improvisations; nor that the most striking parallel he offers for his theory of 'correspondences' in the *Iliad* is Dylan Thomas's 'This day winding down now'; nor that he draws a detailed analogy, in aesthetic, historical, and psychological terms, between Homer's poetry and Geometric Art. He is in every sense a child of his age; and his age, it must be said, is not Homer's. The urge to make patterns is, perhaps, an ineradicable one in the human mind; and for all his ingenuity of exposition, the patterns that Mr Whitman reads into Homer are, by and large, the product of his own passion for symmetry in all things. He might well say, with Sir Thomas Browne, that 'all things began in order, so shall they end, and so shall they begin again, according to the ordainer of order and mysticall Mathematicks of the City of Heaven'.

Mr Whitman makes much play with the *hysteron proteron* device, according to which a sequence of scenes, ideas or images is taken up by the poet and repeated or echoed in reverse order, thus: ABCDEEDCBA—which is, of course, the rhyme scheme of the Dylan Thomas poem mentioned above. A glance at the fascinating tabulated chart which concludes his book shows that Mr Whitman has not only applied this principle to the work as a whole, so that Book I balances Book XXIV, and so on to the five central Books, which apparently defied the process; but that each separate Book has a similar *internal* pattern of its own. It must be said to his credit that Mr Whitman does not attempt, as Myres did, to impose a similar pattern on the *Odyssey*; but this is for a somewhat egregious reason. The *Iliad*, he says, demands such a pattern, being cognate with Geometric Art; the *Odyssey* is a later work, coeval with proto-Attic, where such canons no longer apply. He might with equal probability have claimed the *Odyssey* as Minoan on the evidence of the Cnossos frescoes.

The whole scheme is open to the very gravest objections; and since it is gaining a certain amount of scholarly currency, it may be as well to mention some of them in detail. To begin with, this theory depends on the assumption that the division of Books as we have them goes back to Homer's time, and is not—as generally supposed—a convenient device imposed by Alexandrian scholars. Secondly, such a vast system of correspondences, extending over thousands of lines, is totally at odds with anything we know of oral composition: and Mr Whitman himself insists that Homer did no more than dictate his work, if that. But—and one mentions this as unobtrusively as possible—a comparison of Mr Whitman's *schema* with the text reveals that a good deal of arbitrary selection and manipulation has gone into preserving a symmetrical balance. The present writer, as an experiment, attempted to perform the process (without consulting Mr Whitman's chart) for Books I and XXIV, the star exhibits of the theory, and produced a quite different pair of lists which hardly corresponded at all— except, that is, in one curious numerical sequence. The time-scheme of days in the two books does, precisely, correspond in a *hysteron proteron* pattern; and that is about the only unshakeable piece of evidence which Mr Whitman presents.

The guiding principle behind his thesis is, of course, the analogy with Geometric Art: and this principle is about as misleading, in every respect, as it possibly could be. The history of Geometric does *not* chronicle 'the growth of the Hellenic spirit'; Geometric itself is *not* more advanced than Minoan; the stick-and-triangle figures are *not* 'used as half-abstract elements in a unified and perspicuous design'—shades of Picasso and modern pseudo-primitivism!; the crude leonine 'toothy jaws, glaring eyes, and bristling mane' are *not* evidence of symbolic selectivity but technical incompetence and undeveloped schematism; and nothing is more suggestive of this (though Mr Whitman, still presumably in a Picasso dream, uses it to argue the exact opposite) than the fact that 'the painter shows successive stages of the action as if they were simultaneous, even as Homer often shows simultaneous actions successively'. At one point Mr Whitman quotes Kierke-gaard's remark about the essential subjectivity of truth; and his own work is a notable demonstration of it. The truth of the matter is that Geometric pottery is the only evidence available to us for the period (about the eighth century B.C.) in which the Homeric poems are now generally agreed to have been composed; and we must, it seems, make the most of what we have. It is a thousand pities that this analogical myth has achieved such undeserved prominence: it threatens to open up the old Homeric battles that one had hoped ended for ever, and cast discredit on progress made with great difficulty and in the teeth of entrenched opposition. The trouble is that Mr Whitman's theory has laid its mark on every branch of classical learning he touches in his book: historians will raise their eyebrows at his arguments for an Attic Homer, and linguists at his attempts to demonstrate that 'Ionic is a branch of Attic and not the other way round'. Both contentions are essential for his purposes; and every page of his book demonstrates the overriding powers of an *a priori* concept once it has got a firm grip on its author's mind—however learned, sensitive, or wide-ranging that mind may be. Homer has a unique gift for generating such concepts; and in that fact lies the whole tragedy of the Homeric Question (see note on p. 51).

II. HODGE ON HELICON. *A study of Hesiod and his society*

During the past century our knowledge of early Aegean history has grown almost beyond recognition. Cnossos stands in something more that its original glory ('a poor thing, but Minoan', Sir Arthur Evans remarked of his imaginative handiwork) and the shaftgraves at Mycenae have yielded up their golden treasures. Specialists in Egyptology or Hittite studies have helped to fill in blank spaces on the map of the ancient Mediterranean world. Thanks to social and economic studies such as Mr M. I. Finley's *The World of Odysseus* we now have a pretty clear idea of how Homeric society functioned. But between the high heroic age and the beginning of properly documented Greek history—that is, from about 1000 B.C. to 700 B.C.—fall what are very properly known as the Greek Dark Ages; and about them we know little more than we ever did. This period of anarchy and cultural decline has thrown up no startling archaeological treasures, unless we count Proto-Geometric pottery; for our knowledge of it we still depend, basically, on two sharply contrasting literary texts.

There could hardly be a greater difference of ethics, style, social alignment and subject-matter than we find when we set Homer and Hesiod side by side. Both, most scholars now agree, wrote their works at about the same time: that is, towards the end of the eighth century B.C., when the Greek Dark Ages had nearly run their course. Both composed in the same metre, the epic hexameter. But there the resemblance abruptly ends. Homer looks back to the age of heroic deeds with nostalgic approval. He accepts, whole-heartedly, the social structure which such an age implies: the ritual exchange of gifts, the feudal *oikos*, or baronial Big House, with its self-contained horde of loyal retainers. He glorifies war, and despises trade. His outlook is aristocratic to the *n*th degree, and a radical upstart such as Thersites gets very short shrift at his hands indeed. The noble is the shepherd of his people, as Homer calls him, in more senses than one; he may protect them in battle, but he also fleeces them in taxes to pay for his lavish hospitality. Achilles remarks, among the shades, that rather than be King of all the Dead he would gladly live as—not a slave, which we might expect, but a *day-labourer*. The slave had his place in the Big House; the hired hand was outside it.

Two other points of historical interest we may note about Homer, both of which stem from a common social and psychological pattern. In the first place, he never intrudes his own personality into the poems which survive under his name. Throughout the writing remains anonymous, impersonal even at its most passionate, and free from any trace of introspective self-concern. (It is not hard to see how Wolf and his followers could decide that 'Homer' was a kind of collective folk-saga, the product of that mythical entity the group-mind.) Secondly, his only deliberate references to the mundane or contemporary scene are to be found in his extended similes. Here the aristocratic mask is abruptly dropped, and comic rural realism abounds. But this

37

licence apart, Homer appears as the steadfast *laudator temporis acti*, the self-effacing servant and upholder of *oikos* society. Since that society was much reduced from its former legendary greatness, a re-creation of past heroic glory such as the *Iliad* would both comfort and flatter the squires and barons of Homer's own day. It is, taken all in all, a severely stylized picture, and one which omits precisely those personal details so necessary for any attempt at social reconstruction. Yet, properly handled, it does reveal a great deal about Dark Age upper-class ethics.

When we turn to Hesiod we are in another world. Indeed, so radically opposed to Homer is he on every count, that many have supposed his best-known poem, *The Works and Days,* to be a deliberate counterblast to the Homeric *ethos.* 'We know how to say many false things that seem like true sayings', the Muses inform him, 'but we know also how to speak the truth where we wish to'.[1] Hesiod identifies the Muses, it is fairly clear, with the imaginative faculty; and what he implies in this passage seems to be that Homer presented a false picture, but he, Hesiod, will tell the truth. He has no autobiographical reticence: indeed, almost all we know of him is derived from his own writings. He is the kind of person that the *oikos* preferred to ignore: a Boeotian peasant farmer working his own land, cantankerous, full of wise saws, fiercely critical of authority. He detests war and women with equal fervour, and has a most un-Homeric passion for thrift, hard work, and money. He has a weakness for catalogues and genealogies, and may well have been, as Addison once suggested, the 'oracle of the neighbourhood'. He is superstitious, yet intensely pragmatic, concerned with the harsh here-and-now of economic dearth rather than yearning for battles long ago: 'an individual', as Professor Wade-Gery puts it,[2] 'confronted with a historic situation, like the Athenian Solon a century later'. He is a knowledgeable countryman and a passable astronomer, who by temperament was a kind of early Pre-Socratic.

---

[1] *Theogony* 26ff. All translations are from the excellent new version by Professor Richmond Lattimore (University of Michigan Press, 1959).
[2] *Essays in Greek History* (1958) p.5.

We do not know the name of Hesiod's father; but, as his son tells us, he was a merchant sailor who, because he 'wanted to live like a noble' (a significant aside, this) speculated rather too rashly and went bankrupt. As a result of this setback the family left Cyme in Asia Minor, and emigrated to the district of Thespiae in Boeotia, where they acquired a farm at Ascra on the slopes of Mount Helicon. Hesiod has no love for the place of his birth: he describes it as 'a hole of a village . . . bad in winter, tiresome in summer, and good at no season'. Here, in due course, Hesiod's father died, and left his patrimony to be divided between his two sons, Hesiod himself and the notorious Perses. There is a fragment from the Homeric poem *Margites* which exactly describes Perses: 'He knew many things but knew all badly. . . . The gods had taught him neither to dig nor to plough, nor any other skill; he failed in every craft.'[3] According to his exasperated and thrifty brother, Perses spent his winter days lounging about and gossiping in the warm smithy, while during the summer his life seems to have been one long siesta. When he was in debt and harassed by his own improvidence he would come scrounging at Hesiod's door, begging for a wagon or a pair of oxen. But he had one gift, like many of his kind; and that was for sharp litigation.

It seems clear that Perses not only disputed the terms of his father's will, but bribed the local barons to give him the lion's share of the estate at arbitration. Hesiod's virulence suggests, too, that such dishonest judgments had become common practice. 'Here now is the age of iron', he groans. 'Never by daytime will there be an end to hard work and pain, nor in the night/ To weariness, when the gods will send anxieties to trouble us'. Then comes the famous parable of the Hawk and the Nightingale:[4]

> Now I will tell you a fable for the barons; they understand it.
> This is what the hawk said when he had caught a nightingale
> with spangled neck in his claws and carried her high among the
>   clouds.
> She, spitted on the clawhooks, was wailing pitifully,

[1] Trs. H. G. Evelyn-White, in *Hesiod, The Homeric Hymns and Homerica* (revised ed., 1943) pp. 536–9.
[2] *Works and Days* 202–212 = Lattimore p. 43.

but the hawk, in his masterful manner, gave her an answer:
'What is the matter with you? Why scream? Your master has you.
You shall go wherever I take you, for all your singing.
If I like, I can let you go. If I like, I can eat you for dinner.
He is a fool who tries to match his strength with the stronger.
He will lose his battle, and with the shame will be hurt also.'
So spoke the hawk, the bird who flies so fast on his long wings.

This bitter little fable on the Might-is-Right theme is historically suggestive. It mirrors with some accuracy the faults peculiar to aristocratic rule *in its decline*. Homeric heroes might whip Thersites for his insolence, but their honour would forbid them to give a crooked judgment. The local barons of Thespiae are considerably less scrupulous.

Like so many radical scourges of government, Hesiod very quickly turns his specific complaint into a general attack on corruption. 'There is an outcry when Justice is dragged perforce', he cries, 'when bribe-eating/ Men pull her about, and judge their cases with crooked decision'. He gives the barons a solemn warning: the immortal guardians of Zeus, some thirty thousand in number, rove abroad over the earth and 'have an eye on decrees given and on harsh dealings'. With a touch that anticipates the technique of the hot-gospeller, he exclaims:

The eye of Zeus sees everything. His mind understands all.
He is watching us right now, if he wishes to, nor does he fail
to see what kind of justice this community keeps inside it.

It is easy to see how Charles Elton could write approvingly in 1815 of Hesiod's 'elevated views of a retributive Providence', and Professor Trevor-Roper, somewhat more recently, represent him as a kind of primitive *New Statesman* Socialist, fearlessly laying into privilege, graft, and reactionary authoritarianism.

Unfortunately the truth is neither so simple nor so flattering to Hesiod as might appear at first sight. Hesiod, whatever else he may have been, was no Solon. His sole reason for attacking the barons was because they had cheated *him* of his patrimony: he was peasant through and through. When (as, on internal evidence, seems almost certain) by his persistent agitation he got the verdict reversed, he very quickly changed his tone.[5] In the *Theogony* his early truculence has vanished into thin air. His realism has gone, too: instead of graphic details about his private life on the farm he is busy, as Pindar was later, in working out a creation myth and a table of divine pedigrees that aims to blend tradition and respectability. As Friedrich Solmsen wrote in *Hesiod and Aeschylus* (1949):

> His history of the gods culminates in the ascendency of Zeus, but it provides for the incorporation and integration of some older forces and deities — those whose character allowed it — in the new dispensation. Their continued presence and power are an essential and integral feature of his conception of the new order. While under this order man should certainly honour *Dike*, as Hesiod so emphatically urges his brother, yet should he cease to do things which are *themis*?

Hesiod, in fact, far from being a genuine radical, is a superstitious traditionalist; indeed, once his own cause of grievance has been removed, he is quite ready to change his tone about the local squirearchy. Now he calls them 'respected' or 'temperate barons', 'kingly nobles' who give 'straight decisions'. Between the *Works and Days* and the *Theogony* we can see the classic political swing from Left to Right in its most naked form.[6]

Hesiod is, indeed, one of the most candidly self-revelatory poets in the whole of ancient literature: and on our terms it is a far from flattering self-portrait which he paints. But as a social, moral, and historical testament his poetry is unique. Too seldom do we see any society from the under-side; throughout history the Homeric conventions have, till recent times, almost invariably had the better of it. The common man was either inarticulate or carefully suppressed. But in Hesiod we can see the perennial Aegean farmer, the whole paradigm of sweat and toil and repetitive life that lay, century by century, behind the fine rhetoric and famous battles. For Hesiod there are two Strifes: one is War,

[5] See Wade-Gery, *op. cit.* p. 12.
[6] It is only fair to warn the reader that several scholars believe the *Theogony* to be an earlier composition than the *Works and Days*; but all the evidence is circumstantial, and no final certainty of order is ever likely to be achieved.

which is bad, the other Healthy Competition, which promotes prosperity. 'The neighbour', he writes, 'envies the neighbour who presses on towards wealth.' One can see why Cleomenes of Sparta dismissed Hesiod in angry contempt as a poet fit only for helots.

Hesiod's morality, on close examination, may at first have an ignoble ring about it; but it should serve to remind us that Homeric chivalry—indeed, almost any lofty ethical system—rests *au fond* on some sort of slave or serf economy, and freedom from grinding economic pressure. What is against idleness? The gods resent it. What is the advantage of work? It brings rewards— wealth, divine approval, nobility, honour, the envy of less successful men. 'The man who does evil to another does evil to himself', Hesiod declares, and at first we suspect a moral subtlety; but then we remember those thirty thousand divine spies, and realize that there is a severely practical reason for not committing an offence against your fellow-man. You will be observed; and heavenly retribution is sure to follow. Show yourself pious to the gods 'so they may have a complacent feeling and thought about you'. Cultivate your neighbours; they may come in useful later if you oblige them now. And—a personal *cri de cœur*, this—'When you deal with your brother, be pleasant, but get a witness'. It is all severely practical; but hardly, in Charles Elton's word, elevated.

Yet—to revert for a moment to the fable of the Hawk and the Nightingale—the fact remains that, against all probability, the Nightingale won. Hesiod roused public opinion; and public opinion saw to it that an unjust verdict was reversed. Here we are on the edge of something that recurs again and again in Greek history. As Professor Wade-Gery says,

> There have not been too many ages of the world when public opinion could really control governments. When we remember what Homer thought of such an agitator as Thersites, who spoke up to his betters, we shall recognize the size of Hesiod's achievement. From Hesiod through Solon to Aeschylus and Euripides, the Nightingale was a real power in Greek opinion and behaviour, and the Hawk had to listen.

Viewed in this perspective, it is not, perhaps, so contemptible a thing after all to battle for your own against—dare one be anachronistic for a moment and say the Establishment?

For all his verse-making, Hesiod was, beyond doubt, a genuine countryman: his poetry sprang from his farming. There is no touch of the fake-pastoral *littérateur* in his work. Helicon to him was an all-too-real Greek mountain, swept in winter by biting winds and snows, its soil stubborn and its yield poor. Hesiod tells us the whole cycle of his country year: the felling of wood in autumn for wagons and fresh ploughs; the barn-building and planting, sowing and harvest. A forty-year old hired hand is best for ploughing; he keeps his mind on the job. Spring sailing begins when fig-trees show 'a leaf as big as the print that a crow makes when he walks'. Taboos abound: don't make water facing the sun, or on the road. 'Never, at a happy festival of the gods, cut off the dry from the green on the five-branch plant with shining iron'— that is, never cut your nails during a service. (The characteristic euphemisms and periphrases are to avoid evil demons.) 'Never let a twelve-year-old boy sit on anything not to be moved; better not; it makes a man lose his virility.' Avoid gossip. Do various prescribed tasks on the lucky or appropriate days. Don't be taken in by women; all they want is your barn. Prune and dig and store and winnow; wake early, work long. Honour the gods.

Hesiod saw his own age as a period of moral anarchy when such precepts were largely neglected. When he has finished cursing his feckless brother for dishonesty, he begins preaching rules of good conduct at him. Perses, the glib, improvident dreamer, the harvest-time slug-abed, the importunate idler, is splendidly real: at times (as when Hesiod primly adjures him to 'never be so hard as to mock a man for hateful, heart-eating poverty') we sympathize with the Grasshopper rather than the Ant. But it is all an immeasurable distance from Achilles flame-capped in the trench before Troy, or the funeral games for Hector. This is the stable, unchanging element in history: largely ignored, ever-present, indifferent to war and politics except when they impinge on a limited, personal world. There have always been Hesiods in Greece; there still are; and each one still has a Perses for a brother, and will tell you so, in a richly dramatic narrative style, over the mid-day coffee. The cicadas still shrill in the blistering summer heat, 'when goats are at their fattest, when the wine tastes best,/ women are most lascivious, but the men's strength fails them most'. It is Hesiod, not Homer, who truly lifts a corner of the curtain to show us what life in the Greek Dark Ages was like; and it turns out, unexpectedly, to be very like everyday life anywhere in the Mediterranean, at any era of history. Heroes may come and go, monopolizing the chronicles; but the country remains what it always was.

III. ODYSSEUS TRANSLATED

No figure from the whole rich stock of classical mythology has had a greater influence on European thought and literature than Odysseus. This monolithic wanderer has assumed, through the centuries, a most bewildering and Protean variety of shapes. It took very little time for the prudent, steadfast hero presented by Homer to be metamorphosed into the shifty villain of Sophocles' *Philoctetes*: indeed, his reputation in Hellenistic and Roman times was at a very low ebb. He was indelicate, lachrymose, and too dodgy by half to appeal to Cato's countrymen; and since these also claimed descent from Trojan Aeneas, Odysseus (or Ulysses, as they insisted on calling him) had the additional disadvantage of fighting on the wrong side. Allegorized by the Stoics, denigrated by Virgil, a shabby intriguer in the *Roman de Troie* and a Machiavellian politico in Shakespeare's *Troilus and Cressida*, he has more than justified the application to him by Homer of that most ambiguous epithet, *polytropos*. Etymologically, this word means 'of many turns', which could be and was interpreted as either 'unscrupulous', 'skilled in rhetoric', or 'much-travelled'. But as Professor W. B. Stanford has pointed out, in his admirable book *The Ulysses Theme,* it is only in this century, with the publication of Joyce's *Ulysses* and Nikos Kazantzakis' *Odyssey,*[1] that the mythic

[1] *The Odyssey: A Modern Sequel.* Translation into English Verse, Introduction, Synopsis, and Notes by Kimon Friar. (Secker & Warburg.)

hero has been re-integrated as a comprehensive figure on the Homeric scale.

When we examine, in the light of historical perspective, these various guises which Odysseus has assumed during his long literary career, they fall naturally into two contrasted categories. On the one hand there is the classical Odysseus, whose true goal is Ithaca, the prototype of social responsibility, the husband and father for whom warfare and wandering are an unpleasant necessity, to be dealt with as efficiently as possible. On the other there is the anti-social, romantic, and frequently mystical Odysseus: the yearning exile of du Bellay, Dante's seeker after virtue and knowledge, the pessimistic anarchist of Pascoli or—an obverse of the same coin—d'Annunzio's Nietzschean explorer. This essentially modern figure is perhaps best known to English readers from Tennyson's famous poem; and this is the type of hero whom Kazantzakis has created. As Joyce put it, the distinction is between the centrifugal and the centripetal ideal. Homer's Odysseus is centred on his home; it would strike him as the merest moonshine to pursue an intangible idea over the western horizon, or die in a quest for ultimate truth and reality. Kazantzakis' Odysseus, on the other hand, is a baroque compendium of all the transcendental passions, a synthetic Everyman whose pilgrimage involves him with almost every major religious, ethical, and political system known to man.

At this point we may briefly recapitulate Kazantzakis' plot—if such a word is adequate to describe the narrative movement of his vast symbolic epic. Taking the traditional situation as presented by Homer in Book XXII of the *Odyssey*, he at once re-shapes its conclusion to his own ends. Odysseus, having slain the Suitors, finds his wife a bore and his son an amiable namby-pamby. Appalled by the thought of settling down in Ithaca, his mind yearning for further knowledge and exploration, he sets his affairs in order and leaves the island for ever, with a crew composed of symbolic characters such as Granite, Hardihood, Orpheus, Kentaur, and Captain Clam. Before their departure Telemachus is married off to Nausicaa, and plots to kill his father;

Odysseus is delighted by this manifestation of independence in the boy.

The friends sail first to Sparta, where they find a domestic *ménage* rather like that evoked by Rupert Brooke in his famous sonnet; Menelaus has grown flabby and comfortable, Helen is bored, and the serfs are up in arms. Blond Dorian barbarians, virile and aggressive, threaten the decadent kingdom. After vainly trying to interest Menelaus in joining him on the trail, Odysseus abducts Helen (though without any erotic intent) and takes her off to Crete, where they find Frazerian fertility rites in full swing. There are Holy Harlots, Serpent Sisters, and Mountain Maidens; not to mention priestesses in cow-masks, incest, Lesbianism, bull-jumping, and feasts of raw flesh. To quote from Mr Kimon Friar's Synopsis (which is less bedazzled by the pyrotechnics of exotic metaphor than Kazantzakis' own poetry), 'as Idomeneus steps into the bronze cow, the lords and ladies engage in orgiastic lust throughout the arena, Diktena stuffs Odysseus' mouth with the bull's loins, and both fall into an erotic embrace'. Even Miss Mary Renault at her most colourful hardly matches this kind of ritual junketing. It comes as no surprise when this 'decadent' civilization is wiped out in a holocaust of fire, slaughter, and heftily swung double-axes. When the smoke has cleared away, Hardihood is made King of Crete, Helen is left behind with a barbarian gardener who has put her in the family way, and Odysseus moves on south, to further revolutionary battles in Egypt.

Here, however, Pharaoh proves more than a match for the insurgents, and Odysseus and Co. retreat in disorder upcountry. Their wearisome anabasis is alleviated on occasion by drunken orgies in Negro villages ('black erotic embraces' form a favourite motif for Kazantzakis) and finally they reach that symbolic fastness, the source of the Nile. It is here that Odysseus determines to build his Ideal City; but first he retreats to a mountain cave for communion with himself and God. This section forms a poetic analogue to Kazantzakis' philosophical tract entitled 'Spiritual Exercises (*Askêtikê*), which, significantly, bears the secondary label of *Salvatores Dei*. God, it transpired, is contained in man's own evolutionary nature, a flame struggling to refine and purify the gross human spirit; and Odysseus, after visitations from his three Fates in the shape of Tantalus, Heracles, and Prometheus, transcends first his own ego, then his racial memories, and finally the whole natural order of Creation, Then, fortified by this odd mixed dose of Bergson, Darwin, Jung, and Orthodox monasticism (Kazantzakis, we may recall, spent some time himself as a contemplative on Mount Athos), Odysseus descends, ready for the positive action of building.

The City rises, and proves as syncretic as Odysseus' own spiritual reflections, containing elements of Plato's *Republic,* More's *Utopia,* and St Augustine's *City of God.* On this substratum Kazantzakis then grafts positively Nietzschean precepts concerning the ruthless laws of survival. Evil omens mark the City's inauguration: Odysseus, it turns out, was so busy transcending his ego on the mountain that he failed to notice its volcanic nature. The volcano erupts, and the City is destroyed. This marks the turning-point in Odysseus' journey; he abandons actions for contemplation, and becomes a renowned ascetic, visited by pilgrims and worshipped for his healing powers. He is approached by Temptation in the form—as we might surmise—of a Negro boy. He accepts and embraces the hitherto dreaded image of Death, and proceeds on his journey southward towards the Pole, in the course of which he meets various thinly disguised spiritual leaders from past history, such as Christ and the Buddha.

But these great names, it is clear, are evoked only to be dismissed: it is as though Odysseus (or Kazantzakis) were exorcizing all the demons of civilization and tradition that swarmed stubbornly in his lonely, anarchic soul. Finally God, too, is chased from the temple of Being: Odysseus, alone now in the Arctic snows (whither he has sailed in a coffin-shaped skiff) cries out to the Deity:

'Go pack, you doddering fool! Make way for me to pass!'
Then from his belt he drew an iron sword on whose
broad blade there flashed the sharp-etched threat: "God, I shall slay
you!"

Poor God grew pale and staggered back with buckling knees:
'Alas, I shouldn't have shaped such a dread beast! I'm lost!
I'll run and hide in the vast sky, for the earth's his!'
His red-assed servants ran, his monkeys held him up
and dashed him with rose water to revive his wits,
but his eyes glazed with staring on his last-born son
who with cocked hat and tassel bright as the pole star
flung to the light a gallant and defying song
with words first heard on earth that made the Old Man quake:
he sang of joy, revolt, of freedom, and of bold new roads!

It is at this point that we realize how much Kazantzakis and Joyce had in common. Both were intellectuals trying to struggle out beyond the tangling reins of logic; both, too, were profoundly religious men by upbringing and instinct who were, nevertheless, in deliberate revolt, the one against Orthodoxy, the other against Catholicism. Both ended by cocking a kind of cosmic snook at the God in whom they were unwilling to believe, but could not wholly dismiss.

The final conclusion of Kazantzakis' *Odyssey* is profoundly nihilistic. Not only Death, but a total absence of Hope ('rotten-thighed Hope', as Heracles calls it) must be faced and accepted. Man is nothing and less than nothing; only the savage devouring Flame is real, only Art (in particular Poetry) has the power to survive. The paradoxes of this credo (or non-credo) hardly need emphasizing; they are implicit in Kazantzakis' own position, with its division between passionate action and equally passionate withdrawal, the balance of East and West, Apollo and Dionysus, all fusing in the attitude to which he gave the label of 'the Cretan glance'. As Mr Friar quite rightly observes in his preface, Odysseus is 'a man of mixed motives in a constant state of ethical tension'—a judgment which might on occasion be extended to his creator. To dodge the issue, as Kazantzakis did, by asserting that Hope could only be built on the Abyss of Despair, is the purest sophistry.

Professor Stanford observes that both Bloom and Kazantzakis' Odysseus resemble Aeneas in shouldering all the burdens of Western civilization. It might be equally fair to say that they have been loaded with every characteristic vice of the twentieth-century literary intellectual. This is especially apparent in Kazantzakis' case. The key-note of this vast epic is what might be termed pessimistic syncretism. Odysseus (like Picasso or the young Mr Eliot) is raking through the rubbish-heap of European history, seeing what he can rescue from the burning. He is shopping around, to put it crudely, for a creed, a philosophy, a literary style, even a language in which to express himself. He raids the arsenals of the past like an angry magpie. Dante, d'Annunzio, Pascoli, Tennyson, Yeats, Mann, D. H. Lawrence; Plato, More, Nietzsche, Marx, Freud, Jung, Spengler, Bergson, Buddha; demotic idioms culled indiscriminately from a *periplus* of Greece and the Aegean— all have been ground down, grist to the mill of Kazantzakis' predatory imagination.

Now if ever there was a classic case of poetry, ultimately being justified only by the indivisible sum of its totality, this is it. A prose summary of Kazantzakis' *Odyssey* is fantastic and, in places, ludicrous. Even Mr Friar, when it comes to the dialectic of ideas that sustains these 33,333 lines, is obliged to talk about an eclectic synthesis. As he proved in *Zorba the Greek*, Kazantzakis had the intellectual's characteristic exaggerated admiration for flamboyant physical self-assurance and sexual prowess—a trait which produces some unintentionally comic episodes in the present work. He also had an equally characteristic intellectual yearning for vernacular speech, and gratified it by peppering his text with local terms gathered up geographically at random. It is rather as if an English poet were to reinforce his speech on the same page with Brummagem, Border dialect, Cockney, West Country, and Lallans. The practice may be more admissible in modern Greek, which has still a great deal of plasticity in usage; but it smells of Alexandrianism, the urban artificial desire for peasant simplicity. Kazantzakis may have paid lip-service to the *élan vital*; but one cannot help feeling he was more at home in the mild and decadent world celebrated by Cavafy.

Kazantzakis was, it is true, fighting against the deadening influence of academic fashion when he published his *Odyssey*. In 1938 the literary language was (and still largely remains) the *kathare-vousa*, that artificial pseudo-antique speech which was imposed by a conclave of scholars in an effort to recapture the lost glories of Demosthenes' classic utterance, and purge some five hundred years of Turkish and other accretions from 'the dialect of the tribe'. Feeling ran high over these linguistic nuances; students had rioted in Athens when the *Oresteia* was performed in common speech. Kazantzakis created further scandal by dispensing with accents, and taking as his verse unit a strange seventeen-syllable line to replace the popular fifteen-syllable iambic line of seven beats. All this, together with his penchant for outlandish and polysyllabic adjectives, outraged the Athenian critics who were called upon to judge it, and presented a rare problem to any scholar-poet courageous enough to embark upon the translation of such an immense work.

Mr Kimon Friar has earned the gratitude of all English-speaking students of poetry by the exemplary way in which he has gone about his task. He has wisely shortened Kazantzakis' line to a fifteen-syllable stress-hexameter, similar to that employed in his version of the *Aeneid* by Mr Cecil Day Lewis. Much of the richness and idiosyncratic quality of the original has, inevitably, been lost. English is not a language that takes kindly to polysyllables, as translators from the classics have found out to their cost; and where in Greek (ancient or modern) the star-studded epithet can be used cumulatively, line after line, to strengthen and diversify, the effect in our stubborn Anglo-Saxon is a dilution of poetic intensity. We have to use our adjectives sparingly. Mr Friar is well aware of these problems; he worked over his translation with Kazantzakis himself, section by section, and obtained the Master's *imprimatur* for the initial draft; but, for all his pious devotion and unerring choice of the *mot juste*, he has produced a quieter, more respectable, more 'literary' poem than Kazantzakis' own. Where he attempts to slide into colloquial speech he fairly wriggles with embarrassment. But he has performed, nevertheless, a monumental task, in every sense of the word, and deserves a critical accolade for his scholarship, sensibility, and sheer perseverance.

Where, ultimately, will this epic Leviathan take its place in the roll of European literature? At the moment, one feels, judgment is dazzled by Kazantzakis' sheer verbal virtuosity, the great golden wave of metaphor and rhetoric that surges over the delighted reader's head, and bursts around him in a glittering cascade of symbolic imagery, Zeus-like largesse for every literary Danaë. (Mr Friar spends two pages listing the metaphors applied to the sun alone.) But the doubts remain and multiply when the shower of gold has dispersed. Is not the whole structure a mere unwieldy *tour de force*? Does this so-called 'modern sequel' ever get to grips with contemporary, machine-age Man? Could it not be argued that the ethics veered between nihilism, bogus mysticism, and old-fashioned evolutionary rationalism, with just a *soupçon* of the Laurentian Dark Gods to get the reader excited? In other words, does the poem as a whole have the compulsive ring of truth, or is it an elaborate intellectual charade, a literary game played with potent counters called Love, and Faith, and Hope, and Death? Time will doubtless tell; and meanwhile we may well temper our Dionysiac enthusiasm with a little Apollonian caution.

Note: The great controversy about Sir Arthur Evans' findings at Cnossos, opened in *The Observer* by Professor L. R. Palmer, only became public after this book had gone to press. Whether the discrepancies between Evans' Day Book and his later *Palace of Minos* indicate an old man's carelessness or some less venial aberration is still being fiercely argued. But no one could question the enormous emotional heat which Professor Palmer's revelation generated: *odium academicum* came in by the door, and logic flew out of the window. (See *The Observer*, 3 and 10 July, 1960.) In a year which has also seen Professor Page's brilliant *History and the Homeric Iliad*—not to mention Mr Robert Graves' spirited translation of the *Iliad, The Anger of Achilles* (see the *Times Literary Supplement*, 17 June, 1960, p. 384)—it can hardly be said that interest in Homer shows signs of slackening.

3

Clio Perennis

ASPECTS OF ANCIENT HISTORY

I

Since the beginning of this century several major changes have
taken place in the historian's general attitude to his subject.
The most important new factors were outlined in 1911 by a Swiss
scholar, Eduard Füter, in his *Geschichte der neueren Historiographie*.
Füter saw clearly—and this was perhaps his most valuable
contribution to historical thought—that the changing society of
Europe after the Franco-Prussian War of 1870 had a profound
effect on the *idées reçues* held by subsequent European historians—whatever their chosen period. In other words, he applied the scientific principle of observer-error to history. The
historian was not (as he so often unconsciously assumed himself
to be) an impartial Recording Angel. He was himself conditioned and prejudiced by the flow of history, inescapably
involved in the experiment he was making. History was a
river without banks, where everyone, without exception, had
to swim.

This was what Croce meant when he wrote that all history
is contemporary history, or Collingwood that all history is the
history of ideas. Every historian is at the mercy of his own culture,
tradition, and environment; his attitude to the past will be directly
conditioned by his status or beliefs in the world he inhabits.
Ranke's famous creed, that history should be written *wie es
eigentlich gewesen*—as it actually happened—does not, and cannot,
mean that an objective account of the 'facts' is all that is required.
Even supposing such an ideal to be possible, it would be useless.
Annals are not synonymous with history. Allow for prejudice as

he may, the scholar, in the last resort, has to be a judge. As Professor Barraclough recently insisted:

> We seek, in the end, to know 'what really happened' in order to assess its bearing and meaning for us. . . . The historian, who is intimately acquainted with the matter of history, is (or should be) the person best qualified to assess its bearing. . . . The refusal of the historian to interpret his work does not prevent history from being interpreted; it simply means that interpretation is deprived of qualified criticism, and that the historian's case goes by default.

All history, we may say then, is finally moral history, an extended illustration of the external human struggle with right and wrong. Yet how are these to be assessed? The historian, being human, can only judge morality by the standards he knows (or instinctively assumes), and apply those standards, as judiciously as he can, to the ideas governing those actions which he is studying.

It is not hard to see how the would-be scientific historian, his eyes opened by Füter and others, reached the neutral impasse outlined by Professor Barraclough. To begin with, he was convinced that, before he could master his profession at all, he would have to become proficient in psychology, sociology, political science, biology, and several other equally complex disciplines. Even after this gruelling preliminary training, there was still no guarantee that he would not merely have substituted one set of prejudices for another. No wonder, then, that he so often, despairingly, abandoned any attempt to form value-judgments. What really sapped his nerve was the uneasy awareness of how parochial most historical generalizations tended to be: and here again Füter had blazed the trail. For centuries historians had behaved as though Europe—the *oikoumenê* of antiquity—was the whole world, an adequate base for the formulation of overall laws. In the first decade of this century two factors simultaneously arose to undermine such a view. First, there was the meteoric rise to world stature of China, Japan, and the United States. Next—and perhaps more influential still—came the new sciences of archaeology and anthropology. By revealing ancient civilizations of great achievement and complexity which yet remained outside the traditional stream of European culture, they effectively shattered the Hegelian myth that Europe had a monopoly of progress. By analysing the historical evidence of artifacts, they both forced the historian to take cognizance of the social sciences, and cast grave doubts on the validity of documentary evidence. A document could lie, distort, and conceal; whereas an artifact was an unconscious and therefore much surer guide to the society that produced it.

Such developments were entirely commendable, and have, indeed, revolutionized historical method. Nevertheless, for all that they forced historians—and others—to become more self-conscious, to question their own assumptions and beliefs with greater rigour, they still contained considerable potential dangers. The chief of these is the inevitable temptation to use one or more of the new disciplines as a universal explanation for any and every phenomenon. Marxist historiography, whatever its stimulus-value in the economic field, is no more an absolute substitute for rational critical thought than any other theory. Cultural anthropology is a useful ancillary tool for the historian: it is not a panacea for all historiographical ills, much less an overall substitute for history. The error may be in the first instance semantic: its consequences are incalculable. Insensibly the historian will slip away once more from Füter's hard-won position of self-knowledge. False analogies with biology and physics will lull him into carelessness by convincing him that scientific objectivity is, after all, obtainable. Once again the historical world will fall into the role of patient or corpse, according to the predilection of each new historicist: to be cured or dissected by a superhuman surgeon, mysteriously immune from the diseases he is investigating, and who yet disarms criticism by repeatedly assuring the world that he is as other men. History, *pace* Ford, may not be bunk, but historicism, in any form, almost certainly is.

The great danger then, is scientific complacency. It is still only too easy to impose on the past a total pattern—Catholic or Communist, economic or psychological or sociological—which has no overall relevance to it. The crux of historical method is the necessity to reconcile moral judgments with the essential relativity inherent in history. Ethics and social sanctions no less than religious creeds or acknowledged moralities fluctuate wildly from culture to culture and from one age to the next. Not even the best historian is immune from his unacknowledged, unconscious prejudices. In his last, unfinished book Marc Bloch wrote: 'Whoever lacks the strength, while seated at his desk, to rid his mind of the virus of the present may readily permit its poison to infiltrate even a commentary on the *Iliad* or the *Rama-yana*.'

Many curious and arbitrary conventions continue to delimit historical methodology. Selection and emphasis have always been at the mercy of current *mores*, whether religious, political, or social: terms of reference have inevitably been defined so as to agree with fashionable ideas and concepts. With so essentially subjective a discipline as historical study, which lacks even the quasi-objective framework of the natural sciences, it is hard to see how such an occupational hazard could well be avoided. When the potential field is so enormous, selection cannot be avoided; and every age, not unnaturally, will select aspects of the past which have most relevance to contemporary problems. For example, till recently technology was believed to be irrelevant to history, as were many other collateral subjects; and a good case could be made out for this having been (with reservations) true. That it is quite patently not true today does not necessarily affect the general issue. There was, too, as the late Professor Gordon Childe pointed out, an unspoken 'conviction that war should form a central theme in history'. Seeley, in 1883, could proclaim that 'history is past politics, and present politics future history'. Professor Momigliano has chronicled the long struggle, from the seventeenth century onwards, between professional historians and those amateur antiquarians who were unorthodox enough to prefer 'travel to the emendation of texts, and altogether subordinated literary texts to coins, statues, vases, and inscriptions'. Text-books, as Bloch said, are admirable tools of sclerosis.

Few delusions have proved more dangerous or more pernicious

than the aptly named Catastrophic Theory, which sees kings, Pharaohs, and other such potentates as the single efficient cause of all historical events, and which prompted Pascal's famous remark, that if Cleopatra's nose had been shorter, the shape of the world would have been changed. It seems unlikely, nevertheless, that the present age, for all its enlightenment, will see an end of such theories: they will simply assume a different shape. 'If we wish our civilization to survive', Professor Karl Popper wrote in 1944, 'we must break with the habit of deference to great men'. It is not hard to see what prompted that particular *obiter dictum*: and we should not readily assume that the value-judgment underlying it has any more absolute validity than the historically conditioned hero-worship which it dislodged. The historian today, whatever his chosen field of research, is inevitably affected by the world-shaking events which the last fifty years have produced. He has become acquainted with the totalitarian state at first hand; he knows from bitter experience what a dictator means in terms of human lives. His traditions and theories have been prized loose from the quiet channels of centuries. He understands the brutal realities of torture and total war, which were merely words to his predecessors. (How many nineteenth-century historians, I wonder, ever themselves witnessed such violent and bloody events as they so blandly described, or even heard a shot fired in anger?) His critical faculties have been sharpened to deal with the insidious and all-pervasive weapon of propaganda, and the spread of psychological knowledge has forced him to re-assess his approach to historical motive—just as the spread of Marxism has made him more aware of the economic factors underlying all human action.

We see, then, that the historian's millennium is no nearer than it ever was, that we are, in the last resort, merely better equipped than our ancestors to comprehend certain aspects of the past to which they turned a blind or uncomprehending eye. However, if the present can illuminate the past, it must also, inevitably, distort it. With the multiplication both of sources of evidence and the techniques for its deliberate manipulation, the problem is, indeed, more complicated than ever before. Yet ultimately progress in method *has* been made. If we are assailed by peculiarly virulent temptations in applying our minds to history, we have also acquired a far better equipment to aid us in combating error: the balance works out just in our favour. Scientific methodology may not have eliminated our prejudices, but it has at least taught us to allow for them. Study of semantics has made us sensitive to the nuances of linguistic evidence, and enabled us to recognize the associative emotional aura surrounding such potent words as *feudalism, proletariat, capitalism, democracy,* or even *the Middle Ages.* Comparative anthropology has instilled into our minds the realization that human standards are relative, varying from century to century as well as from country to country. These problems are sharply relevant to the study of ancient, as of more recent history; we ought to consider, first, how the classical scholar has dealt with them, and, second, how they modify our attitude to the ancient historians themselves.

II

It would be idle to pretend that the study of ancient history today is in an altogether satisfactory state. The difficulties confronting the modern historian of the ancient world are, broadly, those with which his mediaeval or contemporary colleague also has to deal: that is, historiographical considerations of the changing human climate. Few classical scholars are seriously interested in problems of historical method; and in two of their three main fields they have, on the whole, been able to side-track conceptual difficulties. Roman historiography remains dominated by the gigantic shadow of Theodor Mommsen; and oriental history, as Professor Momigliano well put it, 'is still in that happy stage in which the almost vertiginous increase of evidence lends plausibility to the convention that thinking is a work of supererogation for the historian'.

But Greek history is devoid of either of these two doubtful advantages; and it is here that doubts have arisen and multiplied—

doubts which, in spite of Mommsen, have equal validity for Rome and for Greece. As long ago as 1872 Fustel de Coulanges foresaw the distortion of historical evidence to partisan ends, a return for the worst motives to those *a priori* methods which Hegel had upheld and Niebuhr condemned. One thinks at once of Droysen, with—in Croce's words—'his lyrical aspiration towards the strong centralized state in his history of Macedonia, that Prussia of Hellas'; of Grote and his admirable but dangerous bias towards democracy—even of the Athenian variety; of Thierry glorifying Jacques Bonhomme, of Mommsen and his obsessional Caesarism. Today—thus upholding the sneer that ancient historians tend to be several jumps behind their more up-to-date counterparts—the arena has been invaded by the champions of Marxism, racialism, determinism, even of psycho-analysis: *a priori* methods have regained at least a foothold in classical studies and archaeology alike. The historical bias during the present century has swung sharply from the politico-religious to the socio-economic. The notion of progress (in any sense of the word) has suffered severe modifications where it has not altogether collapsed. It has become only too easy to sympathize with Droysen's acid complaint that Ranke had 'the objectivity of a eunuch'.

All these phenomena require the student of Greek and Roman history to ask himself some pertinent and searching general questions. During the second half of the nineteenth century, with the upsurge of nationalism in Europe and the absorption of the best classical historians in modern problems, Thucydides and Tacitus were no longer related to living history, but turned over to the dusty mercies of academic *Gelehrter*. Europe, modern Europe, was supposed to have outgrown their problems. Today we know that Thucydides, whatever his faults, could see further than Metternich, and that we have not yet been civilized out of Corcyraean *stasis*. The ancient historians still have a vital task to perform in shaping our historical awareness, and their modern interpreters must shoulder a corresponding responsibility.

Yet, in spite of complicating factors such as Marxism—to which one might add both the theological and existential approaches—classical historiography is still very much in the doldrums. There has always been a tendency to regard authors such as Herodotus and his successors as creators of great literature rather than historical analysts, and to admire them in a somewhat uncritical spirit. In this, as so many other classical fields, we are cramped by the dead hand of traditionalism. To criticize the methodology adopted by such venerable figures savours of iconoclasm; and many modern scholars have skilfully dodged the issue by concentrating on minute areas of research, or compiling strictly factual commentaries, where all value-judgments on the large scale are left in abeyance. Some bolder spirits—Rostovtzeff, Ronald Syme, Ure, M. I. Finley and one or two others—have grappled with contemporary problems in classical historiography: but they would be the first to admit how much remains to be done still.

No one, perhaps, has achieved more in this field than Professor Momigliano; and one of his most permanent achievements has been to clarify the relative positions and functions of historian and antiquary from the Renaissance to the nineteenth century, explaining both the antecedents and the results—which were very far-reaching—of such an odd dualism. For the cause, we must go back to the historiographical attitudes of the Greeks and Romans themselves: to the twin concepts, so alien to us, yet so persistent in their influence, of universalism and moral elevation. As regards the latter, both Cicero and Quintilian took it for granted that history was an *opus oratorium*, a species of moral instruction by example. (Many earlier historians virtually assumed this, even if they did not admit it: a point to which I shall return later.) It is instructive, for instance, to remember how Cato prepared himself for suicide by reading Plato's *Phaedo*. This concept—with the prescribed texts, such as Livy, which accompanied it—was taken over uncritically by the Renaissance, and only finally destroyed by the *Aufklärung*. It may be that ancient historiography is still imperfect; but while this view persisted, historical method in the modern sense simply did not exist.

As for universalism, the *katholikê historia* of Polybius and

Posidonius which regarded history as a cosmology (in their case of the Roman Empire), its implications were to affect such dissimilar *a priori* thinkers as St Augustine, Hegel, Spengler, and Professor Toynbee. Indeed, this concept is at the back of every historical monist who has ever attempted to impose some kind of rhythm or overall predictable pattern on the chaotic mass of human history. There seems an ineradicable urge in the human mind to create myths, patterns, and symbols: an urge from which historians are no more exempt than other men. An eternal order of history suggested by the astronomical movements of the heavenly bodies is about as logical as a horoscope; but this mystical analogy has hypnotized a large number of otherwise intelligent writers: it seems only one degree less arbitrary than pure determinism, what Croce pleasantly described as 'the natural law of the circle in human affairs', or the mediaeval thesis that God willed both the communication-system of the Roman Empire and the spread of that ancient *lingua franca*, the Greek *koinê*, in order to facilitate the dissemination of the Gospel.

Those post-Renaissance scholars who (presumably hypnotized by the magical authority of their written word) elevated the classical historians into the sole—and canonical—sources for classical history did little but cripple the development of the subject for at least a century. Instead of restricting themselves with religious care to the political or military aspects of the subject which their exemplars stressed, and echoing their every opinion with slavishly uncritical fidelity, they would have done better to ponder Polybius' comments on the desirability of utilizing primary evidence wherever available. In fact, while these so-called historians were sedulously transcribing Livy, the foundations of future historical method were actually being laid by the antiquaries: by such men as Sigonio or Fulvio Orsini, who first demonstrated the difference between original and derivative authorities, and from whose researches the sciences of numismatics and epigraphy were later to flower. It is a mark of the peculiar respect accorded the classical historians that this dichotomy prevailed in no other historical field; indeed, it is only in very recent times that classical scholars as a whole have lost their contempt for ancient history as a self-sufficient discipline, let alone for its ancillary aids such as archaeology.

By the end of the seventeenth century however, the situation, if not improved much, was at any rate radically altered. The iron grip of theology was loosening from historical theory; and as a direct result of the reaction there developed that historical Pyrrhonism which opened the way for the philosopher-historians of the Enlightenment. As Dr G. P. Gooch remarks, 'within the lifetime of Fontenelle France passed from the world of Bossuet to the age of Voltaire, from Port-Royal to the *Encyclopédie*'. But, as so often happens in similar circumstances, the revolutionaries lost as much as they gained. For Voltaire and his adherents *érudit* became an unqualified term of abuse, and the scrupulous examination of evidence was swept away in the general holocaust of pedantry. 'Malheur aux détails', Voltaire cried, 'c'est une vermine qui tue les grands ouvrages!' Nor were these savants, after a century which had endured the extremely vocal squabbling of Catholics, Lutherans, Calvinists, and Jansenists, any less aprioristic themselves in their evaluation of ancient religious phenomena. Divination was the invention 'du premier fripon qui rencontra un imbécile',[1] and Plato was decried in favour of Locke. Almost the only writer—certainly the only historian—who completely kept his head in this historiographical maelstrom was Edward Gibbon.

It was Gibbon's great quality (a quality he shares—though he shares little else—with Ranke) to be essentially open-minded and scientific in his approach to historical method. He was well aware that the Voltairean revolution had much on its side, besides being in personal sympathy with its ethical standpoint. He saw that it had broken out of the strait-jacket of political and military

---

[1] This assumption is still liable to appear in unlikely places. A recent *magnum opus* on the history of the Delphic Oracle carries precisely the same implication throughout—though the authors, intent apparently on hedging their bets, are judiciously fair when forced to make any generalizations about the Oracle's authenticity. It is their incidental rationalizations and talk of political deceit which betrays their own basic position.

narrative to analyse such basic elements of civilization as law, religion, education and commerce—an enormous methodological advance on the essentially static concepts of antiquity, and one which opened the way for later analyses of historical and social institutions in dynamic, evolutionary terms. He shared the optimism of the *philosophes* while preserving an antiquary's respect for primary details. His *Decline and Fall* combines the methods of both schools to bridge the gap between past and future; its survival today is a tribute as much to Gibbon's critical eclecticism as to his grand style and sweeping narrative. An incidental result of his *magnum opus* was the unification of antiquarian and historian in one person; and his challenge temporarily defeated *érudit* and *philosophe* alike. As Professor Momigliano says:

> The combination of philosophic history with the antiquarian's method of research became the aim which many of the best historians of the nineteenth century proposed to themselves. It is still the aim that many of us propose to ourselves. It means two difficult things: the constant repression of the *a priori* attitude inherent in the generalizing approach of the philosophic historian and, on the other hand, the avoidance of the antiquarian mentality with its fondness for classification and for irrelevant detail.

But this harmonious balance has seldom been achieved, or long maintained, against the inroads of human frailty. The history of historiography in Europe resembles a pendulum swinging backwards and forwards, from mythopoeia to what Collingwood scornfully termed scissors-and-paste history: action and reaction. It is man's myth-making propensities that hold real danger for the historian, combined with his quite alarming delusions of objectivity: the attempt to reconcile unwelcome evidence with an *a priori* pattern may violate facts and misrepresent the truth, but it is infinitely less dangerous than the firm conviction that no *a priori* convictions exist in the mind at all. Perhaps our critical tools are sharper today, our capacity to discount bias better developed under the challenge of propaganda and semantics: the danger remains. So, too, does the historian's perennial task—to search, with all the knowledge at his disposal, for the elusive truth that somewhere underlies his material. The classical historian more than most can echo those famous lines from *East Coker*:

> And what there is to conquer
> By strength and submission, has already been discovered
> Once or twice, or several times, by men whom one cannot hope
> To emulate—but there is no competition—
> There is only the fight to recover what has been lost
> And found and lost again and again . . .

To each generation, not a new truth, but a fresh facet of that multiple prismatic Truth-in-itself which we can never hope to see whole. It is in that spirit that I now turn to discuss two Greek historians whose influence on their successors was incalculable, and who still have the power to stimulate, provoke and enlighten us today.

III

In the Museo Nazionale of Naples there stands a double bust, of Herodotus and Thucydides: back to back, staring in opposite directions, irreconcilable yet indivisible. The economical sculptor embodies in his work the public opinion of these two historians, an opinion which, with modifications, has largely survived into our own times. Here is Herodotus: a garrulous, credulous collector of sailors' stories and Oriental *novelle*, ahistorical in method, factually inaccurate, superstitious and pietistic, politically innocent, his guiding motto *cherchez la femme et n'oubliez pas le Dieu*. There is Thucydides: the first scientific historian, the embodiment of scrupulous research and painstaking exegesis, impartial to the point of divinity, hovering above the scenes he describes like Hardy's President of the Immortals; indifferent to gods or women, his whole awareness concentrated on Man as the Protagorean centre of the civilized world.

It is a well-known diptych; and the fact that there is hardly a word of truth in it will not prevent its exerting a (probably subconscious) influence on those laymen who today approach

Thucydides and Herodotus for the first time—perhaps via the pleasant new translations offered by the Penguin Classics, which leave Everyman (like his Renaissance forbears) with little more than a plain text on which to base his conclusions. If he has some interest in history, and an ability to come to terms with his own prejudices, Everyman should considerably revise any previous opinions he may have formed. Further, being unencumbered by the influential findings of Victorian scholars, he will assess the material with a lively twentieth-century eye; and if he finds an archetypal familiarity in Thucydidean politics, he will be equally amazed by the unexpected modernity and breadth of Herodotus' historical method.

Let us suppose that (for the sake of chronology) he reads Herodotus first. He is probably familiar with the outline of the Persian Wars that culminated in Salamis and Plataea: how will this Father of History tackle his theme? At first, it appears, in a pleasant but irresponsible way. A cynical story or two about the origins of the Trojan War (*cherchez la femme,* the reader repeats to himself), and, since Persia is to loom large in the narrative, a leisurely disquisition on Persian relations with Lydia. By the sixth book he will be convinced that Herodotus has a digression-neurosis, having reached the beginning of the actual war by way of such diverse subjects as Egyptian burial-customs, Paris and Helen, several studies in *dementia praecox* (Cleomenes, Cambyses), the tribal habits of the Libyans, Scythia and the Amazons, countless amusing tales (including an excellent detective story), the whole regularly punctuated with the sayings of oracles, in which the writer appears to have unshakable faith.

But by the time the reader closes the *Histories* he should have come to see that (as the late Sir John Myres pointed out) the overall scheme has an ineluctable 'pedimental' pattern; that the diverse material is all necessary for the method adopted, and marshalled with extraordinary skill. Herodotus believed (what we take for granted, but in the Periclean Age was revolutionary) that geography, geology, anthropology, and ethnology—though he had no concept of them as sciences in themselves—are of the greatest value for elucidating historical problems. It is easy to pass over the effects of this in the *Histories*, more particularly as it bred no tradition. Thucydides ignored it; so did his successors, both Greek and Roman. It was not resuscitated till after the Renaissance, and even then not—as we have already seen—by scholars and historians so much as antiquaries, and also by the independent tradition that threw up Montaigne and, later, Montesquieu. With the flowering of anthropological method at the turn of this century, and the confirmation by archaeologists or orientalists of many of his more incredible assertions, Herodotus was due for rehabilitation. But public legend dies hard; for too many the Father of History remains the Father of Lies.

Where Herodotus really differs from Thucydides is in personal temperament. So far as general method goes—with one or two significant exceptions—there is little to choose between them. As far as sources went, they were limited by external circumstances. Though both drew to some extent on written material (Herodotus names Hecataeus, and Thucydides Hellanicus) history in the fifth century B.C. was, as has been well said, the autobiography of an age. That is, it depended for its veracity on the evidence of eye-witnesses, and was thus limited largely to the period either of the historian's own life, or that of the immediately preceding generation. Both Herodotus and Thucydides recognized this, and were most painstaking in their collection and verification of facts; but Herodotus cast his net wider. (Thucydides *tells* us he is accurate, which tends to bias us unconsciously in his favour: in the last resort there is always a frightful temptation to take people at their own estimate if they are sufficiently self-assertive.) Where Herodotus saw the epic struggle of nations, Thucydides could only apprehend the tragedy of Homo Politicus: an attitude which explains his popularity with such a writer as Hobbes, who called him the 'most Politick Historiographer that ever writ', and meant it as an unqualified compliment.

Herodotus was, by birth and upbringing, an Ionian, a native of Halicarnassus on the eastern shores of the Aegean. The contact the Ionian Greeks maintained with the peoples of Asia Minor, and the fact that most of their large cities were clearing-houses for East-West trade, produced a cosmopolitanism of outlook, a breadth and tolerance, which are faithfully reflected in Herodotus' historical judgments. Here, we feel, is a man without bile, un-blinkered by a partial or parochial vision; and—curiously—more than Thucydides, a man without prejudices. His Parisian sense of humour, his sophisticated shrewdness—Herodotus' naïvety is a legend spread by the naïve—both spring from his Ionian back-ground no less than his assiduous travels. Indeed, in spite of his *penchant* for Athens, one suspects that the inhabitants of the Greek city-states, with their monadic chauvinism and ineradic-able quarrelsomeness, must have viewed his work with some irritation.

To them, as indeed to us, he was a very untypical Greek. His capacity to appreciate the Persian and other foreign points of view earned him the epithet *philobarbaros* from Plutarch ('wog-lover' would be a fair modern equivalent) in a piece unequivocally entitled *De Malignitate Herodoti*. Greek thought, in fact, was, with truly Hegelian paradoxicality, by its very nature opposed to con-structive historical method. The isolationism of the *polis*, the absence of any large overall political or philosophical system makes the contemporary ancient historian's task hard enough; it renders Herodotus' achievement almost unbelievable. He in-vented, *ex nihilo*, not only the art of history (the jump from the logographer is immeasurable) but also the artistic medium of prose; and he executed the *Histories* in the teeth of a rigorously anti-historical metaphysic which, with the advent of Platonism, closed in triumphantly for hundreds of years.

To understand this we have to remember the circumstances in which he wrote. To be a well-travelled Ionian was not enough; the time as much as the place produced the historian. The *Histories* were written during a period of peace and consolidation, when the afterglow of the Persian Wars still honoured the name at least of Pan-Hellenism. (This may also account in part for Hero-dotus' undoubted weakness where military strategy was con-cerned.) In Athens, Pericles was committed to his imperialist policy of expansion and domination; but war was not yet even the cloud he was later to see rising out of the Peloponnese.

Thus when we criticize Herodotus' apolitical attitude, his confusion over notions of causality, we should never forget the background of his work—or allow our own judgment to be coloured by later and perhaps less valid criteria. Grossly superstitious—in the sense of allowing himself to be duped by politically slanted myth or miracle—he most certainly was not; on the other hand, unlike some of his more arbitrarily rational successors, he was always ready to make allowance for the possible influence of religious belief or divine phenomena on human actions and motives. He accepted mankind as it was, in its multiplicity and confusion; he knew that there was no one thread to lead the historian through his labyrinth in search of truth, that he must unravel the whole tapestry of society before his task was done. Our estimate of his political capacity is bound to be coloured by the obsessive *Machtpolitik* of Thucydides: yet which of them saw the political aspect of history in better proportion? Herodotus had one great advantage, too, often forgotten: he lived in an age which was sure of itself. He had not suffered the psychological shock which war, plague, and personal failure were to bring on his successor. He was, in fact, a scientific humanist born out of his time; he belongs to the pioneering age of Montesquieu or Gibbon.

When our reader turns to the *Peloponnesian War* of Thucydides, he is in another world. 'My work', he reads, 'is not a piece of writing designed to meet the taste of an immediate public, but was done to last for ever.' While reflecting that the claim has been largely justified, he will probably at first find the extremely positive character of the writer a little distasteful. The studied use of the third-person singular should deceive no one: Thucydides is an extremely self-conscious writer—and consequently most interesting when he forgets himself. For example, the deliberate aim at creating an immortal masterpiece, while it argues a strongly developed formal *artistic* sense, also, and just for the same reason, makes the historical method chosen automatically suspect.

When the major aim is creative perfection, involving an overall symmetry of design in the widest sense, truth will almost inevitably be bent to fit the pattern, whether the artist realizes this or not.

From the first page we are in the presence of genius: but whether this genius is literary, historical, or even moral is another matter. After Herodotus' richly variegated narrative, with its neat sociological or psychological digressions, this naked chronicle of political and military action and debate, stripped—according to the author again—of every inessential, becomes very soon irritating: it is a part skilfully disguised as the whole. 'It may well be', Thucydides writes, 'that my history will seem less easy to read because of the absence in it of a romantic element'; and unless the reader is mentally alert he may fail to see just what a question-begging statement this is. It is Thucydides who decides, arbitrarily, what is 'romantic', just as he—equally arbitrarily—decides what, for his purposes, is 'inessential'. Both these pronouncements imply sweeping value-judgments.

Far from maintaining an Olympian balance, we see, Thucydides has a powerful range of prejudices and obsessions which he is at uncommon pains to conceal from his reader. Some are easier to pick out than others—the calculated anti-Herodoteanism, for instance: the significance of the Persian Wars is greatly underestimated. But on almost every page we must struggle to maintain our clarity of judgment under a ceaseless battering from Thucydides' deep-rooted ethical assumptions. These, being static in their essence, will not permit him to treat the movement of history in any developmental, dynamic sense. As Erich Auerbach wrote in *Mimesis,* during a brilliant analysis of ancient historiography:

> When we read Thucydides we get, aside from a continuous account of foreground events, nothing but considerations which are statically aprioristic and ethical in content, on such matters as human nature or fate, and which, though it is true that they are sometimes applied to specific situations, are of an absolute validity in themselves. ... The ethical and rhetorical approach are incompatible with a conception in which reality is a development of forces. Antique historiography gives us neither social history nor economic history

nor cultural history. These can only be inferred indirectly from the data presented.[2]

Over and above this, there is something peculiarly hypnotic about Thucydides—the sort of technique one associates with a persuasive advocate, and which is closely bound up with Thucydides' dramatic force, linguistic subtlety, and sheer emotional impact. (The rhetoric is always most notable when the need for persuasion is greatest.) Sometimes this hypnosis is so strong it enables the reader to overcome the greatest of all stumbling-blocks in the *Peloponnesian War*: the speeches.

'My method has been', Thucydides declares in a famous passage, 'while keeping as closely as possible to the general sense of the words that were actually used, to make the speakers say what, in my opinion, was called for by each situation.' In other words, it is virtually impossible to distinguish between historical *reportage* and the historian's interpretation; the actors are liable to become puppets without a hint given. Nor is it by any means certain that Thucydides *did*, in fact, adhere to the actual speeches, which, in any case, were seldom accurately transcribed. It is extremely suggestive that the Eighth Book, a rough unfinished draft, has no speeches in it whatsoever: it looks as though they were to be inserted afterwards, outside the normal process of historical reconstruction, as illustrations of the author's views on eternal moral problems. This may stimulate great art, but it is hardly good history. Grote argued long ago that the Melian Dialogue contained more imagination than truth, and time has done nothing to refute the charge. With growing uneasiness the reader notes the discrepancies between creative achievement, which is magnificent, and historical relevance, which is frequently questionable. We are so captivated by the dramatic splendours of Pericles' Funeral Oration that we fail to see it, in its context, as a macabre mockery of the military and political situation at the time it was composed: and the question lingers in our mind, whether Thucydides may not have inserted it where he did

[2] A possible exception might be made in the case of Herodotus: see above, pp. 64–5.

precisely with the intention of distracting us from its grim historical background, and reinforcing Pericles' moral stature at a moment when such reinforcement was badly needed.

It was Francis Cornford who first put his finger on the crucial point in Thucydides' psychology. *Thucydides Mythistoricus* has suffered unduly from scholars because it advanced an untenable historical theory about certain specific events; its true value is in its *exposé* of Thucydidean method. Cornford's major hypothesis, now gaining increasingly wide acceptance, was that Thucydides saw the Peloponnesian War as the working out of a fatalistic tragedy, and in fact composed it as such, in more or less Aeschylean terms. One has only to compare the great Messenger Speech from *The Persians* with Thucydides' description of the last battle in Syracuse harbour to see how true this charge is. In Thucydides, Greek thought, having been strained out of its natural mould by the empiricism of Herodotus, returns to monadic absolutism once more.

If the Peloponnesian War was tragedy, it follows that it was also a near-Platonic *paradeigma* of eternal psychological laws; and thus we are faced with a Thucydides whose concept of the supernatural, unknown perhaps to himself, was somewhat more tendentious than his great predecessor's. He was the supreme fatalist: 'the peculiar ironies of chance', as David Grene observes while discussing the political philosophy of Thucydides and Plato, 'inspired him with a kind of horror'. (We remember his treatment of Nicias—not to mention the massacre of Mycalessus.) Together with this comes the increasing certainty that his vaunted impartiality too often consists in his own reassurances and nothing more. For a historian who professes it his business to analyse the *causes* of a war, he is guilty, at the best, of remarkable obscurity: it is not entirely coincidental that no real agreement has ever been reached among modern scholars over just what those causes were. Not only that: he practises the most flagrant *suppressio veri* when it suits him, especially in the matter of the Megarian Decrees. He idolizes Pericles, even though Pericles' policy was directly responsible for the plague which struck them both down; but on the whole he shows a marked bias against the

Alcmaeonidae, and his portrait of Cleon is a vicious, if brilliant, caricature, loaded with political and class prejudice.

Here Hobbes, as we might expect, saw the truth. 'For his opinion touching the government of the State', Hobbes wrote, 'it is manifest that he least of all liked the Democracy. . . . It seemeth that as he was of Regal descent, so he best approved of the *Regal Government*.' Now Thucydides' royal descent was a Thracian one; he owned gold-mines near Pangaeus and his father's name was Olorus. He was connected by blood to Cimon and Miltiades; and thus his partisanship for Pericles was the enthusiasm of a convert from the opposition camp. He saw Pericles, not as the leader of the democracy, but as that almost untranslatable thing, προστάτης τοῦ δήμου — a virtual aristocratic dictator, in whom the qualities of blood and intellect mingled harmoniously. It must have required some casuistry to square this admiration with the conduct of the Peloponnesian War—and, indeed, with its somewhat dubious antecedents.

This historiographical regression from the position achieved by Herodotus does not impair Thucydides' value for us *per se*; but it does mean that the value itself requires re-defining. In particular, warned by Professor Popper's strictures in *The Poverty of Historicism*, we should keep a weather eye open for Thucydides' use of false analogies from other disciplines. In particular, it is an interesting and plausible theory which points to the influence on Thucydidean history of the practice and dialectic of Hippocratic medicine. This not only shows out in such obvious set-pieces as the description of the Plague, but is extended half-metaphorically into less purely physical connexions, such as Thucydides' politico-psychological preoccupation with *stasis* (Corcyra) or *Machtpolitik* (the Melian Dialogue). For this historian, we see, the 'body politic' is a good deal more than a phrase. Like a doctor he is attempting for much of the time to formulate general laws from the evidence of his diagnosis, to prognosticate for the future; and this is grossly to mistake the historian's function. Though as an object-lesson in perennial human psychology these analyses are unrivalled, they have very little to do with history as such.

Le style est l'homme même. The differing qualities of style in Herodotus and Thucydides are immediately striking, and psychologically important. Herodotus has what Dahlmann once called 'that happy and winning style which cannot be attained by any art or pathetic excitement, and is found only where manners are true to nature'; he is an artist in control of his medium and at peace with the world. Thucydides, on the other hand, was a by-word for complexity even in Cicero's time. All who have studied him in the original have been appalled by his packed, thorny, harsh periods, often barely grammatical—the prose of a man straining to express the inexpressible. Besides, Thucydides' style is *suae linguae* as well as *sui generis*: the old Attic which read to Athenians of the fourth century B.C. much as Doughty's *Arabia Deserta* does to us.

In these sharply differing styles the essential difference between Herodotus and Thucydides becomes apparent. One could say that Herodotus was free from disillusion, if that did not imply that disillusion could be equated with reality; or that war (for Thucydides the logical end of all political conflict) was more real a thing than peace. The great pages of tragedy that make up the *Peloponnesian War* were written by a general who failed in his duty and was exiled, who suffered the Plague and yet lived on, neurotic and melancholy, to pen the epitaph on his country, his leader, and his way of life:

> In the strange impersonality of self-sacrifice, in the desperate power and will to create something greater than the reach of a single man's ambition or benevolence, Thucydides found that which he called virtue. (Grene, *op. cit.*)

Herodotus is the true historian: he spreads out the linked chain of past events in all their human and social complexity, setting them against their background of belief, love, custom, intrigue, ambition; amused often, good-humoured and tolerant always, the cheerful guide to foreign territories, the unfamiliar ways of the desert or the steppe. But Thucydides is the psychologist, the chronicler of those

who told their lies too late
Caught in the eternal factions and reactions
Of the city-state.

We recognize our kinship with him; he is of ours and all time in his bitter political obsessions, his sense of the tragic, his instinct for pattern, the crushing inevitability with which he invests his events. To read these two great works is to explore in turn the world and the human heart. But the human heart is only a part of history.

Note: Since the views expressed in the final section of this essay—especially as regards the relative status of Herodotus and Thucydides—have been gaining ground recently (see, e.g. the Introduction to Mr M. I. Finley's *The Greek Historians*) it may be as well to state here that my own piece was written and published in 1954, when, to the best of my knowledge, I was a lone voice crying in a solidly pro-Thucydidean wilderness. I have reprinted it substantially without alterations.

4

The Garden and the Porch

The history of Roman thought is a comparatively neglected subject. Scholars who occupy themselves with ancient philosophy turn, almost inevitably, to Greece; the attention they pay an author is in direct proportion to his originality, and often disregards the historical context in which his work reached fruition. The long shadows of Plato and Aristotle hang over all other philosophers, and very often prejudice the value-judgments and moral assessments which modern scholars make apropos their position in antiquity. But the purely philosophical value of any school of thought, besides being arguable *per se*, bears no direct relation to the light it may throw on its period in more general terms; and an historical document is no less valid through lack of originality. As Professor M. L. Clarke observed, in the preface to his book *The Roman Mind*:

> [The interest of Roman thought] lies not so much in the originality or intrinsic value of the doctrines held as in the fact that particular men held them, and in the relation of the doctrines to the political and literary activities of their adherents. It has often happened in history that ideas have had as powerful an influence outside as within the country of their origin, and it might well be maintained that the Hellenistic philosophies exercised a more important influence in Rome than in the Greek world.

It might indeed; and to this conclusion a rider should be added. Because the two major Hellenistic philosophies *were* Hellenistic, because they were in many ways anti-Platonic, because they were suspected of pragmatic utilitarianism, and modified to serve morally suspect Roman ends—hedonism on the one hand, quiet-

74

ism on the other—their true achievement has till recent times been consistently under-estimated, and, in the case of Epicureanism, actively obscured.

Philosophically, the dominant Roman creed was Stoicism—a Stoicism adapted to accommodate the Roman predilection for family tradition, religious observance, and participation in public life. But this Roman Stoicism had also observed many Epicurean tenets to mitigate its original harshness: the Roman mind, in philosophy no less than religion, had a marked gift for somewhat indiscriminate eclecticism. Epicureanism itself, more dogmatic and sectarian, had made many converts in Italy during the late Republic: its emphasis on personal individualism, its abhorrence of political ambition, its spirit of communal charity, its practical (though not, as is often supposed, utilitarian) ethics—all these appealed strongly to the provincial middle and lower classes. To many thinkers also, after the Civil Wars, a withdrawal from worldly affairs seemed the only possible solution, the only answer to a chaotic state of public moral flux.

But with the coming of the Empire, and Augustus' religious revival, Epicureanism lost ground rapidly to its more pliable rival: the movement towards a socially modified Stoicism is well brought out in the poems of Virgil and Horace. It is difficult to avoid the feeling that philosophy for the Romans meant little more than elaborate justification in theory for the immediate political or psychological *fait accompli*; that their fluctuations in intellectual thought tended to be symptoms rather than causes of social change. Cicero's syncretic vacillations confirm this. The characteristic incapacity—not to say indifference—he shows for original abstract thought led him into some strange predicaments when his borrowed Greek universals clashed with his own pragmatic conservatism.[1] When the Roman found any ethical stumbling block in his philosophy that would not square with his

[1] To take a random example: the Roman urge for personal fame could ill adapt itself to philosophic self-abnegation; and Cicero's compromise is typical. *Philosophiae quidem praecepta noscenda,* he wrote, *vivendum autem civiliter*: 'one should know what philosophy teaches, but live like a gentleman.'

traditional beliefs or way of life, he did not mend his ways; he changed his philosophy to fit the *status quo*. It may be worth while tracing the original outline of his two dominant philosophical systems, and observing what use they were put to at Rome.

Few philosophies can have endured such hostility, neglect, or sheer misrepresentation through the centuries as Epicureanism; few can have more deliberately provoked their opponents into violent and emotional counter-propaganda. When we remember that Epicurus set himself to undermine the foundations of Platonism, at a time when Plato commanded a large majority among literate intellectuals; when we add to this his uncompromising attack on rhetorical education (a most lucrative source of income for the sophist), and his reasoned denial of immortality—then it is not so much the misrepresentation of his tenets which surprises us, as the bare fact of their scattered survival. In the Middle Ages the creed could still arouse the passions of Dante, who devised a particularly grim fate for its adherents in the Sixth Circle of the Inferno; and *apikoros* became a Jewish synonym for unbeliever. The Renaissance found Epicurus largely neglected except in France, where Gassendi, by a curious irony, wrongly took one of his doctrines to mean 'that there is nothing in the intellect which has not been in the senses'—thus earning him a false reputation as an empiricist and, incidentally, providing a platform for Locke and his successors, down to Professor Ayer. It has, indeed, been Epicurus' fate to breed fallacies. Till recent years he was generally regarded as not only an empiricist but a moral invalid, a political nihilist, an enemy of religion, and an ignorant opponent of all culture. These errors were often linguistic in origin: where texts were doubtful they were liable to be interpreted or even emended in favour of a hostile preconception.[2]

---

[2] A study of Usener's *Epicurea* (1887) at once makes this clear. The movement towards rehabilitation was begun by Ettore Bignone in his *L'Aristotele perduto e la formazione filosofica di Epicuro* (1936), developed in 1946 by Father A. J. Festugière's *Épicure et ses Dieux* (English tr. by C. W. Chilton, 1956), and most fully presented by Professor N. W. De Witt in *Epicurus and His Philosophy* (1954). Any future account of Epicureanism will have to reckon with these three works. De Witt is most valuable on questions of pure

It was a troubled and changing world into which, in 341 B.C., Epicurus was born on the island of Samos; a world to be over-shadowed during his youth by the gigantic figure of Alexander. The collapse of the city-state as a political entity had effects extending far beyond the purely political sphere; its psychological effects extended to every aspect of Greek life and conduct. An *ethos* previously geared to the *polis* was disintegrated into indivi-dualism and cosmopolitanism. Theopompus, born only some ten years after Aristotle, commented scathingly on the selfishness, degeneracy, and hedonism which characterized the Athenian of his day. Isocrates' rich prolix rhetoric insensibly passed into scurrilous personal biography. Mythological comedy was re-placed by flashy realism; the parasite, the cook, the greedy *hetaira* now held the mirror up to mankind. Art told the same story: stylized idealism passed by gradual degrees into individualistic portraiture. Parrhasius' 'rose-fed' Theseus was transformed into the 'beef-fed' Theseus of Euphranor.[3]

But there was another, less obvious, yet far more important change. Religion, in the old sense, was undermined; idealism was challenged by scientific method, universality gave way to particu-larism. The loss of one's *polis* meant spiritual, no less than political, disorientation: in the vast cosmopolitan cities which sprang up under the Lagids and Seleucids the Greek had his first true experience of personal solitude. The local gods who protected the *polis* were ill-adapted to succour the individual; they clearly lacked universal validity, as did every aspect of moral or political belief which rested on the city-state as its prime foundation. Ceremony and tradition, as always, long outlasted the inner con-viction on which they depended. The temples remained full; Demosthenes still had a year or two left in which to thunder against the Macedonian. But the civic diehards, for all that they

philosophical interpretation and details of Epicurus' life; while Father Festugière emphasizes the mystical element in his teaching, and presents an excellent account of fourth-century moral and religious problems against their very relevant historical background.

[3] For these changes see further Professor T. B. L. Webster's interesting study, *Art and Literature in Fourth Century Athens* (1956).

had executed Socrates and exiled Aristotle, were fighting a doomed rearguard action. The barriers between Greek and Barbarian were being broken down; cult-associations in honour of foreign gods were springing up, which cut across a devotee's clan or family allegiances. Finally, the despotic monarchies, into which the Greek world was parcelled by the Diadochi after Alexander's death, compelled each individual—a citizen in the full sense no longer—to reconsider his personal ethics.

The first question he now had to ask himself was: 'Must I remain aloof, or act? And if the latter, according to what rules?' It was an agonizing dilemma, exacerbated by what Father Festugière has described as

> an over-refined state of civilization which could only make con-
> sciences more sensitive and, therefore, more uneasy. Man was
> supported no longer, he felt himself to be alone; and in this condition
> he became a prey to scruples, remorse and spiritual disturbances
> which he felt more keenly than before. It would not be long before
> there would be a need for moral direction, before the Sage would be
> essentially a spiritual director.

Yet the redrawing of the Greek political map was not directly responsible for this state of affairs; it merely precipitated an already inevitable crisis. Long before Alexander, the Ionian philosophers had posited a First Cause which it was difficult to reconcile with local gods, as we can see from the satirical verses of Xenophanes:

> Ethiopians tell us the gods are flat-nosed niggers,
> While Thracians swear they have blue eyes and red hair . . .
> And if oxen or horses or lions possessed hands,
> And could draw like men, and like men fashion works of art,
> Then horses would represent God as a horse, and oxen
> As an ox no doubt: each after his own image.   (Frr. 171-2)

In identifying this First Cause with an absolute, unchangeable, Divine Being, beyond all perception, the symbol of truth, good-ness and beauty, the apex of the Ideas, the keystone (as Father Festugière put it) of rational order, Plato—unaware, in all likeli-hood, of what he was doing—drove a psychological wedge between his own concepts and traditional religion, to the latter's detriment. (The notion of local deities as mere manifestations of the single Divine Being could not wholly bridge an ever-widening gap.)

Politically, too, Plato's writings were retrograde: his philosopher-kings were to rule an ideal city-state of which the reality was already passing away. But in the field of cosmology he developed a thesis which was to have enormous influence in the ancient world, and which Epicurus attacked with every weapon at his disposal: the immanence of the Divine Mind in the heavenly bodies, whose movements appeared to embody the ordered planning of a cosmic God. Men who had seen their own world fall in ruins about them now gazed with awe and hope at those majestic constellations, eager to accept a doctrine which, however vulnerable, might restore their faith in a theocentrically ordered universe, and give them a basic pattern round which to shape their lives. This profoundly anti-scientific cosmology, which obscured the pioneering work done by the Ionians and held up the progress of astronomy for centuries, had the one great advantage of offering emotional satisfaction. Truth could follow later.

But for every intellectual thinker capable of grasping the semi-mystical implications of Plato's celestial cosmology—and mentally conditioned to accept its aprioristic premises—there were many ordinary men who remained wretchedly disillusioned, politically cynical, conscious only that the world was out of joint and held no hope of fulfilment for them. They, like many people in our own time, saw intellectual idealism as the root of all evil. Though they were losing their religion, they remained grossly superstitious, as we can see from Theophrastus; and their cynicism manifested itself in a half-sycophantic, half self-mocking worship of their earthly masters—a phenomenon not unparalleled today in, say, the Union of Soviet Writers. When the victorious Demetrius Poliorcetes and his wife entered Athens in 290 B.C. as 'gods made manifest', the prizewinning paean in their honour contained these words:

> The other gods are far away, or they have no ears, or they do not exist, or they pay not the slightest attention to us: but you we see face to face, not in wood or in stone but in truth and reality.

79

Such were the people to whom Epicurus made his appeal, offering them not cold abstractions but a way of life, not philosophers to rule over them but human communion and fellowship, not impalpable yet ineluctable gods, or grim determinism, but freedom from the fear of death, and in life the pursuit of true happiness and pleasure. The original opponents of Epicureanism were not (as is so often assumed from Cicero's evidence) the Stoics, but the Platonists; and indeed it would be hard to find a more striking contrast than the aristocratic, authoritarian Plato, preaching his Ideal State to a select company of exclusively male intellectuals, and the schoolmaster's son from Samos, the 'natural pragmatist', as De Witt put it, 'impatient of all knowledge that lacks relevance to action', who opened his doors to men and women alike, who welcomed courtesans as he would greet great ladies, who recognized pleasure as the *telos* of existence, and life itself as the greatest happiness.

When Epicurus purchased the famous Garden in Athens in 306 B.C. he had already spent some fifteen years meditating on and perfecting his philosophy. An unfortunate experience at Mytilene, where his heretical opinions provoked official action against him, led him thenceforward to teach only in private seclusion; and the violent ends of Demosthenes and Hyperides in Athens, about the time of his military service there, must have reinforced his distaste for the ambitions and follies of political careerism. Yet he did not, as is often supposed, condemn participation in political life out of hand, so much as the pursuit of worldly success which it was liable to involve. 'The wise man on occasion', he wrote—and one cannot but be reminded of Confucius—'will pay court to a monarch. . . . We must explain how best he will guard the end as established by Nature, and how a man will not deliberately from the outset proceed to obtain the offices in the gift of the multitudes.'

Homo sum: humani nihil a me alienum puto: the authentic Epicurean echo sums up his liberal attitude to life. For the rest of his days he taught in the Garden, surrounded by his disciples and cherished friends: unswerving in his dogmatism, loved by his associates, vilified by his philosophical opponents, who were not, in their turn, spared his talent for satirical pamphleteering. He died in 270 B.C. of an agonizing internal disease—his health had always been poor—yet steadfastly happy, conscious of having lived to the full in accordance with his own precepts. The atmosphere of the Garden with its monthly communal feasts—*dulce est desipere in loco*—its voluntary sharing of goods, and its personal devotion to Epicurus himself, more closely resembles that of a religious sect than a philosophical circle. The parallels with the Essenes, or early Christianity, both in practical ethics and general terminology, are quite remarkable. It is, then, the less surprising to learn that Epicurus was honoured after his death as a 'saviour', and that he and his followers wrote letters which bear a curious resemblance to the Pauline Epistles.

Epicurus' philosophy can perhaps best be described as an ethical extension of Democritus' atomic theory, modified to allow for human free will, delimited by the 'controlled experience' natural to pragmatists, and strongly influenced by the Ionian physicists, Aristotle's biological and zoological work, the methods of Euclidean mathematics and, above all, Hippocratic medicine, which crept by image and analogy into most branches of Greek thought.[4] The Hippocratic saying, 'Where there is love of mankind there will be love of healing', finds a direct echo in Epicurus, who declared: 'Vain is the word of that philosophy by which no malady of mankind is healed.' This claim indicates with some accuracy both the scope and the limitations of his creed.

Epicurus, like Democritus, saw the world as being composed solely of atoms and void: a theory which, taken to its logical end, excludes the incorporeal substance, and hence immortality. Yet, paradoxically, the Sage of the Garden was more of a mystic than a materialist in the modern sense; and in substituting Nature for Reason as the norm of experience, and positing Sensations as the only valid criteria from which reason could work he showed himself not so much an empiricist as a pioneer in scientific and psychological method. It was the scientist in him, passionate for truth, that enunciated such principles as these:

4 See above, p. 71, for its influence on Thucydides.

We must not force the facts to fit an impossible explanation. . . .
We must not conduct the study of nature in accordance with empty
assumptions and arbitrary rules but in agreement with the demands
of the phenomena; what our life needs is not subjective theories
nor superficial opinions but the means of living without disturbance.
. . . If we accept one theory and reject another which would fit
the phenomena equally well, it is clear that we are completely
abandoning the sphere of scientific study and drifting into mythology. . . . If a man enters into a struggle with the self-evident testimony of the senses he will never be able to share in true peace of
mind.

This remarkable statement is, in ways, two millennia ahead of
itself. It squarely challenges one of the most dearly cherished
rights of *homo metaphysicus*—aprioristic speculation, the creation of
cosmologies, ethical systems and the rest on a basis of pure
inductive reasoning rather than from a consideration of the
evidence.

The exercise of these principles produced remarkable results.
Released from the cramping bonds of theoretical Platonic Idealism,
Epicurus *observed*, minutely and accurately: we can trace in his
work the embryo study of child-behaviourism, animal psychology,
and archetypal characteristics. Perhaps most valuable of all was
his realization of the close interdependence existing between
emotional and physical phenomena. It is hardly too much to say
(as De Witt does) that he in part at least anticipated the conclusions
of psychosomatic medicine and *Gestalt* psychology.

But when we come to the application of his discoveries in
philosophical terms, it is a different matter. Epicurus found a
sick world, and attempted to heal it: he was an essentially practical
person. Yet he could not wholly escape his own environment.
His pragmatical distaste for Platonic absolutes forced him to
double his role of spiritual healer with that of philosophical
rebel, and thus to attempt the paradoxical step of unseating
Reason by reason. His aims were wholly admirable; his axioms
often invalid. No one could argue with this proto-psychologist
when he preached friendship, tolerance, and the whole life, or
fail to praise his efforts to fortify his disciples against fear of death

and the gods: 'Love', he wrote, 'goes dancing round and round the inhabited earth, veritably shouting to us all to awake to the blessedness of the happy life.'

In De Witt's words, 'as a *design for living* [my italics] Epicureanism is patently suggestive of modern hominism or humanism'. Precisely; but the prevalence of Platonism forced Epicurus to fight that philosophy, in a sense, with its own weapons; and for this his quasi-scientific postulates were ill-adapted. It is easy to pick holes in his Forty Authorized Doctrines and other writings. It has been pointed out that in setting up Nature as a norm he was putting that entity on the same personalized plane as Plato's divine Demiurge; that he confused cause and effect when discussing the atomic fall, and was guilty of special pleading in by-passing Democritean determinism by introducing the famous 'swerve' or *clinamen* to permit free will; that he thus posited a non-purposive First Cause which produced a purposive being, Man. Examples could be multiplied; Epicurus' 'chimerical blend of logic and romanticism', combined with his sharp powers of polemical argument, have involved him in endless controversy, and are largely responsible for his doubtful reputation even today. It is as a practising psychologist and philanthropist rather than as a pure philosopher that he deserves to be remembered.

Both his strength and his weakness are revealed in his treatment of the gods. His basic attitude, surprising as it may seem, was one of deep moral reverence, with a leaning towards traditional formality. His main objection to the Platonic astral theory was that it diminished divine dignity to think of the gods rolling round the sky as balls of fire; and the scientist in him confirmed this by asserting that the celestial bodies *were* balls of fire, and nothing else. The same moral reverence led him to reject all indecency and venality in the gods (together with their illicit offspring the heroes), not to mention prophecy, magic, daemons, and oracles, all of which he condemned as degrading hocus-pocus. (His attitude to the gods is almost identical with that of the arch-conservative Pindar: a surprising juxtaposition.) He observed all festivals and religious occasions scrupulously, and laid special emphasis on the power of adoration to reveal knowledge of the divine nature. It is characteristic of him that while admitting this important element of the *vita contemplativa*, he should at the same time dismiss prayer as mere bribery, *do ut des*; and of course, on his own terms—and ours as well—he was quite right as far as fourth-century Greek prayers in general were concerned.

But—and this reveals the essence of his paradoxical weakness—having admitted the existence of gods, he still has to fit them, somehow, into his dogmatic framework of belief. Thus, since atoms and void are all, the gods must needs be corporeal, though, of course, composed of the finest conceivable atoms: they exist at the summit of a sequence in which man forms the next link and have to be graded themselves to ensure reasonable continuity. As the supreme good is *ataraxia*—emotional peace, undisturbed calm, and tranquillity—then the gods, who must by definition be supremely happy, cannot occupy themselves with the affairs of men, or suffer any of the more unpleasant emotions. (This gave great scope to the Christian apologist Lactantius: by a neat disjunctive syllogism he argued that the absence of some emotions in perfect beings implied the absence of all; and that this *per se* implied non-existence.) It might also be argued that since men are required to love one another, the gods should be assumed to do likewise, with a perfect love beyond all understanding; but there is no suggestion of this. Epicurus himself, with strict logic, never called the gods immortal; his followers were not so strongminded. There is a fascinating clash here between religious traditionalism and scientific method.

Further instances of this sort could be given; but it is more profitable to concentrate on the practical and ethical side of Epicurus' teaching. Here he shows at his best—though no doubt the epithet 'utilitarian' will always be used against him in a pejorative sense. As De Witt rightly said, 'the very name of pleasure is quick to accumulate a semantic load of disapproval'. Plato's four cardinal virtues, so closely integrated with an obsolescent political system, Epicurus found insufficient: his entire trend was away from the civic towards the social and personal virtues. Honesty he placed above all, whether in public or private dealings; there was to be no servility or personal surrender of standards. Honesty 'was destroyed by the study of rhetoric and dialectic. It was opposed to sycophancy in politics, obsequiousness in court life, smugness and hypocrisy in private life.' Faith—based on the certainty of knowledge—came next; and its opposite was not Pyrrhonic scepticism so much as uncertainty. Friendship (with a surprisingly practical flavour about it), suavity, considerateness, 'hope for the future, gratitude for the past, patience to endure the present'—these are the Epicurean's virtues; and his great goals peace of soul and love of mankind.

It is hardly surprising that several of the early Christian Fathers, such as Arnobius and Lactantius, were steeped in Epicureanism, nor that St Augustine—saving always its views on immortality—spoke of it so highly; perhaps it is not impossible (yet another paradox!) that it facilitated the spread of Christianity. It cannot have been hard for an Epicurean to become a Christian. Epicurus hinted at a life in the spirit: it was the great final doctrine of Redemption which eluded him. His inner dissatisfaction with the old religion, far from implying militant atheism, hinted at unanswered religious needs. But the standards he set were too high for a Roman audience. It is doubtful whether the higher qualities of Epicureanism survived their transplantation to Italian soil. The creed was immensely popular, during the last two centuries of the Republic, with provincials (especially in the Greek-influenced South) and individualistic intellectuals; but it seems clear that its appeal for them lay partly in its allowance for hedonism (the Roman notion of true pleasure differed somewhat from the Greek) and partly in its religious radicalism. Similarly with the concept of 'friendship': φιλία and *amicitia* are worlds apart in many of their implications.

It was without doubt the publication of Lucretius' *De Rerum Natura* that first turned official opinion against Epicureanism in Rome—and perhaps with some excuse. The accusations of irresponsibility, civic indifference, lack of moral conscience, and contempt for tradition may well have been justified. The Roman temperament was not well equipped to practise a demanding form of spiritual individualism; and once this purity of doctrine had been abandoned, Epicureanism was extremely vulnerable to social or political sanctions. To Augustus, struggling with programmes of reform in an atmosphere of war-weariness and moral exhaustion, it must have seemed a pernicious creed, a mere refuge for *fainéant* nihilists and godless radicals. Cicero's attacks provided him with welcome ammunition against the Epicurean pleasure-principle; and by the end of his reign it had been driven underground and almost destroyed. Yet, to quote De Witt once more, Epicureanism 'spread more widely, penetrated deeper, and left a permanent stain beneath the Stoic varnish'. It was Stoicism, however, that ousted it as a working philosophy.

Of all the creeds and philosophies which flourished in antiquity, Stoicism is considerably the most elusive. Ask any two reasonably well-read men what doctrines they associate with the name of Plato, and the odds are that their replies, if not identical, will at least bear some generic resemblance to one another. Extend your enquiry to the Stoics and you will be lucky to get a philosophically valid reply at all, let alone any basic agreement. Stoicism had an extremely chequered career: being intimately affected by changing historical conditions, it underwent more radical modifications than most of its rivals. Like the Roman Empire, with which it is generally associated, it contained the seeds of its own corruption from the beginning: indeed, in its later and most influential manifestations, it can hardly be considered as a philosophy at all. By the time of Epictetus and Marcus Aurelius it had become, to all intents and purposes, little more than a psychological therapeutic, a private bulwark against the ravages of spiritual and political *Angst* under an immutably autocratic *régime*.

Thus a sharp distinction has to be made between Stoicism properly considered, the philosophy formulated in the Hellenistic era by Zeno of Citium, and the adaptation of Stoic ethics to the requirements of the Roman upper classes from the late Republic onwards. Yet even in the beginning Stoicism, complete with its cosmology, its detailed apparatus of dialectical method, its tripartite division into Logic, Physics (including theology and psychology!) and Ethics, has the air of emerging to fill an historical vacuum rather than as a genuine contribution to the history of thought. It is eclectic, makeshift, and riddled with contradictions. Behind it lies, not the unifying power of a great and original mind, but the shadow of social transition. The city state was dead; the new cosmopolitan, as we have seen, was adrift in a new world, without guidance, the prey to conflicting desires and fears. Epicurus in the Garden had offered one solution; Zeno, as he paced the colonnades of the Porch (Stoa), propounded another. In Edwyn Bevan's striking words:

> Some ring-wall must be built against chaos. High over the place where Zeno talked could be descried the wall, built generations before, under the terror of a Persian attack, built in haste of the materials which lay to hand, the drums of columns fitted together, just as they were, with the more regular stones. That heroic wall still looks over the roofs of modern Athens. To Zeno it might have been a parable of his own teaching.

When Zeno first came to Athens, we are told, he went the rounds of the philosophical schools to see what they had to offer him. But though he absorbed a good deal—more than some scholars have been prepared to admit—both from the Lyceum and the Academy, neither satisfied him entirely. Plato's theories were too rarefied to admit of a wide practical application; they lacked the reassuring solidity that the ordinary man needed at this juncture in history. The Sceptics—those logical positivists of antiquity—had undermined the comforting belief that absolute knowledge was, ultimately, attainable. The old gods, the old cosmologies were equally under fire. What men demanded, above all, was reassurance, guidance, a scale of values. It is a dilemma which we today can at once recognize.

It is impossible to disentangle Zeno's teaching with any degree of certainty from its development by his successors, such as Cleanthes or the laborious Chrysippus; but it seems—despite its emphasis on sovereign Reason—to have had more than a touch of

Eastern 'prophetic' methods about it. There is a persistent tradition, often denied today, that Zeno was a Phoenician; and certain features of his doctrine—in particular his monism and his ideal of inner tranquillity—have an oriental rather than a Greek flavour about them. There are curious verbal echoes, too, of the Bhagavadgita. But any attempt to isolate and identify such potential sources specifically is bound to end in failure; moreover, it tends to distract one's attention from the very real debt that Zeno owed to earlier Greek thought.

To counter the Sceptics, Zeno constructed an elaborate epistemology, of which the central core was the assertion that true knowledge *was* in fact attainable, and that on such knowledge all true virtue was based. He posited a sharp and real dichotomy between virtue and vice, without any degrees of compromise between them. As a concession, however, he allowed that certain actions, though morally neutral, might be treated as 'advantageous' or 'disadvantageous', and that the philosopher could, for practical purposes, take account of these without loss of virtue.

Under the heading of Physics Zeno considered not only physics, as the Greeks understood the term—that is, a consistent account of the universe—but also metaphysics, psychology, physiology, anthropology, and such religious or theological questions as Providence and free will, the existence and nature of the gods, the operations of chance and the problem of evil. (It is no accident that Tyche, or Chance personified, was one of the most popular deities in the fourth century B.C.) It was on this groundwork that his more general ethical propositions rested. Here he was forced to reconcile a number of obstinately incompatible elements. His physics were basically deterministic, but his ethics allowed for the play of free will; and in the field of religion, having started from premises that were *au fond* revolutionary and atheistic, he was compelled to compromise with the traditional demand for a theocentric universe.

Zeno thought of the world, as the early Ionians had done, in primarily hylozoic terms: a living entity, harmonious in all its parts, of which man was the microcosm and 'nature' (*physis*) the guiding principle. By identifying *physis* with God he reconciled his monistic theory with the natural immanence in the phenomenal world of a divine Creator, and still left himself free to clear away what he termed mere superstition. But his boldest decision was taken over the eternal problem presented by the existence of evil in a world supposedly ruled by a Creator both omniscient and morally impeccable. Though he argued skilfully towards a compromise, in the last resort he was prepared to limit divine knowledge in order to save divine morality.

Zeno's cosmology was both unoriginal and depressingly retrograde. Two major scientific discoveries currently in the air—the concept of the heliocentric universe, and the notion of the earth's rotation—he opposed on the old reactionary grounds that they were 'humiliating to human self-esteem'. Historically it is not hard to see why. A few decades after the publication of the Copernican theory Pascal could write that 'le silence éternel de ces espaces infinis m'effraie'; to Zeno it was imperative that Man should once more find his bearings at the centre of a stable, comprehensive universe.

It was on this presupposition that his major ethical precept—that we should live 'consistently with nature'—depended for its psychological validity; it provided a link between his fundamental, if syncretic, philosophy and those pithy aphorisms designed to help the man-in-the-street with his everyday conduct. And such a link was necessary, because a marked discrepancy appeared (and increased as time went on) between Stoic theory and Stoic practice. For example, it is clear that in theory the Stoic ideal society 'calls for a revolt against nationalism, antiquity, custom, pride and prejudice; and a new construction based upon universal reason and individual liberty'.[5] Yet in practice men were advised to take part in festivals and public gatherings, to make themselves useful members of their existing society. In the Republic of Zeno, his ideal constitution, women were to be held in common; yet the practising Stoic was recommended to marry and bring up children. Examples could be multiplied. Thus a dual standard of

[5] Quoted from E. V. Arnold, *Roman Stoicism* (1911; new ed. 1958).

allegiance developed in Stoicism; which meant in turn that its doctrines were slowly modified to suit changing conditions. Its steady decay as a philosophy was matched by its increasing spread, at a lower level, as a guide to conduct.

At first sight this might seem an uncompromising creed for the Roman nobility of the second century B.C. to fasten on with such eagerness.[6] Politically conservative to the point of blind chauvinism, attached by strong emotional bonds to traditional observances in religion and social conduct, they could hardly be expected to embrace a doctrine founded on the disagreeable notions of internationalism, inner tranquillity, and disregard, within limits, for social status. On the other hand there was a great deal in Stoicism which could, without too much difficulty, be adapted to Roman needs; and those needs had become pressing. In the pliant hands of Panaetius and Posidinius Zeno's philosophy was transformed into a moral stiffener for a spiritually bankrupt Roman aristocracy:

> Thus strong will and assured conviction are no longer required; the door is thrown open for convention, opportunism and respectability. The daring moral theories and bold paradoxes of the founders of Stoicism tend to disappear from sight, and are replaced by shrewd good sense and worldly wisdom: in short, by the doctrine of 'making the best of both worlds'. . . . It was from this standpoint that Stoicism so rapidly won its way with the Roman nobility of the last century of the Republic. (Arnold, *op. cit.*)

What did these Romans find in Stoicism that proved so congenial to them? In the first place, that indefinable quality which they called *humanitas*, the civilized ethic which through internal corruption and rapid acquisition of foreign wealth they were in danger of losing altogether. In an age of civil strife, too, there was a subtle appeal in the doctrine of *ecpyrosis,* which taught that the world would be destroyed by fire, the slate wiped clean and a new start made—an apocalyptic notion that has turned up since at

6 While the impact of Epicureanism was widespread, Stoicism initially was confined to a social and intellectual minority, largely in Rome. See De Witt, p. 340.

various crises of world history. By a certain amount of Peripatetic casuistry they also convinced themselves that the Stoics' 'mixed constitution' vindicated their own Republican system; they approved the rule which encouraged family solidarity; and they were quick to find in their own history examples of rugged virtue which they could square with Stoic principles. They concluded that Zeno's God 'treats good men as a Roman father his children, giving them a stern training, that they may grown in virtue', etc. By such devices the new Greek philosophy was grafted on to the old national stump of *patria potestas* and ancestral tradition; and the result was that symbolic figure of Republican Stoicism, Cato of Utica.

Cato shows us the best side of this hybrid creed; and the point is worth emphasizing. For some time now historians who are never tired of enlarging on the undoubted corruption of the Roman Republic have simultaneously contrived to dismiss Cato, with some contempt, as a reactionary Blimp: two opinions which it is a little hard to reconcile in moral terms. As a boy he demanded a sword from his tutor, Sarpedon, in order to kill Sulla. His taste for rigid justice and self-denial lent special colour to his studies in Stoicism, which he conducted under Antipater of Tyre. Where others rode, he walked. His dress was modest, his appetites negligible; he even gave away his wife to a friend, though he took her back after the friend's death. When he attended the theatre, such was his puritan probity that the strip-tease girls put on their clothes. Yes, a comic figure; but he was the only man who had the courage to speak out, on moral grounds, against Caesar's imperial self-aggrandisement in Gaul. It was all very well for Mommsen to declare that 'Caesar, wherever he came forward as a destroyer, only carried out the pronounced verdict of historical development'; we have heard that particular pernicious argument before.

Those who complain of corruption are in no position to gibe at Cato. Their only logical course is to smear him with the easy charge of political hypocrisy; and they will have quite a job to make the charge stick. (His famous remark about bribery sometimes being necessary for the good of the Republic is an implicit condemnation of his colleagues rather than Machiavellian cynicism.) We should remember, too, that it was not till the nineteenth century that Cato declined into a figure of fun; and today, when our own attitude to the law of nations needs overhauling rather badly, we may well reconsider some of the moral values for which he stood. Cato may come into his own yet: *virtus*, *libertas*, and *fides* (that much-abused trilogy) still have real meaning today, and reflect back a new light on the period when they were employed. Then as now, men such as Cato were in a minority —and as time went by not only did the minority shrink, but the Stoic principles they professed became insensibly corrupted.

The quality in Stoicism which perhaps appealed to Romans most of all, and which still remains most closely associated with the creed in popular thought, was an essentially negative one: self-restraint. Again, in all likelihood, on Eastern principles, Zeno had taught that the philosopher must totally free himself from such feelings as pity or grief; he may act benevolently, yet (and here the Greek in Zeno reasserted itself) according to the dictates of Reason alone. Virtue is its own sufficiency:

> The wise man, even though (by those circumstances which he cannot control, and which in this connexion we call 'the play of fortune') he gain no 'advantage' at all but suffers dishonour, captivity, mutilation and death, still possesses the supreme good, still is as completely happy as though he enjoyed all things. (Arnold, *op. cit.*)

It follows that courage (which forms one aspect of virtue) displays itself most laudably in the face of tyranny and death. Life is never worth preserving at the cost of dishonour, and under certain conditions the Stoic may without fear put an end to his existence. The relevance of such principles to Imperial Rome is not very far to seek.

The Republicans took Stoicism like a shot in the arm to restore their damaged moral probity; the post-Augustans used it as an anaesthetizing drug, which enabled them to co-exist with the oppressive régime they felt themselves powerless to change or destroy. It saved their spiritual dignity, and gave them some measure of inner self-assurance; they could die at an Emperor's whim with their faith still intact. But such hardy souls were in a minority. All too often Stoicism was perverted by time-servers and place-seekers to justify or exculpate their own despicable conduct. Before the death of Nero it had largely degenerated into a mere handbook of ethical and moral etiquette, a convenient substitute for personal decisions. Politically it had kept abreast of the times (though still tinged with enough archaic Republican virtue to preserve the illusion of stern integrity); and in any case, what had suited the cosmopolitan post-Alexandrian Greek world would, modified still further, find a ready audience in Imperial Rome. Chrysippus had conveniently laid down that the wise man might without compunction pay court to emperors and monarchs; and Seneca for one was not slow to take the hint.

The weaknesses of this compromising creed are at once revealed when put to the test of public life. Seneca's career reveals just how far casuistry and compromise can go in an intelligentsia that has lost all moral self-respect; it offers an unpleasant but most telling gloss on the development of the Roman character, and a salutary reminder of the dangers inherent in the continual sacrifice of principles to expedience. The deadly gap widens between reality and abstraction, truth, and literature: nothing crystallizes this better than the juxtaposition of Seneca's high-flown ethical writings and his disgusting yet pitiable life. There is a perpetual fugal contrast between his noble principles and his almost ludicrously subservient trimming. He preached poverty, yet owned millions, much of it obtained by exorbitant usury. Far from showing a Stoic indifference to misfortune or success, he grovelled in exile and flattered at Court. Having begun his official career as Nero's guardian and moral tutor, he ended it as his accomplice in murder. At the best he was an idealist corrupted by power-politics, a morally schizoid rhetorician; at the worst, a greedy and unprincipled hypocrite. Plato refused to compromise with the tyrant Dionysius; Seneca had no such qualms.

The truth is that Roman Stoicism was less well adapted to the vicissitudes of public life than the Epicureanism it supplanted;

and this is the last and greatest paradox of the two philosophies. Stoicism was *au fond* a quietist faith, which lacked the spiritual intransigence of uncorrupted Epicurean doctrine. In its syncretic, Romanized form it made too many concessions, attempted to reconcile too much, and ended by becoming a philosophy of expediency, entirely at the mercy of each individual who practised it. It is no coincidence that the most admirable Stoics under the Empire were not the professional intellectuals, writers, or philosophers (who, to a greater or lesser degree, were adept at squaring a degenerate life with idealistic literary pronouncements) but morally self-reliant men of action, such as Helvidius Priscus or Marcus Aurelius. The doctrine that virtue is the only good, coupled with the belief that all the world except the wise man (i.e. the Stoic) is insane,[7] offered peculiar comfort to the politically impotent or oppressed. This was hardly a philosophy of revolution; yet it has been asserted that Stoicism formed the moral backbone of Republican resistance against the Imperial autocracy. Some Stoics were certainly persecuted; yet they were not persecuted for their Stoicism, but their sedition; nor were they seditious in the first place because of their Stoic beliefs.

The Stoic movement, as Villeneuve pointed out, was well-established in Rome before Augustus' time. It did not spring up as a supporting ideology for anti-Imperial revolutionaries and diehard Republicans: on the contrary, it offered a convenient alternative to any form of direct political action, and in that sense was a contributory cause to the moral failure of nerve which characterizes so many well-born Roman intellectuals during the critical formative years of the Julio-Claudian and Flavian dynasties. Studying it, we can see how inextricably the threads of literature, social life, and political belief are interwoven, and perhaps understand something of the forces that made Silver Latin literature—with the extraordinary exceptions of Petronius

[7] Cf. Czeslaw Milosz, *The Captive Mind,* who cites S. Witkiewicz's novel *Insatiability* (1932) for the new Stoicism in pill form, used by members of an occupied satellite nation. These pills, known as Murti-Bing, made the user 'serene and happy . . . He lived in the midst of his compatriots like a healthy individual surrounded by madmen'.

and Apuleius—so utterly remote from contemporary reality. When literature is treated, not as an integral part of life, an expression of society, but as an escapist alternative to living, it becomes sterile, artificial, and ultimately meaningless. When a society loses its moral independence, when it preaches one thing and practises another, its philosophy degenerates into contemptible compromises and dead aphorisms. So it was in Rome. From the historical viewpoint Roman Stoicism is infinitely revealing: its progressive corruption contains the whole paradigm of those tumultuous centuries between the Gracchi and the Antonines. Today we, of all people, can understand and sympathize with those anguished, impotent intellectuals; yet we cannot afford to condone their choice.

5

Imperial Caesar

This twentieth century has not been overkind to the myth of the Great Captains. The gilt is wearing a little thin today on Alexander and Hercules: and who would now try to make a hero out of Lysander? Hector, perhaps, still moves us in England; but then we have always had a weakness for noble failures and the heroic last stand. Julius Caesar stands somewhere between these two extremes: both his achievements and his nobility have taken on an ambivalent quality with time. The bimillennium of his death, celebrated a year or so ago, did not exactly produce a full or over-enthusiastic memorial press. Things would have been very different if he had died a hundred years earlier. What a paean of praise would have rung out from the Germany of the Hohen-zollerns, and from that other empire on which the sun, so far, had never set!

In order to understand Caesar we have to see him against the background of the Republic, long obsolescent, which he finally destroyed. Today, perhaps, we are in a better position to appreciate the collapse of that political and social fabric than any of our immediate predecessors. As Professor R. E. Smith observed, in that stimulating, heterodox little book *The Failure of the Roman Republic*:

> The fifty years before the First World War were quite alien to the Republic's crisis; men lived in a stable world, where law and order stretched to its uttermost bounds, and where difference or dis-agreement was resolved according to the claims of sweet reason. . . . We live in less certain times; all that they assumed as permanent

we have either lost or fear to lose at any time. . . . It is what I may call the spiritual element which we see to be so important, transcending far political or economic issues.

Both Caesar and his period have a great deal in common with the public figures and institutions which have so profoundly affected our own lives. Propaganda, *Lebensraum,* military dictatorship—we know them as our great-grandfathers could never hope to do.

At the same time our peculiar position explains the slump observable today in Caesar's reputation. If Hitler and Mussolini help to clarify our understanding of Caesar, they also fill us with an instinctive repugnance for their infinitely greater prototype. We find the hero-worshipping attitude of Goethe, Nietzsche, or Mommsen immoral and offensive; yet, by the same token, the inescapable historical parallels lead us to re-examine Caesar in the light of recent events. In 1953, for instance, Michel Rambaud published a thesis entitled *L'Art de Déformation historique dans les Commentaires de César*—a fairly self-explanatory title. We should not forget that he began it in 1944, when France was still under German occupation: this contemporary circumstance must have sharpened his mind for the problem as nothing else could have done.

Perhaps the old-fashioned idea of history providing moral *exempla* is due for a revival. As Miss Lily Ross Taylor has written 'for the generation which has read *Mein Kampf* and has seen Hitler's ruthless execution of the designs for domination . . . of which he provided a blue-print long in advance, the rise of a dictator to power has a peculiar fascination'. No less fascinating are the various estimates which Caesar has provoked through the ages: many of them are as alarming as they are unexpected. But they all, as we might expect, faithfully mirror the convictions and desires of those who put them forward. All, that is, except Caesar's own self-portrait. 'To study Caesar's method of writing,' M. Rambaud declared, 'is to study the man himself.' Is it? How can we separate Caesar the writer from Caesar the apologist, the general from the revolutionary, the politician from the propagandist? To what extent, indeed, may it be said that posterity has believed more or less what Caesar wanted it to believe?

Caesar's posthumous evolution into a myth (like Alexander before him and Charlemagne afterwards) was at least partially due to his own deliberate policy during his lifetime. Aphorisms like *veni, vidi, vici* or 'Caesar's wife must be above suspicion' hint at the man with an eye to future generations. This myth was by no means destroyed when monkish chronicles and mediaeval superstition gave way to apparently rational historiography; nor has it altogether lost its force today. A German writer called Gundolf, who in 1925 felt acutely the need for a strong man to over-ride what he called 'small-town morality', described this phenomenon very well as

> an energetic myth, a permanent motive to which the mass adheres and which the mass elaborates upon. These solidify vague conceptions into figures, notions into judgments and formulas; and though they may rarely create the language of history, they often create its legends and proverbs.

Such an accumulated tradition cannot but have its effect, whether consciously or not, upon the historians who inherit it; and they in their turn disseminate the myth in a different form. Few, I imagine, would dissent from Professor Butterfield's claim[1] that 'the nineteenth-century myth of romantic nationalism would appear to have been born of historical study.'

Our picture of Caesar ultimately derives from three main sources of evidence—his own works, Cicero's letters and speeches, and the portrait left us by Sallust. From 'the agreements and contradictions between these three' all the rest springs. Already, then, we are on sticky ground. Caesar's *Commentaries* were almost certainly intended to impress the Senatorial class in Rome; he had learnt by the examples of Sulla and Marius that this was a section of public opinion which even a potential dictator ignored at his peril. On this basis we can further infer that the abortive campaigns in Germany and Britain were largely undertaken for publicity purposes. Ultima Thule had a fine romantic ring in Rome, and the twenty days' thanksgiving granted by a grateful government shows

[1] H. Butterfield: *Man on his Past* (1955) p. 30.

that Caesar gauged his men well. We should not forget, however, that on this occasion Cato voiced a memorable protest: 'Caesar', he declared, 'ought to be delivered up to the Usipetes and Tenchtheri [German tribes] to prevent the gods from visiting upon Rome his violation of the law of nations in seizing the sacred persons of ambassadors.' Even at this stage in the Republic's history, moral sensibilities were not entirely blunted.

By the time Suetonius and Plutarch came to compile their *Lives* of Caesar, the myth was already firmly established. The cult of Divus Julius, with its echoes of Alexander, was in full swing. The diarists and gossip-mongers of both factions had leisure to embroider the truth to their hearts' content. Even in the Augustan poets Caesar, as has been pleasantly observed, 'disappears in his own halo, and his name becomes synonymous with a constellation'. Livy, Appian, Dio Cassius, Diodorus, Velleius Paterculus, and the rest all derive ultimately from either Caesar's own self-portrait or the less favourable Republican criticisms put forward by Cicero. Sallust has depersonalized Caesar with rhetoric, and reduced him to the type of the ambitious *megalourgos*; it was left for Appian to draw the first detailed comparison of him with Alexander. The portrait rapidly became a formalized *eikon*; the Caesar-myth, reluctantly or enthusiastically, was generally accepted. Even those with Republican sympathies, such as Tacitus or the Elder Pliny, could give Caesar generous praise, dividing their opinions (as Cicero had done) between personal, aesthetic approval, and political or moral condemnation.

But it was Plutarch and Lucan who between them finally crystallized the image which would remain intact for centuries, and influence countless later writers. Plutarch's unique gift is that of selecting significant anecdotes, and presenting them in such a way that they become symbolic projections of a myth. Sulla's prophecy that in Caesar many Mariuses were concealed; the glimpse of Caesar sighing before Alexander's statue, lamenting that at his age Alexander had conquered the world, while he himself had as yet done nothing; the dark hour before the crossing of the Rubicon; the Ides of March with their portents and horrors

—all this builds up a legend which lifts its protagonist out of history into myth. Such a concept of the Civil Wars is reinforced, from another angle, by Lucan in his *Pharsalia*: he is not so much an anti-Caesarian propagandist, a fashionable anachronistic Republican, as a man obsessed by greatness as such. He lifts the whole struggle on to a supra-human, cosmic plane, not unlike that of Hardy's *Dynasts*, where the characters are merely puppets fulfilling some vast blind destiny. From Plutarch descends the Shakespearian concept of Caesar; from Lucan's dark satanic *Uebermensch* the line runs through Dante, Corneille, Goethe, Hugo, and Nietzsche.

In the early Middle Ages little was left of Caesar but his name and office; the rest was myth. It was not enough that he was actually the father of Caesarion by Cleopatra; legend also credited him with liaisons even more exotic, such as that with the fairy Morgana, on whom he was believed to have sired Oberon. The name of Caesar, however, persisted; Kaiser and Czar are, of course, both corruptions of it. Statues and coins gave substance to the imagined personality. In his official capacity he continued to be remembered for three things, which sometimes merged, but were never quite lost beneath the mythic accretions. He was the divine founder of the *imperium*; he was a law-giver; and he was the conqueror of the West.

By the time of Dante and Frederick II, Caesar's historical personality was beginning to return, and the more fantastic aspects of the myth to be forgotten. But it was—of all people— Petrarch who re-established him as an historical figure in the modern sense. The Renaissance humanists, no less than their ambitious and worldly patrons, badly needed a secular hero from antiquity to offset the mediaeval Church against which they were reacting— much as Brougham, Bentham or Darwin in the nineteenth century turned to science, or utilitarianism, or evolutionary biology to replace their loss of faith. Petrarch's exhaustive, hagiolatric biography, which drew on almost all the available sources, gave them what they were looking for. Sigismondo Malatesta consciously modelled himself on Caesar; Cesare Borgia is even supposed to have believed himself a reincarnation of the dead Imperator. The Emperor Charles V was acutely conscious of what Caesarism meant, and planned his career in that knowledge. Catholic orthodoxy, however, necessitated some trifling modifications to the original concept; after the Battle of Mühlberg Charles remarked, with ambivalent modesty: 'I came, I saw, God conquered.'

Now began that intimate association between the historical assessment of Caesar and the justification of modern monarchy or dictatorship which has lasted down to our own times. In 1578 Schiapollaria wrote his *Vita di Cesare*, largely to publicize the Hapsburg monarchy; a politico-moral tract full, as Gundolf puts it, of 'bromidic remarks and oratorical digressions'. Caesar's propaganda was being put to good use. To the Court poets of Louis XIV he was an ideal exemplar; La Rochefoucauld saw him as the Great Man above any moral or physical restraint. His disciple Vauvenargues modified this concept in ominously familiar terms: Caesar was 'the magnanimous soul which must expand and which becomes a crime and a disaster only by reason of the world's resistance'. How foolish and selfish of the world thus to deny genius its due *Lebensraum*!

So the way was paved for the development of the *Führerprinzip*. De Bury dedicated his biography of Caesar to Mme Pompadour, and Secondo his to the Bourbon King of Naples; Herder set history as a throne above morality or metaphysics, and placed Caesar on it; Goethe idealized him, Napoleon and Frederick of Prussia learnt highly practical lessons from his life. The Prussian jackboot echoed the tramp of the legions, and Mommsen wrote his wildly approving panegyric. Under the Hohenzollerns, Cesare Borgia's old motto was renewed: *Aut Caesar, aut nihil*![2] Macaulay could describe Caesar as the finest gentleman, the most humane conqueror, and the most popular politician that the world has ever known; a view shared (with some reservations) by the late Lord Tweedsmuir—who was, one recalls, one of Lord Milner's young

[2] Cf. a revealing anonymous pamphlet, published under this title in Berlin in 1862.

men in South Africa before becoming a distinguished pro-consul in the Imperial tradition.

Finally, with the advent of Fascism in Italy, the wheel came full circle; Caesar received such gross adulation as only Romans—in his time or ours—know how to bestow. Out of many examples we may select the biography by Guarnieri, written in 1936 (or, as he prefers, the fourteenth year of the Fascist Era). Till now, he declared, the time had not been ripe for a full appreciation of Caesar: 'solamente il Fascismo poteva farci rivivere la romanità in tutta la sua potenza, in tutta la sua gloria e in tutto il suo suggestivo splendore'. There follows a nauseating comparison of Caesar and Mussolini, not to the latter's entire disadvantage. *Plus ça change*; Marius, one recalls, was hailed as a second Romulus after Vercellae.

But from quite early times there had been a firm political and moral opposition to the Caesar-myth. German Lutheranism instinctively stood out against his glamour; Hans Sachs, the cobbler-poet, drew him as a rapacious monster, who drove his way to supremacy 'by means of cunning, force, ruin and malice'. Bacon, whose acidly detached study is still worth reading, observed, with commendable meiosis, that 'he was, no doubt, of a very noble mind; yet such as aimed more at his particular advancement that at any merits for the common good'. Pascal declared tartly that one might forgive Alexander the undertaking of the conquest of the world as a youthful excess, but that Caesar was old enough to know better. It was, however, Montesquieu who first, in the *Esprit des Lois*, formulated the notion that a leader is responsible to society for his actions, and must be judged accordingly. He opened the way for more extreme antagonists such as Rousseau and Boileau, who denounced Caesar without reservation as a bloodthirsty destroyer.[3]

---

[3] Cf. in this country the *Life* published anonymously in 1846 by the Religious Tract Society, esp. pp. vi–vii: 'The selfishness of his ambition, his recklessness of human life, his contempt of national liberty, his rapacity, his arrogance, his sensual and luxurious prodigality, cannot but awaken every feeling of sorrowful and righteous indignation . . . To those who condemn all war, shrinking from conquerors as from fiends, the life of Caesar presents little more than a series of murderous tragedies.'

The most obvious test case over one's historical and moral attitude to Caesar is his behaviour in Gaul. Montesquieu, who could excuse Alexander on the grounds that he had opened up a new world of commerce and *Kultur*, found no such mitigation for Caesar. He condemned the Gallic campaign as wanton aggression. It was left for Hegel to point out that the conquest of Gaul marked the beginning of Western Europe as such, and for Mommsen and Ranke to suggest that it 'expanded and maintained world civilization': a peculiarly specious plea. It must be said that French historians, if no one else, have shown themselves singularly ungrateful for the benefits thus conferred; and when we re-read the *De Bello Gallico*, even Caesar's own apologia fails to enlist our support for the calculated deception and brutality it reveals.

In the first campaign against the Helvetii, in 58 B.C., out of an estimated 368,000 Helvetii only 110,000 returned home; and of the original figure 92,000, no more, had been fighting men; the total had included women and children. On the capture of Avaricum, the modern Bourges, in 52 B.C., every inhabitant was butchered. We read of hand-loppings, torture, wholesale enslavement. This, it may be objected, was the practice of ancient warfare. But that right of nations which Cato defended could hardly extend to wanton aggression for personal ends. It seems abundantly clear that Caesar's main object in fighting the Gallic Wars was to build up a strong army and so maintain his own position in Rome. [4]

Caesar's much-vaunted clemency can be dated, with some confidence, to 51 B.C., no earlier. He was by then beginning to learn the simple political adage that conciliation pays better in the long run than brutality; and with Pompey moving every day further towards the aristocratic party, and Crassus dead at Carrhae, it was essential that he should be free to return to Italy. His record of mercy in the Civil Wars was simply a proof of his farsightedness. It was more convenient for his purposes to make friends than enemies, especially when those friends could be of use

[4] This view is upheld by Rambaud, and by Gérard Walter in his recent biography (*Caesar*. Tr. Emma Craufurd, 1953).

to him. So long as he got his own way, he was prepared to be a magnanimous gentleman. It is, I feel, only ironic justice that one of the factors that must have influenced his assassins was their impotent resentment of his patronizing mercy. As Mr Alfred Duggan has percipiently remarked,[5] 'he was merciful, and his rule was not oppressive; but he made no efforts to spare the feelings of his nominal equals'.

Today we are, I think, swinging back to a position roughly comparable with that taken up by Montesquieu. The Nazi and Fascist *régimes*—not to mention the personality-cult of Stalin in Russia—have discredited not only the Great Man theory of history popularized by Carlyle, but also de Gobineau's Aryan myth and other such nationalist aberrations. Furthermore, the whole nineteenth-century concept of Imperialism is undergoing a radical moral revaluation. Such revaluations can, of course, produce regrettable *bêtises* among historians—those, I mean, who have proposed, in Professor Marsh's words, that Caesar 'should have modified the system of slavery, invented representative government, or set up some form of Socialism'. Nevertheless, Marxism and its ancillary economic disciplines have given us a fresh angle from which to examine the events leading up to Caesar's *coup*.

It can, of course, be argued that the present denigration of Caesar's achievements is as much influenced by contemporary events—perhaps more so—than the adulation he received from our forefathers. That is almost certainly true. It may also be urged that the historian's job is to discover the truth, not set himself up as a latter-day Rhadamanthus. But even the discovery of truth involves implicit moral judgments. In working out what Caesar did, and why, we are bound to produce a verdict on his motives. Why did he invade Gaul? Why did he cross the Rubicon? It is not enough to analyse the immediate historical causality of these events, and avoid the moral issue by saying that Caesar had no option but to behave as he did. Will, whatever the historians may say, is free. Was he—as many, Mommsen included, have supposed

[5] A. Duggan, *Julius Caesar* (1955) p. 174.

—gifted with a kind of divine prescience, that enabled him to fore-see the necessity of a military dictatorship to clear up the physical mess and spiritual failure left by the obsolete Republican system? Was he at bottom driven by personal ambition or a desire to better the lot of his country?

It is, I think, a proof of his enduring vitality, if nothing else, that these questions are almost impossible to answer in an im-partial frame of mind. Moral rectitude is far from precluding historical bias. Often truth and prejudice, insight and anachron-ism, are hopelessly blended. In a sense both Caesar's detractors and his apologists are right: they are talking about different things, on a different basis of values. There is a great deal about Caesar, considered *in vacuo*, which commands our instant admiration. He was, undoubtedly, a genius: statesman, general, law-giver, jurist, orator, historian, philologist, mathematician, and architect. If the criterion of virtue is success, Caesar is *sans pareil*: his judgment was almost faultless, his execution efficient to a degree.

But is success in fact the sole criterion? As Dr Marañon has reminded us, there is a marked tendency among historians, if a man is efficient, to forgive him all else for that alone. And when we turn to motive, though the historical situation does much to palliate Caesar's actions, it cannot conceal the naked fact that all he did was in furtherance of his personal ambition. Those who see in him an agent of that *ignis fatuus,* historical necessity, must con-sole themselves with the knowledge that 'the movements sup-posedly initiated by great men very seldom coincided with what they intended, and often far surpassed in extension anything they could have foreseen'. Of no historical figure can this be more truly said than of Caesar.

It would not, I think, be altogether unfair to say that he began as a second Marius and ended as a second Sulla; one thing we can-not but observe is how much the memory of his two great predecessors influenced him, and how much he learnt from their successes and mistakes. His life exhibits the classic swing from left to right of an ambitious and unscrupulous politician: from Marius and the *populares* to Sulla's position of absolute authority.

There was hardly a trick employed by Sulla or Marius—or, for that matter, by the Gracchi and their successors—which Caesar did not use at some time in his life: political marriage, legislation by violence, mass bribery of the populace, and so on. It is true that his first overtly illegal act was not till 59 B.C., the year in which (like Gracchus before him) he carried an agrarian law by force, and ignored the protests and vetoes of his fellow-consul. But this means nothing. He was ready to use legal channels as long as they served his needs; when they failed him, he overstepped them without a qualm. And his whole early career bears this out. As Erik Satie said in another context: 'M. Ravel has refused the Legion of Honour. But all his music accepts it.'

To say that such conduct was accepted practice in Republican Rome is no argument of extenuation; there was always a Cato to speak out grimly against the abuse of moral values in the pursuit of ambition. The whole of Caesar's slow, relentless struggle to absolute mastery of Rome seems to have been willed from the beginning: he would be a Sulla but not (as he said) commit the folly of resigning his dictatorship as Sulla had done. The only doubtful problem we have to consider is how far he was justified by events. And here, whether we wish it or no, we are largely thrown back on those moral judgments which the historian tends to treat as secondary to his main duty.

It is undeniably true that quite early in his career the chauvinist obstruction of a caste-ridden Senate placed Caesar in the awkward position of having either to abandon his ambitions or, from the moral viewpoint, treat Roman law and tradition as a dead letter. Professor Smith has put the dilemma in a nutshell: 'Caesar', he writes, 'was a genius, and a well-ordered State should be able to employ its great men fruitfully. If Caesar climbed to power by opposition to the nobles, it was because he could never have succeeded without it.'[6] '*Hoc voluerunt*!' Caesar exclaimed, surveying the bodies of his enemies strewn over the battlefield after Pharsalus: 'they asked for it!'

Precisely; but the question of his justification still remains.

[6] *Op. cit.* p. 117; cf. p. 102.

Because the nobility were an exclusive, snobbish clique who ran the Empire as a private estate for their own benefit, was Caesar justified in over-riding his country's laws—however ill-administered—and plunging Rome into revolution and civil war? There are others of whom the question could be asked: Sertorius, Caius Gracchus, that strange figure Saturninus. And this, in the context of the Republic's decline, raises another thorny problem: if traditional moral and legal sanctions have been rendered obsolete by events, how is the way ever to be opened for change, if not revolution? Can it not be argued that Caesar took the only possible course by which Roman government could be re-established on a working basis?

Given the sitation as it was when he crossed the Rubicon, this is of course true; no less true than the fact that Pompey's career (for instance) was technically far more illegal than Caesar's, and our attitude to him modified by his abject failure rather than his moral obliquity. But here, once again, we are making a judgment of expediency: we should not forget that it was due to Caesar's own choice of career, no less than the Senate's obstinacy, that the Rubicon had to be crossed at all. There was no compulsion on him, in the last resort, to be where he was. Obsolete laws (as we have seen in this country) can be modified without recourse to civil war, and ambition does not necessarily imply corruption.

Quis iustius induit arma? Lucan asked; and answered his own question with the religious *cliché*, *scire nefas*. We today may well for *nefas* substitute *impossibile*. And indeed, the real tragedy may be that there is, in fact, no answer to the question; that the motives of both parties were equally contemptible. That, I must confess, is my personal reaction to these abominable and chaotic times: a plague o' both your houses. 'No man' (to quote Professor Smith again) 'marches against his ideals; if a Roman army was prepared to march on Rome, it was because Rome stood for nothing that won their loyalty.' *Aut Caesar, aut nihil*: Caesar, by his very ruthlessness, made himself indispensable to the State he had largely been responsible for disrupting. This cannot, in the last resort, justify his actions at the bar of history. When one has given all due praise to his extraordinary qualities as a man of action, one is still left with the regret that they were, for whatever reason, so miserably employed, and that the Caesarian legend had so malign an influence on later ages. His career offers a perennial warning, today more than ever, against the dangers of *Machtpolitik,* insatiable ambition, the erection of expediency into a principle over-riding morality and the law of nations. It was Mr T. S. Eliot—again, a poet and moralist, not an historian—who most memorably crystallized the tragic dilemma which faced Caesar and Sulla alike. In *Murder in the Cathedral* he wrote:

> *The last temptation is the greatest treason:*
> *To do the right deed for the wrong reason.*

Note: Those interested in pursuing this subject further may be referred to Professor Arnaldo Momigliano's admirable article 'Per un riesame della storia dell' idea di Cesarismo' in the *Rivista Storica Italiana 68* (1956) pp. 220–229 now reprinted in *Secondo Contributo alla Storia degli Studi Classici* (Rome, 1960) pp. 273–282. This article also contains an exhaustive bibliography.

6

Venus Clerke Ovyde

The mysterious fluctuations of literary taste throughout recorded history can seldom have treated an author so capriciously as Ovid. No classical poet, with the exception of Virgil, survived so triumphantly (after a temporary moral eclipse) into the Middle Ages and the Renaissance. No notable classical writer of any description, with the possible exception of Seneca, has fallen so low in critical estimation from his original pinnacle of fame. In general we may say that Goethe and Molière were the last major writers to treat Ovid with that admiration and serious respect he had aroused among countless earlier generations; and that the Romantic Movement was largely responsible for the death-blow to his reputation. For the past century only isolated voices have been raised in Ovid's defence: he has been dismissed by countless scholars and critics as frivolous, facile, heartless, immoral, shallow, rhetorical, insincere, and possessed of a fatal fluency which precluded him from ever leaving well alone. Though Ripert could claim, with characteristic generosity, 'en vérité Ovide est encore, en ce début du xxᵉ siècle, un poète d'actualité,' the general unanimity of opinion has resulted, I fancy, in his being condemned rather more often than he is read.

Hermann Fraenkel, in a study of the poet as stimulating as it is heterodox, wrote:

> This settled state of affairs itself invites question. However valid a critical judgment may have been in the first place, it will lose some of its cogency with each reiteration, and by the time it has become a truism it has little truth left in it. . . . Unchallenged perseverance in a belief leads to complacent over-simplification.

Here is an extremely healthy attitude. It may not be entirely coincidental that the status of Ovid is being discussed once more when Dryden and Pope are back in fashion, when wit and elegance are once more at a premium; but we have to recognize that Ovid's reputation, secure for nearly two thousand years, presumes the existence in his work of high qualities in their own right, rather than a minor talent to be elevated by some accidental and passing fashion. His nineteenth-century eclipse must be considered in relation to his cumulative reputation; and immediately one begins to examine his claims in detail it becomes apparent that though he may be disliked he cannot be dismissed.

Ovid himself would not be in the least surprised to learn that he was still remembered. At the end of his most ambitious poem, the *Metamorphoses*, he wrote confidently:[1]

> And now I have finished a work which neither divine wrath
> Nor fire nor sword nor corrosive age shall destroy.
> Let the day predestined to close my life's uncertain span
> Come when it will. Only this human body
> Is forfeit to it; my finer self will soar
> Immortal over the towering constellations,
> My name be cut deep and indelible into the future.
> Wherever Roman dominion spreads over conquered lands
> Men's lips will speak me; and through all the ages
> —If a poet may trust his prophetic gift—I will live.

It is true; he has lived. His conventional prediction has been triumphantly justified. The poet whom the Goliards made their own—what better name for the twelfth-century Renaissance than the *aetas Ovidiana*?—was no mere frigid Court poetaster. Dante placed Ovid among the *quattro grand'ombre*; Chaucer borrowed from him extensively. Petrarch and Boccaccio, though both renouncing him in their old age—it is significant that he has always been a young man's poet—were steeped in him in their youth. Du Bellay and the Pléiade, Cervantes, Montaigne (who read the *Metamorphoses* for pleasure as a child) Drayton and, above all, Shakespeare—the list of those indebted to him is as long as it is distinguished. 'Is it not possible', enquires Mr L. P. Wilkinson,

[1] All translations, except where otherwise stated, are by the author.

in *Ovid Recalled*, 'that a poet who could say so much to Shakespeare, Milton, and Goethe, may still be able to say more than we have realized, even to us?'

It is clear that any reassessment of Ovid today will have to deal carefully and objectively with problems of literary and historical perspective. In particular, it will need to attack three major questions. There must be, in the first place, a presentation of the poet's life and work unencumbered by those neo-Baroque accretions, both stylistic and conceptual, which the eighteenth century fathered on him; next, his themes and methods must be related to the social and historical context of Augustan Rome; lastly, some attempt must be made to solve the problem of his recent critical decline, to form a purely literary judgment of his poetic achievement: 'instead of disparaging him for not displaying the intellectual passion of a Lucretius, the religious patriotism of a Virgil or the moral purpose of a Horace, we should be grateful that he realized his own limitations and chose a subject in which the qualities he did have could find scope'. Yet these limitations, as we shall see, were not entirely of the poet's own choosing.

In his own life-time he was the equivalent of a best-seller—which is perhaps why Roman critics were somewhat off-hand with him. Quintilian, for example, wrote:

> Ovid is flippant and licentious even in his serious poetry, and far too fond of indulging his technical virtuosity. Some of his work, however, deserves praise. His tragedy *Medea* shows, in my opinion, to what heights he might have attained if he had been prepared to discipline his talents rather than indulge them.

The *Medea*, as if in answer to Quintilian, is one of the very few Ovidian works that have failed to survive. But Quintilian is the model for all future attacks. Ovid is *lascivus*, which implies both flippancy and wantonness. He has a euphuistic passion for rhetorical flights of fancy. His immorality, his lack of seriousness, his overflown rococo style: these are the points that are hammered home again and again. Roger Bacon writes of 'the fables and mad quirks of Ovid and other such poets, where every kind of heresy and immorality is propounded'. Petrarch described him as 'a most talented man, but of a wanton and lubricious, indeed a feminine cast of mind', while even in the Renaissance Savonarola spoke contemptuously of 'Ovid the story-teller, Ovid the madman'.

It is true that till the nineteenth century Ovid's popularity far outstripped such criticisms: but this popularity was not alto gether due, originally at least, to pure literary merit. The Middle Ages allegorized him, moralized him, and gave his works almost gospel credence. He provided a vast storehouse of ancient mythology in easily construable Latin. He was quoted by doctors as a serious authority on erotic psychology. He was an excellent narrator in an age that lacked novelists. These factors (as Mr Wilkinson suggests) also hint at some of the reasons for his later decline. After the spread of vernacular handbooks on the classical myths, and the development of the forerunners of the novel, Ovid fell from supremacy as a source-book for mythology and erotica alike. He lost ground, too, with the increasing popularity of Greek literature; puritan morals militated against him; the Romantic Movement depreciated his stock still further by labelling him a prosaic and cynical versifier, devoid of all true poetic inspiration.

Here they broke ground with the Augustans, who still regarded Ovid in some sense as a psychological authority and master of description. Dryden could write:

> If the imitation of Nature be the business of a poet, I know no author who can justly be compared with ours, especially in the description of the passions. . . . I will appeal to any man who has read this poet, whether he finds not the natural emotion of the same passion in himself, which the Poet describes in feigned Persons?

Emotional *mores* change as rapidly as social conventions; and today, while we may cavil at the close and misleading association of Ovid with the eighteenth century, we would probably on this point agree with Dryden. But Romantic critics, who had somewhat different notions of morality and love, answered his rhetorical question with a resounding 'no'. Their attitude, and that of the nineteenth century in general, is well summed up in the words of a French history of Latin literature popular at the time:

> Ovid wrote a book of love poems without being in love, a

mythological poem without understanding mythology; a poem on national themes without the inspiration of a Roman spirit; and a collection of elegiac plaints without the impulse of genuine feeling. His sole attachment is to smart society, and his removal from that society is the cause of his grief in the poems of exile.

Even so liberal a critic as Macaulay, who had a great affection for Ovid, could not entirely avoid the familiar tone of moral condescension. He hints, too, at the objection most commonly sustained against Ovid to this day: that he lacks poetic *seriousness*:

> He seems to have been a very good fellow; rather too fond of women; a flatterer and a coward; but kind and generous, and free from envy, though a man of letters sufficiently vain of his literary performances. . . . The love, which he has reduced to a system, was little more than the mere sexual appetite, heightened by the art of dress, manner and conversation. This was an excellent subject for a man so witty and so heartless.

Ovid is certainly not a romantic poet as we understand the word; but he was very far from being heartless. He was a passionate realist, who would have found the ideals and ethics of the Troubadours totally incomprehensible, and if he were alive today would agree strongly (I imagine) with the central thesis of Denis de Rougemont's *Passion and Society*. In a word, he antedates the Romantic Ideal (a point often forgotten in dealing with ancient erotic poetry) and his frank acceptance of physical pleasure as an end in itself is well brought out in this poem from the *Amores*, written when he was about twenty:[2]

> Sultry it was, and the day had passed its noon-tide:
>   I laid my limbs for ease upon my bed.
> One shutter closed, the other was half-open;
>   What light came through was such as you find in woods,
> or a glow like dusk's, the sun just disappearing,
>   or like night just gone, and daylight not yet here.
> It was such a light as would suit a shy young lady
>   whose modesty still hopes to find some shade—
> And, in fact, Corinna came, in a flowing tunic,
>   and her fair hair loose on each side of her neck;
> The very spit of the way that high Semiramis
>   sought her bed, or Lais her many men.

2 Translation by Mr G. S. Fraser.

I ripped her gown off—not that it veiled her greatly,
    but struggle she did to be covered by it still;
she fought me off, not hoping to conquer:
    and of course I won, since she did not wish to win.
She stood before me with her thin gown fallen:
    in all her body I could find no flaw.
What shoulders I saw (and I touched them, too), what arms,
    and her paps' roundness—how fit they were to be pressed!
What a level plain, under trim breasts, her belly!
    what grand, great flanks; and what a youthful thigh!
Need I catalogue details? I saw nothing unlovely,
    and her naked body I pressed to my naked own.
Write the rest for yourselves! Tired at last, we slept quietly.
    May such a noontide often come my way!

It is important to appreciate that Ovid, for all his surface simplicity, is in fact a complex and difficult poet. There are the usual stumbling-blocks of language, literary convention, and historical perspective; but, over and above these considerations, it is difficult for us to look at Ovid as an essentially *Roman* poet, because he is so overlaid in our minds with misleading English accretions. His 'sweet witty soul' lives not only in 'mellifluous and honey-tongued Shakespeare', but in ten thousand Augustan couplets as well. We see Ovid today through a haze of unjustified assumptions and bad translations. We have to get behind modern notions of love and morality, rhymed distichs, and Renaissance euphuisms: we must clear our minds of something more than cant. Ovid's poetry has flowed out into the broad delta of European literature: we must go back and explore the river at its source, without preconceptions. We must judge Ovid, both as poet and man, in the context of his own age.

Here, indeed, we are fortunate, for Ovid tells us a good deal about himself.

You of a later age, would you know who I was, your gay
    poet of tender loves? Then learn the truth.
Sulmo is my homeland, where chill hill-streams make lush
    our pastures, and Rome is a hundred miles away . . .

His childhood surroundings affected Ovid's visual imagery to a remarkable degree. As a man he was a city-dweller, and later an

exile; he has the sharply-coloured nostalgia, the slightly sentimental eye for scenery which characterize the urban poet. A
Times correspondent in 1930 wrote of Sulmo, the modern Sul-
mona:

> As we came down among the plots and fields, the Ovidian
> qualities of the landscape became apparent—the bright colouring,
> the firm contrasts, the engaging detail. Far above the snow was so
> white and the rocks so brown; below, the vines and the young
> corn were so green, the fields of lucerne so purple, the poplars so
> tall, and the grass starred with such golden flowers. . . . It took us
> back to the days of our elegiacs, when all hills were sunny and the
> shade of the ilex ever black over cool streams, and when pentam-
> eters ended smoothly to the sound of falling waters.

That is the setting; but the time is equally important:

> Here was I born, in the year both consuls met their fate
> at Antony's hands, and Mutina was besieged.

Born, that is, in 43 B.C., too late to take part in the convulsive
Civil Wars which finally destroyed the Republic and established
Augustus; born to a disillusioned post-war generation, despising
violence, yet guilty at not having fought; born when the State
religion was crumbling, the old morals giving way to cynical
individualism. Mr Wilkinson and others have noted the literary
changes that he heralded—the general substitution of elegiac
for hexameter, the increasing discipline and formalization of
language, prosody and thought under the stultifying influence
of rhetoric, the influx of *cliché* and convention, the refuge
taken in Greek mythology from the 'corruption and banality of
modern life'—yet have drawn no general conclusions from such
a melancholy catalogue. Why is it, when we open a schoolroom
Ovid or a Latin Gradus, that we feel a vague unease at the smooth
phrases, as worn as an old penny, lacking any immediacy of
feeling, that can so easily be fitted into harmless, conventional
patterns, and obstinately deny any depth of association to the
surface sense they form? What is the key to the emptiness and
insincerity we feel today at the heart of so much of Ovid's work,
and which forms such a startling contrast to the original power
which infuses his more personal poems?

To find the answer we have to remember the historical background. Augustus, however civil a despot, was only too conscious of the powers of propaganda and censorship which an autocrat must wield if he is to survive. In the first flush of peace after long internal conflict Virgil and Horace could write, with honest and honourable gratitude, of the blessings conferred by the *Pax Augusta*; but by Ovid's hey-day that brief golden hour was past. Ovid's tragedy is that of an individualist whose every instinct was diametrically opposed to the political propaganda, the artificial resurgence of State Religion, the puritan sumptuary laws which the Emperor imposed on a morally shattered city. His final and irrevocable exile can be taken as a symbol of his entire life. He was denied his natural heritage of free and undirected thought: that denial was to corrupt language and themes simultaneously, and to have repercussions that continued long after his death, bringing about the swift degradation and collapse of Roman literature in a welter of vapid rhetoric and unreal conceits.

In this lamentable historical condition can be found the ultimate cause of almost everything that baffles, irritates, and alienates us in so much of Ovid's work: the inflated rhetoric, the artificial antiquarianism, the sterile and contrived attitude to human relationships. It enables us to understand his passion for syntactical patterns and sophistic parody, to penetrate beyond his assumption of moral nullity, his stock themes and interminable catalogues, his alarming verbal juggleries. The hyperbole falls into place; the underlying bitterness of the *Heroides*, the disgust that permeates the smart dialectic of the *Remedia Amoris*, the Alexandrian pathos over children, now take on a deeper significance. Ovid's ideal beau—depilated, deodorized, dandified, beringed—becomes an all-too-well-known protest against an intolerable emotional climate.

He had the additional disadvantage of being born a natural poet in a city which still despised literature as a full-time occupation. Hermann Fraenkel puts this predicament with great force and clarity:

> In Rome, poetry had no proper standing because the spirit had

none. . . . At best, poetry would be called upon to glorify the nation and to propagandize its true virtues. Any poet whose work was un-related to practical purposes because it was exclusively devoted to the concerns of the mind and heart, saw the fruits of his earnest endeavours classified as playthings. . . . Thus he established for his creations a setting of their own, apart from normality. . . . A very considerable part of the great Augustan poetry is erotic, and the reason is that the lover's world, while it offered a suitable habitat for free poetry to thrive in, yet at the same time was situated not without, but within the Roman actualities.

Ovid was temperamentally an artist, an individualist for whom the grandiose Roman social myth had few attractions; and to temperament he added that innate talent which he could not control, much less suppress:

> My brother from his green years had the speaker's bent,
>   He was born to the clash of words in a public court;
> But I as a boy already delighted in the divine,
>   and subtly the Muse was seducing me to her work.
> My father would say: 'Why choose this profitless career?
>   Homer himself left no inheritance.'
> Moved by his plea, I abandoned Helicon
>   And struggled to write without poetic form;
> But a poem, spontaneously, would shape itself to metre—
>   Whatever I tried to write, turned into verse.

Hardly surprisingly, Ovid joined Propertius' literary circle while still in his 'teens. Such groups met sometimes over dinner, sometimes after luncheon, in a private room reserved for the occasion. During these meetings literature or philosophy would be discussed in theory, and members' work be read aloud. Their main purpose was to analyse each others' work at leisure, and criticize it, ruthlessly and honestly, before publication. These elegiac poets, conscious perhaps of being an intellectual minority, cultivated true pedantic Alexandrianism. They wrote didactic poems along the lines of Callimachus or Nicander, and filled them with obscure mythological allusions, ingenious technical conceits —anything, in fact, that was safely remote from the dangerous material that lay all around them in Rome.

It was a subtle and satisfying form of literary escapism; and its

one outlet into immediate reality was through the private microcosm of the passionate love-affair, which threw up countless
poems to pseudonymous Cynthias or Delias. (This withholding of
names is more than a mere literary device: it was symptomatic of a
social atmosphere we know today only too well.) Such poems, too,
could only be addressed to a mistress, never to a wife: a convention which tells us as much about Roman social values as about
Roman elegiac formulae.

These influences Ovid absorbed: now he only needed a personal
spark to fire his own emotional and poetic self-discovery:

> When first I read my earliest poems in public
>   my beard had only been shaved once or twice;
> *She* fires my genius, who now is a Roman by-word
>   because of those verses—the girl I have called Corinna.

Who was Corinna? No one knows, and her identity is unimportant. She certainly was not, as was once believed, Augustus's
daughter Julia. On the other hand, it is hard to believe those
scholars who suppose her to have been a figment of Ovid's
imagination. We have already met her at siesta-time; that poem
does not bear the stamp of mere literary fantasy. The *Amores*,
indeed, have been consistently under-rated by critics who, for one
reason and another, doubt their sincerity. Some complain that
they are intellectually shallow, presumably in the belief that Ovid
ought to have paved the way for Donne. Others, nurtured in the
lap of modern sentiment, refuse to believe that their author
understood what he was talking about: here, they proclaim in
effect, is the voice not of love but of mere concupiscence. Appreciation of the poems has always been bedevilled by such *a priori*
value-judgments.

Grant Showerman is fairly representative of this trend. 'The
reader', he tells us, 'will not look to the *Amores* for profundity of
any sort, whether of thought or emotion. Except in a general way,
they are not even the expression of personal experience, to say
nothing of depth of passion.' This seems to me the very dia-
metrical opposite of the truth. These youthful poems possess a
passion, an honesty, an *immediacy* from which Ovid steadily moved

A DISGUISED AUTOBIOGRAPHY

away in his later work, and which he only partially recaptured in
the poems of exile. Revised, and cut from five books to three
by the author, they still offer a remarkable guide to Ovid's
emotional and poetic development. In places they have the air of
a *roman à clef*, a disguised autobiographical novel. First there is
Ovid as the social butterfly, the heart-whole Don Juan. Here he is
giving advice to his mistress on her conduct at a dinner-party,
where both her husband and Ovid himself will be present:

> Arrive before your husband—though I don't see what can be
>   done
>   if you *do* arrive first—but still, arrive before him.
> When he sits down, join him with wifely modesty—
>   but touch my foot discreetly as you pass by!
> Watch for my nods and meaningful expressions,
>   catch each stealthy sign, return it to me:
> My brows will speak to you in silent eloquence,
>   my fingers, dipped in wine, form secret words.
> When the thought of our wanton love-making stirs in your
>   heart, touch your flushed cheek with elegant thumb . . .
> When you wish your husband the ills he so richly deserves
>   lay your hands on the table as if in prayer . . .

We find the same advice transferred to a more artificial and
didactic context afterwards in the *Ars Amatoria*: Ovid admitted
there that experience had been his guide. But this carefree initial
mood is subtly modified later in the *Amores*, where Ovid betrays
the symptoms of the psychopathic rake, insatiate and revolted by
turns:

> The hunter pursues his flying quarry only to leave it
>   when caught, and ever strains to the prey ahead; . . .
> I am sick of desire, my ardours ebb, a dark
>   vortex of misery wrenches at my mind;
> Yet like some hard-mouthed horse that bolts with its master,
>   foaming over the bit, quite out of control,
> Is the turning gale of desire that grips me again
>   when flushed Love draws his too familiar sword.

The impact of Corinna on Ovid is as devastating and obsessional
as that of Lesbia on Catullus or Cynthia on Propertius. His
diffused passions are now focussed as though in a burning-glass,

and his poems attain a corresponding height of intensity. We follow the affair through all its fluctuations of triumph and hopelessness. Corinna clearly understood Ovid well: she played him like a fish, keeping herself always a little elusive. She objected to his writing tragedy, or epic, or, indeed, anything but love elegies —and here we can admire her judgment. In the end he capitulated completely:

> Take me, dear heart, on whatever terms you will:
> Lay down your laws, be the mistress of my desires.

But Corinna, like Lesbia, tired of her lover, and left him— supreme insult—for a soldier. Even after two millennia the anguish and shock of Ovid's loss communicates itself to us. Marlowe, who as an undergraduate turned the *Amores* into heroic couplets —thus setting an unfortunate fashion which is still with us—still catches superbly the violent conflict in the poet's mind:

> Long have I borne much, mad thy faults me make:
> Dishonest love, my wearied brest forsake.
> Now have I freed my selfe, and fled the chaine,
> And what I have borne, shame to beare againe . . .
> Leave thy once powerful wordes, and flatteries;
> I am not as I was before, unwise.
> Now love and hate my light brest each way move,
> But victory, I thinke, will hap to love . . .
> I flie her lust, but follow beauties creature;
> I loath her manners, love her bodies feature.
> Not with thee, nor without thee can I live,
> And doubt to which desire the palme to give.
> Or lesse faire, or lesse lewd would thou mightst bee;
> Beauty with lewdnesse doth right ill agree.

'I am not as I was before, unwise': despite the hesitations, that line marks a key-point in Ovid's development. It seems clear that henceforward the poet of immediacy, of direct experience, gives way to the witty, detached, cynical, didactic teacher of erotic technique. Psychologically it is an all too understandable transition. In the *Amores* we see Ovid face to face; his emotions are stripped bare. In particular we can sense his feelings of guilt and inferiority: the constant use of military imagery for affairs of love, the constant mocking depreciation of the 'lame' elegiac as opposed to the heroic hexameter. From now on, however, he retreats behind an impregnable mask of wit, scholarship, and Alexandrian conceits. The process is gradual, yet clearly marked.

The *Heroides*, his next work, takes up a half-way position between immediacy and didacticism. By a neat device these poems apply his personal knowledge of feminine psychology to a series of classic situations. Various famous mythological women— Penelope, Briseis, Dido, Oenone—write stylized, and agonized, letters to their inconstant lovers. Perhaps it is not an accident that almost every plea is hopeless—and that the reader knows this. Typical (though in this case the story did have an eventual happy ending) are these lines from Penelope to Ulysses:[3]

> Your Penelope writes to you, long-delaying Ulysses—
>   yet send no letter home, come home yourself!
> Tall Troy is down now, loathed of Danaan daughters:
>   Was Troy, was Priam worth the cost to me?
> Long since that adulterer's ship sought Lacedaemonia:
>   Would the mad waters had then whelmed him down!
> I should not have lain cold on a lonely couch then,
>   not be grumbling, stranded, now at my long slow days:
> Nor as, sighing, I seek to cozen the night's vastness
>   would the hanging web weary my widowed hands . . .
> For what can it matter to me that by your sinews
>   Troy has been torn, and where was a wall is a plain,
> if here I must wait, as I waited, Troy standing,
>   and my man to the end of time must be my lack?
> Smashed for others, for me Pergamum stands, still,
>   though the victor plough it with a plundered ox,
> though where Troy was, fields are, and grains ripe for
>   reaping
>   spring from a soil made fat with Phrygian blood,
> though the ploughshare strike at the bones of half-buried
>   bodies
>   and the tall grasses cover their ruined homes.
> You won; and you are not here; and they will not tell me,
>   hard-hearted man, what keeps you—and keeps you where!

It is possible to select extracts from the *Heroides* which for

[3] Translation by Mr G. S. Fraser.

depth of emotion and density of poetic texture still equal anything in the *Amores*. But to read them in bulk is quite another matter. This test, seldom applied to Ovid, is highly revealing. Brilliant at first, the *Heroides* soon pall. They are repetitious; the tricks are worked too often, and worked self-consciously. Alexandrianism begins to rear its head. While the poetic force is diluted, the rhetorical devices and mythological parallels increase. Robbed of felt experience, Ovid's ungovernable verbal facility began to get the better of him. It is just this quality, however, which commended the *Heroides* to the Renaissance. In 1516 Guido Morillonius wrote a tribute which today we cannot but find a little two-edged:

> Ye Gods, what manifold learning do they display, and how they twinkle with sprightly wit! If Horace gave his vote for one who could combine the profitable and the pleasant, none, methinks, can excel Ovid in this art. He has so mingled the serious with honey-sweet fiction and fiction with the serious, that 'tis hard telling whether he offers us more pleasure than profit or more profit than pleasure.

It was the pedant Holofernes whom Shakespeare credited with the famous judgment: 'For the elegance, facility and golden cadence of poetry . . . Ovidius Naso was the man: and why, indeed, Naso but for smelling out the odoriferous flowers of fancy, the jerks of invention?'

At this point, while still a young man, Ovid deliberately abandoned the writing of love-poetry—and, indeed, all poetry—for about nine years. When he confronts us again it is as a mature poet of forty; and what he offers us then is the *Art of Love*. The metamorphosis is remarkable. Gone are the violent passions of the *Amores* and *Heroides*. Instead we see the Ovid we all know by repute—witty, cynical, man-of-the-world, offering a textbook of seduction to young gallants. Henry Fielding, who paraphrased the *Art of Love* into prose, has caught the mood admirably:

> If in so learned an Age as this, when Arts and Sciences are risen to such perfection, there be any Gentleman unskilled in the Art of Loving, let him come to my School; where, if he hath any Genius, he will soon become an Adept; For I would by no means have any

young Gentleman think, that Erudition in unnecessary upon this Occasion. . . . Rules are necessary even to make a good Coachman, as those Gentlemen who have the Ambition to excel this way very well know. Now it hath pleased Venus to place me in the Coach-Box: what a Captain is to a Ship, or the Driver to his Chariot, that am I to Love.

It is no accident that this version represents the *Ars* so well. More and more of Ovid's verse during this middle period is mere metrified prose: this is partly because the *Ars*, the *Fasti,* and a great deal of the *Metamorphoses* are didactic poems, or parodies of didactic poems. Originally such works were written in verse simply for mnemonic purposes: they contained facts or precepts which had to be remembered. Hesiod's *Works and Days* is a good example. They are not essentially poems as we understand poetry, whatever their incidental literary merit. Yet even such metrical treatises sometimes show genuine poetic inspiration, inseparable from the structure and thought. Empedocles offers a good example of this—and Ovid was a poet to his finger-tips.

What had happened? Had the break with Corinna crippled his creative talent in some psychological sense? It is possible, but this would not supply an adequate answer in itself. Had his natural talent simply dried up? This seems improbable in the case of a man whose every utterance transformed itself into verse. It seems more likely that, for whatever reason, it was deliberately suppressed. Yet nothing—though the sincerity and thematic honesty might be denied—could ever damp down Ovid's metrical fluency. He could have turned the consul-lists into elegiacs; on occasion, when he came to write the *Fasti*, he nearly did.

At all events, in the *Art of Love* Ovid has his emotions—poetic or personal—very firmly under control. The poem appears as the testament of a witty, fashionable urban *rentier*, an aesthete deliberately turning his back on Republican *gravitas* and social responsibility:

> Let others delight in tradition: I am glad I was born
> Into these times, this congenial today.
> Not for the stubborn gold we mine, or the rare shells
> gathered for our delight on foreign shores;

> Not for the marble quarried from crumbling mountains,
>   not for the palaces pier-built over the bay—
> But for refinement and culture, which have banished
>   the tasteless crudeness of our forefathers.

The *Art of Love*, besides being a poetic retrogression, thus en-
dangered Ovid politically. It was the basic cause of his later
banishment. Nothing could have run more flatly counter to the
Emperor's plans for regenerating the Republican spirit. Augustus
aimed to bring back the old yeoman virtues: strict personal
morality, stable and fertile marriages, worship of the State gods,
pursuit of the agricultural ideal. In the *Art of Love* Ovid, on the
other hand, proclaims himself a modernist, a city-lover, an anti-
Establishment individualist, and a professor of extra-marital
seduction. About religion he had this to say:

> The existence of gods is expedient; therefore let us
> Believe they exist, and perform them traditional rites—

a piece of cynicism which came too near the political truth of the
matter to please Augustus.

From the moment of the work's publication, and immense
popular success, Ovid must have been a marked man. Augustus'
own attitude to literature, as Suetonius tells us, was hardly
sympathetic to heterodoxy of this sort: it was, in the public
sense, strictly utilitarian, and formed a useful adjunct to the
Emperor's propaganda service:

> Augustus in his Greek and Latin reading sought for nothing so
> keenly as precepts and examples of salutary application to the
> commonwealth or to individuals. These he copied word for word,
> and, suiting the admonition to particular requirements, would fre-
> quently dispatch to his captains and provincial governors, or to
> magistrates at Rome.

It seems impossible that the Emperor's displeasure could have
hung over Ovid's head for ten years before his banishment
without Ovid being very well aware of it. Rome was a small
society at the higher level, and Ovid moved at its very centre.
This suggests a reason for the course his writing took during the
period which followed the *Art of Love*: he was desperately trying
to restore himself to official favour.

First came the *Remedia Amoris,* his official recantation of the *Ars*: but its counter-suggestions would hardly have satisfied even the least captious of critics:

> My advice, then, is to take two mistresses at once;
> (He's a strong man who can manage more than two);
> Divided attention that wanders between them both
> Leads each desire to sap the other's strength.

Perhaps he underestimated the gravity of the situation when it was conveyed to him that a palinode was necessary: at all events the two large works that followed both chose safer subjects and treated them in an eminently orthodox fashion. Ovid at this stage of his career rather suggests the picture of Frank Harris struggling with a Government-sponsored biography.

The works in question were those two varied and imposing edifices, the *Fasti* and the *Metamorphoses.* Both were unfinished when Ovid went into exile. Both contain highly complimentary references to the Imperial family. Both steer very clear of contemporary politics, social *mores*, or aesthetic individualism; and both strain after that somewhat lapidary major form which in Rome was the hallmark of poetic seriousness. The *Metamorphoses* retreats—as Alexandrian poets had done under similar circumstances—to the safe world of Greek mythology. The *Fasti* is more positive in intention: it is Ovid's hopeless attempt to prove himself at one stroke patriot, antiquarian, and a devotee of Rome's religious totems. But as Fraenkel pleasantly puts it, 'that sweet nostalgia for pristine things which actuates the antiquarian did not come to him naturally'.

Mr Wilkinson sums up the *Fasti* as 'a jumble of astronomy, history, legend, religion, superstition, scholarship, guesswork, and antiquarian lore. The ingenious transitions of the *Metamorphoses* are not attempted, but the right to pass over one item and elaborate another at whim is maintained.' The formal structure, in fact, is artificial, externally imposed. A versified calendar of the first six months of the Roman year could hardly avoid this, it is true; but Ovid never showed himself capable of controlling large-scale composition. His talent was all for the miniature, the short elegy. The main interest of the *Fasti* is for the antiquarian, not for the student of poetry. It has seldom been translated. John Gower's seventeenth-century couplets catch something of its gnomic, half-humorous sententiousness:

> Why is a Barley-Bean-Cake, you will say,
> And lard of Pork now eaten on this day?
> This ancient Nymph loves best her ancient Fare;
> And (plain) for farre-fetched dainties doth not care.
> Fish in those dayes about did safely play:
> On sands the Oyster unrespected lay . . .
> Pork was the meat; with pork their feasts were filled;
> And Earth did only Beans and Barley yield.
> These mix'd whoever eats upon this day,
> He'll be the haler all the yeare, they say.

Ovid was too urban, too civilized and sceptical by nature to catch the numinous quality of these ancient country superstitions. Virgil did it; but Virgil was himself by instinct a countryman. Ovid, like Heine or Byron, is always laughing slyly at his own high seriousness; he could not believe in the theme which he so piously and politically undertook. Occasionally the *Fasti* do flash out into poetry; but the central impulse is lacking:

> To Parents' tombs now orisons they pay,
> And on friends' urns some little offrings lay.
> Small things please ghosts; in Styx none greedy be;
> Gods for great gifts accept true piety.

The *Metamorphoses*, on the other hand, is always being translated (still most often into heroic couplets) and is generally acclaimed as Ovid's major achievement. It has influenced not only European literature, but also European art, more than almost any other ancient work. Sixteenth-century tapestry workers, artists such as Filarete and Raphael, Titian, Bernini, or Rubens, all drew from this vast treasure-house.[4] Alone of his works, too, it is

[4] This fact must be connected with Ovid's remarkable visual sense. It is likely that his youthful visit to Athens left him with strong memories of the statues and paintings he saw there; that his brilliant landscapes are functionally connected with such works as the Pompeian wall-paintings, whose terms they so consistently echo. Just as Mr T. R. Henn has traced the influence on Yeat's poetry of his assiduous gallery-visiting, so we may infer a similar source of inspiration in Ovid.

composed in the epic hexameter. The Elizabethan translator Golding wrote of it:

> For this do learned persons deeme of Ovid's present worke:
> That in no one of all his bookes the which he wrote do lurke
> Mo darke and secret mysteries, mo counselles wise and sage,
> Mo good ensamples, mo reproofes of vice in youth and age.

All this is quite true; though perhaps we would judge the poem by less purely moral criteria. It is certainly the most Alexandrian of Ovid's works: a rag-bag of myth and legend, in which tiny epics are here and there embedded, an index to Ovid's natural creative length, and a quarry for the anthologist, who can cut away self-contained fragments to illustrate Ovid's growing taste for the fantastic, the semi-allegorical, the proto-baroque. Here is his description of the Palace of the Sun, given as an introduction to the Phaethon legend:

> The Palace of the Sun reared up on roof-tall pillars,
> Alive with caustic gold, harsh bronze that burns like fire,
> And the gables above them were diapered with ivory,
> The bridal pair of doors all branched with lightning silver.
> But the hand's skill was subtler than these glistering elements:
> For in high relief on the doors wry-footed Mulciber
> Had carved the waters that dandle the middle earth,
> The land's contour and the low profile of the skies.
> This sea held all the cerulean gods, held musical Triton,
> Held Proteus flickering through a thousand shapes, Aegeon
> With one gross hand hooped over two massy whales;
> Held Doris, that sea-lady, with her shoals of daughters
> Marbling the waters, or on rocks stately sitting,
> The sun threading through green eddies of their hair,
> Or bareback riding on fishes. Each with a different face,
> But muted and refined to the haunting difference of sisters;
> And carved on the land itself men, cities, animals, trees,
> Rivers and nymphs and Gods of the countryside,
> And above them all one glowing blazon of the sky,
> And to left and right six signs of the Zodiac. [5]

This passage offers an excellent instance of Ovid's visual emphasis, his *penchant* for describing a recognizable *picture*.

[5] Translation by Mr Iain Fletcher.

The real failure, as with the *Fasti*, lies in the overall structure: an art-gallery is not formally coherent. Once again Ovid was defeated by a major opus. There are about a hundred and seventy legends of metamorphosis treated here, in no less than fifteen books. No poem of epic structure could sustain so many un-related climaxes: each legend seems no sooner begun than it is artificially resolved by a transformation scene. To confuse matters further, Ovid, who had a very lively sense of the absurd, fre-quently punctures his own myth with superb and deliberate bathos, as in the legend of Arethusa:

> On my beleagured limbs an icy sweat sprang out,
> Dark drops rained down from the whole of my body; my footsteps
> Left puddles behind them, dew lay thick in my hair—
> And swifter than words can tell, I became a spring.

It has been suggested that Ovid's interest in metamorphosis sprang from an obsession with 'the phenomena of insecure and fleeting identity.' This may well be true; he lived in a world of changing *mores*, which his own career reflected. He suggests at one point, with typical egocentricity, that the *Metamorphoses* is a self-portrait in macrocosm. But this does not make the *Metamorphoses* a unified poem: the parts remain obstinately greater than the whole, the virtues incidental rather than organic. Swift narrative, sharp visual images, a most un-Roman feeling for fluid planes of reality—all are here; yet they only coalesce in brief, detached episodes. Perhaps the most successful and most characteristic of these is the strange wooing of Hermaphroditus by Salmacis—the water-nymph who is simultaneously a humanized naiad and the pool she inhabits:

> Clapping his flanks with hollowed palms, he dived
> Quickly into the pool, and swimming arm-over-arm
> Gleamed through the crystal water, an ivory figurine
> Or virgin lily sheathed in glass. 'He is mine,
> Mine!' cried the nymph, 'I have won!' Off flew her dress,
> And naked she plunged to join him, gripped him struggling
> Breast to breast, kissed his writhing lips, clung hard
> This way and that to the boy's resistant body

Till her coiling limbs had him prisoner: so the serpent
Caught aloft in an eagle's talons, thrashes round
His captor's head and legs, lassoos those widespread
Wings with his tail; and so lithe ivy enlaces
Vast tree-trunks, so the polyp its submarine prey
With suckered tentacles crowding from every side . . .
In such a clinging embrace their members merged,
Boy and nymph no longer, a double being,
Not male, not female, yet with the parts of both.

How would Ovid have escaped from this creative cul-de-sac if he had remained in Rome? It is a question which those who condemn the poems of exile out of hand might well ask themselves. His urge to write was as strong as ever; his technical virtuosity was at its peak. Only the heart of the matter was wanting: a congenial theme, sincerity of emotion, individual passion. If the poems of his middle period are still worth reading in the original today, it is at least as much for their sheer verbal and metrical skill as for his subject-matter.

Here, indeed, his genius has proved a positive handicap: too great, too effortless, the verbal and rhetorical dexterity he displays has earned him a bad reputation—especially in this country, where amateurs are at a premium, perfection of any kind is automatically suspect, and the writer is expected to pretend, modestly, that every line has cost him untold effort. Ovid's rhythms, it is said, are mechanical, his epithets *cliché*-ridden. He is regularly compared, to his detriment, with his great predecessors. Where in his verse, it is asked, will one find the great hammer-strokes of Lucretius, the enjambed, architectonic Virgilian period, the freshness of Catullus, the sharp mosaic patterns that make the Horatian odes so memorable?

The truth is that Ovid was capable, in places, of rising to them all: but never for long. In any case he was aiming at a quite different kind of target, and his verbal texture reflects this. It is true that both his prosody and his vocabulary, when viewed in the perspective of his total output, seem to us over-schematized and unoriginal in comparison with earlier writers. His unelided, prevalently dactylic hexameters lack Virgil's depth and plangency:

he cannot build a period. His elegiacs are less striking, less verbally and rhythmically adventurous than those of Propertius—yet the *Amores* at least show an equal passion. As I have already suggested, it seems clear that the basic reason for his apparent superficiality— especially in those poems composed immediately before his exile— was the later Augustan censorship, which had a psychologically crippling effect on originality of language as well as expression.[6]

If this theory be correct, we should expect to find Ovid's most consistently satisfactory verbal imagery in the *Amores*, and to a lesser extent in the poems of exile and, perhaps, the *Heroides*. This is actually the case. The dull *gradus* epithet, the flat rhythm, the artificial trope all become most obtrusive in his middle period, the period which produced the *Fasti*, the *Ars Amatoria*, the *Remedia Amoris* and the *Metamorphoses*. Here he also suffers from the inability to conceive at length. In short poems his visual and emotional lyricism, his crystalline precision of phrase, his Propertian Hellenisms, his Virgilian assonance and onomatopoeia, his Horatian verbal patterns all find their proper, restricted place. Over a long stretch the effect is both vulgar and tedious: it is as though one were to decorate a house-front with diamonds. The epithets lapse into *cliché*, the delicate, self-contained couplets bore us by their intolerably repetitive perfection. The same applies to his under-enjambed, over-dactylic hexameters. Only over brief stretches, both technically and emotionally, is the necessary density achieved. Narcissus, for instance, contemplating his own beloved reflection in the water, is made to exclaim:

> This is I, I know it; my reflection cannot cheat me;
> I burn with love of myself, both kindle and suffer the flame;
> What shall I do? Ask or be asked? And ask for what?
> What I long for I have; possession has dispossessed me.

There is a Virgilian force in the original hexameters which Ovid could not long sustain: in the pronominal juxtapositions, the verbal patterns, the assonances, the cumulative force of alliterated c's, f's, and m's:

---

[6] For a further general discussion of this point see below, pp. 163ff, and especially the passage by George Orwell there quoted.

Iste ego sum, sensi; nec me mea fallit imago;
uror amore mei, flammas moveoque feroque.
quid faciam? roger anne rogem? quid deinde rogabo?
quod cupio mecum est: inopem me copia fecit.

Here the emotional force, sharpened by Ovid's own undoubted narcissism, with its faintly schizophrenic undertones, matches the technical skill. It is not always so. Ovid is seldom far from the edge of rhetorical conceit, cleverness for cleverness' sake. All too often he slips over; as Seneca said, he never knew when to let well alone. He resembles a powerful dynamo with an insufficient load: he is liable to thrash himself to pieces on trivialities. Brilliance without content, rhetoric without passion, rapidly turn monotonous. The tricks repeat themselves; the mood, as Dryden saw, becomes fixed and tepid: 'Ovid, with all his sweetness, has little variety of numbers and sound: he is always, as it were, upon the hand-gallop, and his verse runs upon carpet-ground.'

It took a personal crisis—long-delayed, yet inevitable—to resolve his dilemma. In A.D. 8, at the age of fifty, Ovid was exiled by Augustus to the Black Sea port of Tomi—now Constanza in the Rumanian Dobrudja. The cause of his banishment is given as the *Art of Love*, coupled with some private indiscretion, the nature of which remains obscure. The fruits of his exile were the *Tristia* and the *Epistulae ex Ponto*, or *Black Sea Letters*. External events had forced Ovid back at last to personal, immediate poetry—though now the driving impulse was not love but obsessional self-pity and nostalgia. Here is how, from exile, he describes his final hours in Rome:[7]

> The memory has not died—it still returns to torment me—
>   Of those black hours which were my last in Rome.
> Even now, when I think again of that night
>   Which closed, like an iron door, upon all I love most dearly
> My eyes are stung with tears.
>   When the sun rose, I was to be an exile
> By Caesar's command driven forth
>   Beyond the furthest frontiers of Italy.

[7] Translation by Mr Ian Scott-Kilvert.

The time was short, yet I could not make ready,
  My heart was numbed with despair, my spirit failed me;
I could not think of slaves, of companions for the journey,
  Of possessions, of clothes, of any comfort for my exile.
I was stunned, as a man hurled to the ground by a thunderbolt,
  Who lives, but has no feeling.
At last the very pain brought back my senses;
  I said goodbye, for the last time, to the few who came,
One or two, no more, of all the friends I had.
  My wife clung to me, and seeing the bitter tears
Roll down her innocent cheek, I could not hold back my own . . .
  It seemed that Death was suddenly a visitor to our house;
I heard men, women, and children cry aloud,
  There was weeping in every room, such a wild clamour of
    despair
As might have echoed above the roofs of burning Troy.
  Later, when every sound had sunk to silence,
And the moon's chariot drove out from the black arch of night,
  I gazed by her light upon the gleaming Capitol
That loomed above our house, yet could not shield us,
  And spoke aloud:
You gods that dwell by my home, you temples
  That I shall never see again, Protectors
Of the high-built destiny of Rome,
  This greeting I give now must last for ever.

The poems from exile, no less than the *Amores,* have suffered
from irrelevant moral criticism—but of a different and crueller
kind. In England they have been disparaged for two main reasons.
First, Ovid refuses to take his punishment like a gentleman.
He complains in loud and undignified tones. He fails to maintain
a stiff upper lip. Second, and arising from this, is his undisguised
sycophancy. He grovels abjectly to Augustus. He indulges in gross
flattery in the hope of recall. It is all, we are made to feel, a little
repellent, and best dismissed with Gibbon's bland, oblique irony:

> The nine books of Poetical Epistles, which Ovid composed during
> the seven first years of his melancholy exile, possess, besides the
> merit of elegance, a double value. They exhibit a picture of the human
> mind under very singular circumstances; and they contain many
> curious observations, which no Roman, except Ovid, could have an
> opportunity of making.

Today we are better acquainted with the realities of exile, and more charitable towards its victims. Yet it is hard to clear our minds of such long-standing moral preconceptions, to appreciate that the *Tristia* contains poetry more immediate, more deeply felt, more fully realized than anything Ovid had written since the *Amores*:

> In that land now gay boys and girls are plucking
>   violets that spring wild down country lanes;
> Meadows are stippled and rich now with rainbow flowers,
>   young birds are breaking into their first spring song;
> Under the eaves now swallows bicker and build
>   dark midget nests;
> Now from their mothering furrows the first green spikes
>   spring, and unfold each tender tip.
> Now in vineyards the world over shoots are bursting
>   (But the vine grows far from these barren shores);
> Now in orchards upcountry blossom is heavy on boughs
>   (But trees grow far from these barren lands).

Exile has its own language and imagery, its recurrent wish-fulfilments, its aching obsession with lost everyday things of home or countryside. Few poets have used the symbols of this private, suffering world with such power and economy as Ovid. Yet these poems, taken as a whole, remain difficult reading, as all repetitive and obsessional poetry is bound to do. No one knew this better than Ovid himself. Wistfully he wrote:

> Now I am out of words, I have asked the same thing so often;
>   Now I feel shame for my endless, hopeless prayers.
> You must all be wearied by these monotonous poems—
>   Certainly you have learned by heart what I want
> And know the contents of each fresh letter before
>   you break the seal that keeps its privacy.

Like the *Amores*, the poems from exile, read as a whole, form an autobiographical sequence. At first Ovid is stunned and sick; he refuses fully to believe what has happened, or to accept his surroundings. Then he rallies, with volatile optimism; there is energetic canvassing through his wife and friends for a reprieve. But no reprieve comes. The tone changes to a frightened,

uncertain querulousness. Age, illness, brutal conditions, hopelessness are all taking their toll. Finally Ovid makes his grim peace
with Tomi, accepts it as his last home.

His exile had lasted ten years when he died, and his closing
words in the *Black Sea Letters* are a reproof to his later moral
critics no less than his living enemies:

> Ah Malice, sheath your bloody claws, let the exile sleep,
> 　do not scatter my ashes after death!
> I have lost all; only bare life remains to quicken
> 　the substance and knowledge of my pain.
> What pleasure do you get from stabbing these dead limbs?
> 　There is no space in me now for another wound.

Ovid's phases of popularity and neglect have been largely due to
para-literary considerations; thus while the *Amores* and *Tristia*
have been unduly depreciated, both the *Metamorphoses* and the
Ars Amatoria have undergone a process of artificial poetic infla-
tion. I suspect, however, that the biggest stumbling-block to our
appreciation of Ovid—certainly for the reader who deals with
him entirely through translations—is the heroic couplet into
which he is still regularly turned, and with which he is almost
indissolubly associated. This at once imposes on his work a
purely factitious eighteenth-century character; such a verse-form,
besides thus identifying Ovid in the reader's mind with English
Augustanism, seems indefensible from even a purely prosodic
and aesthetic point of view.

The stiffly balanced, disjunctive antithesis of the rhymed
distich is in direct conflict with the flexible long-and-short
characteristic of the elegiac (and even more so, of course, with
the rapid, falling rhythm of the hexameter).[8] Ovid himself was
obsessed by the *un*equal measure, the lame pentameter; 'Let my
verse rise in six feet', he wrote, 'and fall back in five'. To represent
the elegiac by two iambic lines of equal length, rhymed and
stopped, is misleading in every possible way. The first, and
perhaps most remarkable attempt to break down this unfortunate

---

[8] For fuller discussion of this point see below, 'Some Versions of Aeschylus', esp. pp. 201–2.

convention was made by Hermann Fraenkel, in the passages he quoted for illustration. He adapted the Day Lewis six-beat stress-hexameter for the elegiac couplet by following it up with a similar five-beat line, usually catalectic: a device which was subsequently adopted by Professor Richmond Lattimore for translating Greek elegists such as Theognis, and has been used in the present essay on most occasions. Fraenkel's experiment was arrestingly successful: at one stroke all the Drydenish associations were sloughed off. The monotonous well-turned complaints of the poems from exile (*quid lacrimas, odiose senex?*) suddenly regained a pristine freshness and dignity; one might almost be reading a frontier elegy from the Chinese.

Here, then, is my personal verdict on Ovid. He wrote his most valid and immediate poetry in the *Amores* and the poems of exile. Most of what came in between, whatever its incidental virtues, was a progressive retreat from poetic honesty into Alexandrian pedantry and politically-inspired escapism or trimming. His technical skill, his wit, his sense of the absurd, his psychological acuteness, his gift for empathy, his intensely personal vision—all these should recommend him to modern poets. Like them too, his bent was for the short piece; when he attempted a long poem he crashed in glittering fragments. His final tragedy is very much a tragedy of our own times; his poetry gains greatly from translation into an idiom familiar to the contemporary reader and shorn of misleading historical overtones. Though on nearly every page we may lament the waste of his superb technical abilities on unreal, trivial or sterile themes, nevertheless, again and again, his true qualities shine indomitably through the protective carapace of fashion and wit under which he so long concealed himself. Let the final comment be his characteristic own:

> Although this age is rich in noble poets
>   Fame has not grudged my gifts renown.
> Many excelled me: I know it. Yet I am quoted
>   As much as they, and most read throughout the world.
> Which I was it triumphed? True poet or fashion's pander?
>   Either way, generous reader, it is you I must thank.

7

Two Gentlemen of Rome

THE ELDER AND THE YOUNGER PLINY

To most of us—even, I suspect, to many classical scholars—the Elder and Younger Pliny are nebulous, mildly eccentric figures, hovering on the fringes of Roman history, only brought into the limelight by accident. We know that the Elder Pliny was killed—an early martyr to the scientific spirit—while observing the eruption of Vesuvius in A.D. 79, the same eruption that preserved Pompeii. We may laugh over that fantastic *omnium gatherum* the *Natural History*. But how many of us have read it? As for the nephew, he remains fixed in our minds as a fussy Governor of Bithynia, who corresponded with Trajan about the political implications of the Christian religion.[1] Yet in their lives and in their works, both uncle and nephew provide important evidence about the critical social period through which they lived.

We are inclined to imagine—it is an understandable, but fatal, mistake—that the ancient world was socially static: that not only in dress, diet, and language, but also public behaviour, there was little to choose between Periclean Athens and Hellenistic Alexandria, between Republican and Imperial Rome. In reality, constant, radical changes occurred—as radical as those in England between the sixteenth and eighteenth centuries—and the pattern of political and private life varied from generation to generation. The Elder Pliny, born in Tiberius' reign, must have met men who

[1] *Letters* 10.96: 'I could discover nothing more than depraved and excessive superstition.' Trajan's reply contains a noteworthy comment on the use of anonymous informers: 'It is introducing a very dangerous precedent, and by no means agreeable to the spirit of the age.' Yet his successor Hadrian made use of the secret police and the *agent provocateur*.

remembered the Republic; he lived on through the eventful years of Caligula and Nero; he survived the 'year of the Four Emperors', and died a month or two later than Vespasian. The period during which he flourished coincides with a gross outburst of licentious luxury which in his nephew's time, under Nerva and Trajan, had largely abated.

But it was the suppression of the Republican government, after years of bloody anarchy, and its replacement by an autocratic Emperor, that most profoundly affected the Roman way of life during the first century A.D. However hard Augustus might strive to maintain the polite fiction of joint rule with the Senate, the ultimate authority was himself; and Romans, who had found the very name of King abhorrent, now bowed before an Imperial master. Hitherto their ambitions had found an outlet in political or military achievement. Now Senate and Forum could offer little but the empty simulacrum of power; and ambition was perilously liable to be interpreted as *lèse-majesté*. New outlets had to be found.

The cult of litigation was one answer. The Romans had always been legally minded; and the advocate's profession was one of the few that a nobly born citizen could practise without stigma. Under the Empire, the number of law-suits swelled astronomically; both Augustus and Vespasian had to deal with chronic congestion in the courts. Throughout the century Forum and Basilica re-echoed to the speeches of pleaders, the barracking of the public, and the raucous clamour of professional *claqueurs*. Both Plinies, among their other duties, practised at the bar. The nephew, who specialized in inheritance cases, has left us a vivid picture of the crowded court-room, the interminable rhetorical haranguing, the poor acoustics, the packed crowds of onlookers. Under the arcades of the Julian Basilica, where Pliny held his briefs, have been found roughly scratched draught-boards: we can imagine the idlers killing time between cases.

In Republican times, the major preoccupation of a well-born Roman had been *negotium*—public affairs—because he had good expectation of taking an active and influential part in them: he might, with luck and judgment, achieve the supreme power of the consulship. The *porcus Epicuri*, who contracted out of public life, was morally inferior. But when, under the Emperors, the civic horizon abruptly contracted, the character of *negotium* altered. A magistrate was now little more than an Imperial servant; oratory was robbed of its political force; law became increasingly a matter of private suits. Thus the appeal of *negotium* was considerably lessened. It still drew its honest servants, among them the two Plinies; but more and more the Senatorial and Equestrian classes, financially independent, politically impotent, were turning to the claims of *otium*—leisure intelligently used. Cicero was one of the first to suggest that *otium* should be devoted to literary pursuits; but he has doubts about it as a full-time occupation. By A.D. 100 the position has altered considerably. The Younger Pliny regards public duties as a tiresome burden that keep him from his true interests: the pursuit of learning in rural seclusion. Rome is crowded with *ardeliones*—social butterflies with nothing to do but kill time and meddle in other people's affairs. It is an age of aesthetic *rentiers*.

The temptation was almost irresistible. For over a century wealth and luxury had tumbled into the Roman's lap: provinces from Asia to Spain supplied him with gold, *objets d'art*, and an inexhaustible market of skilled or unskilled slaves. Now, bored by irresponsibility, aesthetically immature, juridical rather than creative by temperament, he laboriously set about imitating the literary, philosophical and artistic tastes of the Greeks he had benevolently subjugated. If the Emperor overshadowed Rome politically, Greece did so culturally: the impact of Greek literature had stunted the organic growth of Roman writing, and left sprouting only the branch labelled 'satire'.

Conscious of their own inferiority, yet fiercely resenting it—as Lucretius had pointed out, Latin was inadequate to express Greek philosophical thought—Roman *littérateurs* spent half their time slavishly imitating Greek models, and the rest abusing and sneering at the Greeks, their slippery adaptability, their deceit and greed, their thoroughly un-Roman morals. For a short period in the Golden Age of Augustus, Rome found her individual voice, which expressed thanksgiving for peace after a century of internecine conflict, and an epic sense of her own destiny to rule the nations. But, all too soon, the *Aeneid* and the great Horatian odes themselves became classics, to be imitated and expounded: the creative impulse had died—as it always dies—under an autocratic censorship.

Roman writers now had leisure, but lacked inspiration. Granted their social and political condition, it is hard to see what else could be expected of them but Alexandrian epic, occasional verses, polite correspondence (tastefully edited for publication), lampoons, memoirs, scissors-and-paste works of scholarship. The political gag could only be removed when dealing with condemned figures of the past; the venomous assaults on the dead by Lucan, Tacitus, and Juvenal reveal the immense restraints under which they laboured. It is a melancholy spectacle, but not without its parallels. What is surprising is the degree to which the sense of public duty still persisted. Nothing corrects Tacitus' lurid canvas better than the lives of the Plinies; notorious exceptions—such as Sejanus—tend to overshadow the honest rule.

Neither the Elder Pliny nor his adopted nephew was native to Rome; and this is characteristic. It was Rome, as a political and moral centre, that had so signally degenerated during the Social and Civil Wars: conservative rural Italy, cut off by poor communications, retained a far stronger feeling for the antique virtues[2]—a fact that Augustus was quick to recognize. During the following years, the prejudice against countrymen and provincials who rose to high office was steadily broken down: Trajan himself was a Spaniard. Such men increasingly carried the main burden of Imperial administration; and the Plinies were typical of them. They belonged to the Equestrian nobility; and, while this rank offered important posts in its own right (including the Governorship of Egypt), the Younger Pliny could, and did, ascend from it to the Senatorial *cursus honorum*. His uncle was more modest—and too busy. Within the Imperial framework, however, they both still upheld the Republican tradition of public service combined with fruitful leisure.

[2] Cf. R. E. Smith, *The Failure of the Roman Republic* (1955), pp. 140ff.

Whatever their personal foibles, the background to their daily life was much the same for uncle and for nephew. Augustus had boasted that he found Rome brick and left her marble; certainly during the first century A.D. Rome's physical appearance considerably altered. It was an age of construction and expansion. New baths and theatres and temples, huge blocks of flats many storeys high, all pointed to an increase of both wealth and population; yet the fire service remained hopelessly inadequate, the water-supply irregular, and sanitation primitive. The 'clients' who wanted to pay their early morning respects on patron or advocate, thronging his *atrium* from the small hours, would have picked their way through dark and filthy streets—there was no system of street lighting—and would later return to rickety tenements and inadequate meals of pulse-porridge and cheap vegetables.[3]

From our point of view, the picture of a gentleman's life, whether under Nero or Trajan, presents an odd blend of luxury and extreme discomfort. The main article of furniture remained the bed; there were few chairs—though the Younger Pliny kept some in a private chamber for his special friends—and practically no tables as we understand the word today. Lighting was poor, glass for windows non-existent, soap as such unheard of. Even at the height of excess during Nero's reign, standards of dress were comparatively simple and uniform. One needed many changes of clothes—often several a day in summer. We hear of scarlet cloaks and gay evening dinner-robes; but there is nothing to compare with the peacock exuberance of the Renaissance. Roman luxury mainly manifested itself in rare food, spices, jewellery, and, above all, in the enjoyment of country estates.

We should not forget that most of the Roman's day was spent out of doors: that the average *rentier*, or official off duty, drifted from courts to Forum, from Forum to baths, paying visits, passing time in the gymnasium, gossiping, perhaps witnessing a will or listening to a literary recital. Only in the evening would he return home to entertain his friends at dinner, with music or

3 The Romans were, indeed, vegetarians by nature; soldiers complained when compelled to eat meat by the exigencies of a campaign.

dancers during the meal and a philosophical discussion to follow it. The Younger Pliny several times expresses his desire to escape from this stultifying social round: it must, indeed, have been even more exhausting than legal practice.

Against such purposeless dilettantism, his uncle set an example of hard work and rectitude that it would be hard to surpass, whatever reservations we may have about its ultimate value. Not content with procuratorships in Spain and Africa, a cavalry command during the German Wars, and a place on Vespasian's Privy Council, this corpulent, asthmatic old man contrived, at the same time, to be a prodigious polymath. Up at midnight, or a little later in winter, only pausing for meals and a short nap, he would work on until the evening—reading, excerpting, cross-indexing. He was read to in the bath and at dinner; and he was very short with those who wasted precious moments that might have added to his store of knowledge. His vast labours filled his more indolent nephew with a mixture of awe and guilt.

Yet he remains a pathetic—and by no means isolated—phenomenon. Polymaths were a feature of the age; there was an emotional need for them, as Varro had already proved a century earlier. With the crushing weight of Greek thought hanging over their numbed brains, the Romans—practical, pragmatic, at sea among universals and abstracts—took the inevitable step towards self-improvement that such people always take: they acquired facts. Never, perhaps, have the magic virtues of knowledge for its own sake been so highly prized. This 'immense register' (as Gibbon described the *Natural History*) 'where Pliny has deposited the discoveries, the arts and the errors of mankind' is a monument to its age, no less than to its industrious compiler.

What are we to make of the man himself? As a scholar, he is third-rate; he totally lacks the capacity to synthetize; and his work gives the impression of having been shovelled together by some delirious magpie. As a person, he must have been somewhat trying. He was probably a bachelor—we hear of no wife, and had he one, she could probably not have stood the pace he set—but his generosity was as well-marked as his tetchiness. Most of his works are lost to us: the treatise on the javelin, the history of the German Wars, the linguistic studies he wrote under Nero, when any more controversial subject was highly dangerous. He is full of old Catonic saws: he fulminates against Greek doctors, Persian magicians, all new-fangled foreign tricks. Somewhat rhetorically —it was a commonplace of the schools—he attacks the modern craze for wealth. He was crusty, bull-headed, an indefatigable *laudator temporis acti*; and, like most such, his moral indignation remained untempered by economic insight. His eccentric life reveals one answer—a not wholly unworthy answer—to the age's cultural and spiritual poverty.

The Younger Pliny, who was eighteen when his uncle died, tells us far more about himself than any other Roman except Cicero. We know the details of his career: he came to Rome from Comum, studied under Quintilian and, as we have noticed, practised with some success at the bar. He walked warily during Domitian's reign; under Nerva and Trajan his rise was rapid. Praetor, Treasury official, *consul suffectus* (for two months only), Augur, President of the Tiber Conservancy Board—it is a solid and respectable progression. But, in A.D. 111, Trajan, having noticed his talent for accountancy, sent him out to Bithynia as Governor, with a special commission to overhaul the province's chaotic finances. He went willingly enough: honour was all. He never saw Rome again. About three years later he died, probably in Nicaea; his last recorded letter is an apology for using the Imperial posting system to send his wife home.

The life from which Trajan plucked him at the age of fifty was a full and pleasant one. His legal duties he found irksome; but they by no means occupied his whole time: for example, he always conscientiously abandoned them when holding an official post. He was happily married (for the third time), though his wife Calpurnia was liable to miscarriages, and their childlessness caused him some distress. Comparatively poor by Roman standards, he was still worth something in the neighbourhood of £200,000 when he died, and could always afford to be generous with his debtors. He spent a great deal of his time away from Rome, especially in the summer. From July onwards, the sweltering, malarial atmosphere of the City drove the leisured out to their cool and tranquil country estates; Rome emptied like Edwardian Mayfair, and only slaves and the *plebs urbana*, ill-doctored and uncared-for, were left to die of tertiary fevers, plague, dysentery, or plain malnutrition. Every respectable citizen—which meant every wealthy citizen, Eques or noble—had not one but several country 'villas'. Pliny himself possessed properties in Etruria, at Laurentum and, naturally, on Lake Como.

He was never happier than when in retreat at one of these country houses; and in his correspondence he has left us detailed descriptions of them—almost the only evidence in our possession. The many rooms are carefully designed to catch the sun and avoid cold winds; the baths are luxuriously appointed; the gardens and terraces are laid out with myrtles and plane-trees; the walks are lined with box hedges, trimmed by the topiarist into animal shapes, or, characteristically, the letters forming Pliny's name. There are vine-shaded corners where fountains play, and arbours where in summer a few guests can dine *al fresco*; from a window of the Como villa one can fish in the lake.

Here, when free from official or legal duties, Pliny passed his days: hunting occasionally (though he took writing tablets with him as well as a boar-spear), correcting his speeches, reading the classics like any eighteenth-century gentleman, dabbling in poetry, writing interminable letters to friends or relations. These letters reveal him in all his moods. He emerges as a mild Stoic who believed in ghosts: warm-hearted, finicky, a self-deprecating collector of antiques, a devoted, if uninspired, *littérateur*. In some ways, his *mores* (we perceive after a little) differ remarkably from ours. His notions of friendship appear mercenary; he gives the impression of inordinate vanity.

Neither of these assumptions is altogether just. As Mlle A. M. Guillemin points out:[4] '*l'amitié romaine entre intellectuels est austère et pratique . . . la critique est essentiellement une fonction de l'amitié.*' Roman friendship had been, and remained, an extremely formalized

---

[4] *Pline et la vie littéraire de son temps* (1929), p. 22.

and well-graded relationship, untouched by the sentimental considerations that we attach to the word *amicitia*. Its aim was mutual assistance to public *gloria*; and its ritual resembled modern diplomatic protocol. The *beneficium*, or present, whatever form it took, was an acknowledged gesture, for which one returned thanks publicly, and which the donor took a legitimate pride and pleasure in bestowing. Under the Republic, *beneficia* largely consisted of recommendations for political or military promotion; but, when Pliny wrote, these were being turned (as we might expect) into more personal and innocuous channels. Panegyrics on one's literary friends, the hope of literary immortality after death—such are the aspirations that now occupy men's minds. It was just as much in order to ask favours for oneself—from a 'friend' entitled and obliged by protocol to give them—as for one's *protégé*. On these terms, much of Pliny's supposed vanity emerges as a more or less legitimate convention.

We also observe the protocol of *amicitia* at work in Pliny's literary circle, which lightened so many of his leisure hours in Rome. These private literary clubs were numerous; and they seem scarcely to have overlapped. Pliny and Tacitus, two close friends, were the leading figures in their own, which numbered about fifty in all. Besides Suetonius, the only other notable member was Martial; and he seems to have been an *amicus minor* on the fringe of the group, tolerated but patronized. Juvenal, an exact contemporary, is—not altogether surprisingly—never mentioned. Silius Italicus had his own circle at Naples; Statius belonged to a set that gathered at the house of Lucan's widow.

Pliny's circle would sometimes meet over dinner, sometimes after luncheon, in a private room reserved for such occasions. During these meetings, literature or philosophy would be discussed in theory—style and rhetoric tended to bulk larger than originality of subject-matter—and members' work be read aloud. But their main function was to analyse each other's work at leisure, and criticize it, ruthlessly and honestly, before publication. This technique—'admonition, exhortation, objurgation'—was an extension of the normal responsibilities inherent in *amicitia*: it was equally applicable to one's friend or his writings. The Romans lacked false pretensions as much as they lacked false modesty.[5]

Such a life, for all its resting solidly on slavery[6] and financial independence, retains a certain dignity if judged by the standards of its own times. Pliny was an honest lawyer and a conscientious magistrate; his lack of original creative ability cannot disguise his very real love of literature. In Bithynia he shows at a disadvantage: he missed the self-confidence that marks a successful administrator, although, under the Imperial aegis, it was probably better to be tediously safe than fatally sorry. He is always peppering the Emperor with routine questions. 'As I have your permission, Sir, to address myself to you in all my doubts . . . ' is the ominous beginning of one letter; and we can forgive Trajan those brief and often acid replies which his Governor preserved with dutiful *pietas*.

So the Younger Pliny—young no longer—fades out of history, far away from his Tuscan estates and from the villas on Lake Como which, in an unwontedly skittish moment, he had christened 'Tragedy' and 'Comedy'. He had adequately fulfilled his modest ambitions; he had done the State some service. He was generous to his native town, which he never forgot; he established a fund for the education of free-born children, built new public baths, presented and endowed a library. His character was softer than his uncle's; his amiability merges into the ineffectual; his literary tastes often smack of pedantry. He was an ordinary, moderately intelligent, highly honest man, living in an age that cramped what talents he possessed into a rigid mould. When we remember the world he inhabited, we are not so much

[5] These conventions do much to explain the tone of Pliny's notoriously unreadable *Panegyric* on Trajan: there is as much discreet 'admonition' as fulsome praise in it. The entire concept of *amicitia* betrays a strong epicurean influence, both as regards its utilitarian basis and the rule of honest mutual criticism. Cf. A. J. Festugière, *Epicurus and His Gods* (1955), p. 37; and N. W. De Witt, *Epicurus and His Philosophy* (1954).

[6] As an advocate, Pliny would be attended to the courts by at least eight slaves; his household retinue would be far larger, forming an almost self-contained community.

tolerant of his subservience as amazed at the integrity and sense of purpose with which he conducted his career. It is all too seldom that ancient history permits us so intimate a glimpse into its characters' private lives. Great actors occupy the stage; yet we rarely see them, as we do Cicero and Pliny, *en déshabillé*. When we know that a man suffers from weak eyes, and composes in the dark: that he declaims speeches not only to improve his style but to strengthen his digestion: that he likes talking literature after supper with his servants, and corrects his briefs before retiring to bed—then the ancient world and our own leap together across the centuries.

8

Roman Satire and Roman Society

I. THE REPUBLICAN TRADITION

'Satire at least', Quintilian declared, 'is wholly Roman.' This melancholy half-truth has been dutifully echoed by generations of scholars, who were, perhaps, not primarily concerned with the moral or sociological implications it contained. But what in fact did Quintilian mean? Hardly that Rome had a monopoly over the satirical vein; Horace could claim with some plausibility that the Roman satire derived entirely from Athenian Old Comedy. Quintilian was a rhetorical literary critic; and what he meant was that Rome was unique in promoting satire into a distinct literary *genre*, with its own form and conventions. He might have added that the satire was Rome's sole original contribution to the history of literature. It did not occur to him—as it should to us—that this phenomenon reflected gravely on the society which threw it into such peculiar prominence.

In considering Roman satire today, we are handicapped by the radically different moral and ethical assumptions which lie behind the Christian tradition. Sex, for example, remains for us a primarily moral issue; to the Roman it was a social one. There are frequent attacks on homosexuality by the satirists; but it is never once even suggested that this constitutes a moral crime. The emotions betrayed are physical repulsion at an act which defies natural biological laws; social condemnation of a practice which falls away from the stern standards of self-restraint imposed in earlier times;[1] and half-envious anger at those who contrive to

[1] Martial (*Epigrams* 11.104) credits the worthies of the Early Republic with certain abnormal marital practices; but as he was attempting to justify his own homosexual tastes, his evidence may be discounted. Yet it is instructive that his final court of appeal (whether on false evidence or not) was that of the *antiqui mores*.

avoid the normal public and private responsibilities contingent upon marriage. It is tempting, but fruitless, to cast the shadow of Original Sin over the Roman social scene, and then charge Roman satirists with spiritual nihilism for being apparently indifferent to it. Our notions concerning slavery or physical cruelty likewise must be modified when evaluating contemporary criticisms of a world which took both for granted as part of the natural order.

Yet, when all such allowances have been made it is still difficult to see Rome's history through the satirists' eyes without experiencing a certain horror—not so much at the tediously repetitive list of vulgar excesses, but the moral vacuum which they imply; not so much at misguided beliefs as a total absence of beliefs, and empty materialism that reaches the proportions of a national neurosis. Wealth is the sole criterion: 'money first, virtue second', Horace wrote, 'everything at Rome has its price'. Juvenal echoes him. At one end of the scale the miser, at the other the spendthrift, linked by a common insatiable itch for acquisition: the spendthrift must gather gold-dust if only for the pleasure of seeing it run through his fingers. An unpleasant manifestation of this financial obsession was legacy-hunting—involving as it did flattery, sexual exploitation, domestic intrigue, sharp litigation, and an occasional discreet murder. Petronius wrote:[2]

> In this city the pursuit of learning is not esteemed, eloquence has no place, economy and a pure life do not win their reward in honour: know that the whole of the men you see in this city are divided into two classes. They are either the prey of legacy-hunting or legacy-hunters themselves. In this city no one brings up children,[3] because anyone who has heirs of his own stock is never invited to dinner or the theatre. . . .

The paradox of Rome is that of a nation whose ruling passion was money, but whose educated classes nevertheless ignored and

[2] *Satiricon,* 116 (tr. M. Heseltine). Petronius wrote in the 1st century A.D.; the practice, though mentioned by Republican authors, had not then attained the proportions it was to assume under the Empire.

[3] The justice of this remark may be deduced from the energetic efforts made by Augustus and the early Emperors to maintain the free birth-rate, by such time-honoured bribes as privileges for those with three or more children, and by sanctions against bachelors.

despised the means by which their money was made. Such an attitude was not dissimilar to that of the landed gentry in England for several decades after the Industrial Revolution: it is the credo of the agricultural aristocrat, who accepts profits but refuses to adjust his concepts to new conditions. Professor Highet's strictures on Juvenal can profitably be given a wider application here:

> Since his ideal is the farm which supports its owner in modest comfort (or the estates which make a man a Knight), he does not realize that Italy now lives by imports. And he will not understand that the Greco-Roman world was built up by the efforts of the shrewd, energetic, competent men who made harbours, highways, aqueducts, drainage-systems and baths; who cleared the forests and set up the trade-routes; who exchanged the products of the far parts of the globe and ventured on innumerable dangerous voyages.

Rome and Italy as a whole, had been—and remained by nature —a nation of peasant-farmers: shrewd, greedy, harsh, hard-working, ignorant of the wider aspects of commerce and trade, earthy in their philosophy and ethics. When successful wars against Carthage, Greece, and other Mediterranean powers brought an enormous increase in national wealth as well as considerable territorial expansion, these men remained fixed in their immemorial ways. They continued to govern a growing empire by methods barely adequate for a rural municipality. In poverty or wealth, the Roman—patrician or plebeian—remained a peasant. His vices were peasants' vices on the grand scale. His stubborn belief in agriculture as the only legitimate source of wealth did not prevent him speculating, if it technically excluded him from trade. Like many modern investors, he accumulated shares with only the haziest notion of the economic realities that underlay his fairy gold. He despised the merchants on whom his unearned income largely rested; and frittered away the bullion acquired by second-century conquest in wasteful imports of luxuries from the East. He had no notion of balance of trade, nor of long-term investment.

Now the Romans who wielded this power, the men whom the

satirists persistently attack, directly or by implication, were the members of the Senatorial or Equestrian classes. Till the close of the Republic, Rome was largely governed by a handful of old-established families, jealous of intrusion, immensely conservative, the repositories of all national tradition. If the Eques could command his rank with a down payment of 400,000 sesterces, the would-be magistrate had to look to his ancestors. Some 'new men' broke through the barrier; and the death-roll of the Civil Wars made entry progressively easier. But for many hundred years it was these privileged, chauvinist, aristocratic peasants who both profited from Rome's good fortune and dictated how that fortune should be used.

Inevitably, like the Spartans in similar circumstances, they were corrupted by success. They had responsibility thrust upon them, and temptation in its train; they reacted as peasants might be expected to react. This influential minority, whose grim self-control had once exceeded that of the men they ruled, now launched themselves on a tidal wave of self-indulgence. Small wonder that the satirist was to remind them that authority resided in the person, and that neither worth, virtue or power were guaranteed by a mere hallful of ancestral portraits. Yet for the traditionalist his ancestral genealogy had almost magical powers. If his vices were peasant vices writ large, his touchstone of virtue was the *mos maiorum*. His only panacea for his own ills was a pathetic nostalgia for the rugged peasant virtues of his ancestors. He looked eternally over his shoulder to the past, blind to the conditions that had broken down its stability; and the satirists who criticized him were no wiser than he. They too shared this Rousseauish vision of an idealized antiquity, and castigated their contemporaries for having inexplicably fallen away from it.

One influence which, from the sociological point of view, they quite justifiably suspected was that of Greek philosophy and culture. The educated slaves released among these pragmatic overlords constituted a redoubtable intellectual Fifth Column. 'The nobles in 200 B.C.', Professor R. E. Smith tells us, 'had eaten the apple of knowledge, and knew themselves to be culturally

naked.' The virus took only too easily. A stultifying system of
Greek mythology and literary conventions, which had no relevance to Italian traditions or needs, was henceforward imposed on
Roman literature. This both killed immediacy of theme, and
effectively banished the vernacular from the written page.
Between life and letters a vast barrier of artificiality, rhetoric and
convention was erected, which was not to be completely lowered
till Petronius defied all the rules by writing the *Satiricon*.

Such are the men—the ruling class of the Republic and early
Empire—who form the main targets for Roman satire. Their
character remains surprisingly constant from age to age. Only in
one respect do we find them undergoing a deep psychological
change. Until Horace's day, with the machinery of Republican
government still working, however corruptly, satirists could
write more or less as they pleased. (It is interesting that Varro
stayed in Athens during Sulla's dictatorship.) Under the Empire,
with its censorship and secret informers, with supreme power
vested in one man, a swift descent into subservience becomes
remarkable.[4] The satirist remains; but he is forced to find an
oblique outlet for his spleen, a mask behind which to conceal his
open criticism. If the Republican tradition stood for anything
apart from reactionary fossilization, the maintenance of the social
fabric by precedent rather than principle, it was for these things:
public service, devotion to the State, honest dealing, freedom of
speech, physical courage, personal dignity and honour. In the
days of Ennius and Lucilius such rights and virtues are still
present. By Varro's time they are passing away; we see them
finally lost during Horace's lifetime.

To take a random example, under the Republic the split between soldier and civilian, which was complete by Juvenal's
time (*c.* A.D. 100),[5] was still practically non-existent. Ennius served
as a centurion; Lucilius campaigned in Spain with Scipio; Varro,

[4] Cf. the illuminating story told by Aulus Gellius, *Noctes Atticae*, 13.13;
and G. Boissier, *Étude sur la vie et les ouvrages de M. T. Varro* (1861) pp. 12–13.
[5] Highet, *op. cit.* p. 159. As he rightly points out, this was a vital factor in
the final fall of the Empire.

despite his scholarly habits, won the *corona navalis*—a decoration which carried all the *cachet* of the V.C., and was far less frequently awarded. Even Horace had been a military tribune (however undistinguished) in Brutus' army. This sense of civic responsibility shows an abrupt decline under the Empire. The poor, irresponsible, professional writer then appears. Ennius, Lucilius, and Varro were Republicans: citizens first, writers second. Horace, who bridges the transitional period between Republic and Empire, displays in his career the metamorphosis from public independence to officially-sponsored subservience.

But all Roman satirists, Republican or Imperial, have one thing in common; none of them (with the doubtful exception of Petronius) were Roman-born. Mostly they came from Italian provincial towns; Seneca and Martial were Spaniards. Thus their standpoint is both externalized and more conservative than the average; they judge Rome with alien or provincial eyes against the severer and more old-fashioned rural standards of their own impressionable childhoods. This may partly explain why their criticisms in general remain so remarkably constant throughout three centuries and more—from 200 B.C. to A.D. 130, when Juvenal probably died. Greed, luxury, gross acquisitiveness, lechery, excess in every form: in all cases they are the vices of the peasant—aristocrat or *parvenu*—uneasily urbanized and confronted with undreamed-of abundance.

Gluttony is both the most persistent and the most prominent manifestation of Roman self-indulgence. It is also the most notorious. Every reader has heard of those fantastic banquets, given while the bulk of the population were at bare subsistence level—the sturgeon and the oysters, the rich wine cooled in snow, the boars and sucking-pigs and kickshaws. The revolting practice of vomiting *in mediis rebus* in order to prolong sheer sensation beyond normal capacity can have few parallels. One suspects a hereditary peasant trait here also. Today's rich *rentiers* were descended from yesterday's struggling farmers; instinctively they guzzled the plenty to hand in fear of tomorrow's potential leanness. There is, too, the exhibitionism of the *parvenu*: my banquet has more courses than yours; you may have mullet, but my mullet is the largest ever. 'Give me sensation and yet again sensation', wrote Louis MacNeice of a not altogether dissimilar generation; it is a fair summary of Roman hopes and desires from the late Republic onwards.

The Republican satirists thus had a wide field open before them. But as we read their work it rapidly becomes apparent that they are neither unacknowledged legislators nor true moral judges: they are far too closely enmeshed with the civilization and way of life which they apparently condemn. There is an ambivalent love-hate relationship between them and the trends they are satirizing. Of the four names we know it is the rich landowner, Varro, who puts his finger most closely on the weaknesses and foibles of his own class; but even he looks backwards rather than to the future, to the fading myth of the agricultural Golden Age.

It is, of course, impossible to expect radical criticism from satirists who can conceive no other possible palliative for present ills than a return to the *antiqui mores*. George Orwell observed of Dickens that he did not wish to abolish the Bumbles; he merely wanted bigger, better, kindlier Bumbles. Similarly in Rome; it never occurred to a Roman satirist to suggest that the patron-client system was inherently vicious or degrading; he merely wanted more perquisites for the clients.[6] The Roman satirist, one sees, is more liable to be moved by personal or party interest than public concern—even under the Republic. Abstract principles elude him; the profit motive is never far distant. Practical advantage is all. One of the few references to the provincials, advising leniency in their treatment, makes it clear that compelling political motives lie behind the precept. The passage [7] includes these words:

> You despise perchance, and deservedly, the unwarlike Rhodian and the scented Corinthian; what harm will their resined youths do you, or the smooth legs of the entire breed? But keep clear of rugged

[6] Martial and Juvenal were *clientes* themselves, and proportionately more interested in the subject than any of their predecessors. The inference seems clear.

[7] Juvenal 8.87–124, esp. 112–8. Tr. G. G. Ramsay.

Spain, avoid the land of Gaul and the Dalmatian shore; spare, too, these harvesters [i.e. in Egypt and Africa] who fill the belly of a city that has no leisure save for the Circus and the play. . . .

Thus a materialist civilization is presented to us through the eyes of largely materialist critics. This perhaps may explain why even the earliest Republican satirists foreshadow in embryo all the most characteristic vices of the Empire. If they condemn physical excess, the indulgence of every appetite, their condemnation is quantitative, not qualitative; they do not envisage any radically different way of life, but merely plead for moderation in an *ethos* they have no real desire to revolutionize.

The origins of satire (like the origins of Greek tragedy) are shrouded in mystery; they probably derive from country drama liberally spiced with crude abuse and modified by infusions of Greek political wit—the parabases of Aristophanes, Hipponax's savage iambics. The literary form first crystallizes with Ennius— better known to us as an epic poet than a satirist—of whose six books of satire, written with 'a direct and censorious bearing on public morals and politics', we only possess a few tantalizing fragments.[8] Yet these have great value in that they are our sole evidence for the tone of satire during the period following the second war against Carthage, after 200 B.C., when wealth and power first began to corrupt Rome. The immediate and inescapable truth apparent is that Ennius' social criticisms set the exact pattern to which every satirist in the future was to adhere: charges of gluttony and corruption, advice to preserve the old traditional farming morality. The Republic, it seems, was already spiritually bankrupt, even if financially solvent as never before.

With Caius Lucilius, generally regarded by his immediate successors as the true father of Roman satire, we are on firmer ground; nearly one thousand three hundred fragments from thirty books are preserved. He 'lashed the city', we are told by Persius; and Juvenal goes further in detail: 'Whenever Lucilius in a blaze of passion roars upon a man with drawn sword, the bearer,

---

[8] See E. H. Warmington, *Remains of Old Latin* (1928) Vol. I, pp. xviiff and 383–395, where the fragments are translated.

whose mind is chilled with crimes, blushes while his heartstrings sweat with unspoken guilt'.[9] It is easy, but misleading, to assume from this a definite moral standpoint; but fragments and corroborative evidence make it quite clear that Lucilius was not so much a moralist as a party pamphleteer, determined in his outlook by a personal allegiance to the powerful Scipionic Circle, which probably protected him as a resident alien. At the same time his attitude was not (as was the case with Martial, Juvenal, and even Horace) dictated by financial considerations: he seems to have been a well-to-do landowner, with estates in southern Italy, Sicily, and Sardinia.

This fact may go some way to explain Lucilius' ambiguous political position. At first sight one would have expected him to be a strong, if not a revolutionary radical. He was writing at the exact period when Tiberius and Caius Gracchus were challenging the Senate's authority and proposing their radical, Greek-inspired schemes for redistribution of land to the common people. He also lived through the disgraceful and corrupt war against Jugurtha.[10] Surely one might have expected a satirist in his position to show some progressive principles?

Certain fragments, indeed, give superficial support to such a notion. 'Something important—the people's health and prosperity—this is Lucilius' greeting imparted to verses such as he can write, and all this with heartiness and earnestness.' 'Corn has failed: the people get no bread.' A revealing sequence oᶠ fragments attacks the nobility: 'Wickedness and wantonness and prodigality take hold of these men. . . . They thought they could sin unpunished and that it was easy to repulse their enemies by virtue of their high birth. . . . They look upon [the common folk] as attacking their property and passing into it by marriage.' But closer analysis shows that Lucilius' attacks were in fact restricted to Scipio's enemies (who often supported the Gracchi in their popular movement) and his praise reserved for Scipio's friends

[9] Persius, *Sat.* 1.114–5; Juvenal 1.165–7, tr. G. G. Ramsay.
[10] For the strong financial interests of the business community in North Africa *vide* H. Hill, *The Roman Middle Classes* (1952) pp. 61–4, 116ff.

(who equally often opposed them). And as a large land-owner himself Lucilius had little personal sympathy with the Gracchan agrarian reforms.

This lack of a moral centre is also apparent in his more general pronouncements: his shafts are launched at random, as the fancy takes him. He satirizes the current passion for things Greek but is soaked in Hellenisms himself. He is equally contemptuous of clients ('troops for hire', 'munch-murderers') and their patrons. He castigates women's lax morals and lasciviousness, but is ready with a crudely practical Roman solution—the brothel—to the ineradicable sexual urge. At the same time he has a vivid turn of phrase (the *nouveaux riches* are 'those whom riches promote, whose frowsy little heads riches anoint'), and gives us some valuable sociological information: he is the first, for example, to chronicle both the growing prevalence of male homosexuality ('beardless hermaphrodites, bearded he-whores'), and the epicene, boyish ideal among women. He sets the fashion for all successors—the loose hexameter, the indiscriminate yet conventional attacks, the autobiographical details, the wide range of subject-matter, the direct, button-holing approach to the reader. His gusto and virulence tend to make one forget, in his own words, 'what a void exists in the heart of things'.

When we come to Varro, that distinguished and prolific polymath whose life stretched from the Jugurthine War (116 B.C.) to the Republic's final fall, we glimpse what Roman satire, given different conditions, might have become. Varro, it is true, says similar things to Lucilius, and is equally nostalgic for the *ancien régime*.[11] But he is an incomparably better and more original writer; wittier, less inhibited, Rome's nearest approach to Swift, with a firm grasp of vernacular that rivals Belli's nineteenth-century Trastevere invective. He yearned for the thrift and good husbandry of the Old Republic, the age when 'religion was sacred

[11] He was criticized for 'mulling over the past', and denied the charge (fr. 505); but his own work admits it beyond doubt. The fragments are edited by F. Buecheler (5th ed. 1912). To the best of my knowledge they have never been translated into English.

and all things were chaste', when men never shaved and women could watch the pot and spin their wool simultaneously.

His attacks on luxury and gluttony have a vivid and detailed immediacy of treatment, almost unique in Roman literature: 'Let Jupiter send a fiery thunderbolt through the roof of the fishmarket, that great Rome and the gluttons' great gullets may tremble. . . . Hungry spendthrifts are burning up Rome as a rabble fires a corn-granary.' He knew that mere wealth could never relieve the soul of its anxieties; and unlike most of his contemporaries he had a lively horror of cruelty, bloodshed, and the terror of the sword. His plea for patriotism has common sense as well as dignity: 'If any man destroy his country, his greater parent [i.e. by engaging in civil war], he is guilty, from partisan selfishness, of the crime of the self-castrator, or the man who corrupts children. . . . '

Yet Varro's own life betrays the hollowness of his words, however sincere they might be. Like his friend and contemporary Cicero, he was caught up in a clash of political ambitions that revealed only too clearly the Roman inability to take a firm stand on moral principle. He sided with Pompey against Caesar when the Civil Wars broke on Italy: with the Republican Senate's man against the would-be Dictator. He satirized the First Triumvirate in a vicious sketch entitled *The Three-Headed Monster*. Yet when Pompey failed, Varro surrendered his Spanish legions peaceably enough to Caesar; and after Caesar's victory he cheerfully accepted a post as Chief Librarian from the Dictator's hands. After Caesar's death he retired altogether from the struggle into scholarship. He had not (within the meaning of the Act) stained his hands in civil war; but he had contracted out of the struggle, as the Epicureans did, for the benefits of a quiet private existence. He was not a coward—his early military career proves that amply; he was simply not equipped to deal with a ruthless world of *Realpolitik*.

Nevertheless, Varro possessed a sharply original talent, strangely modern in its methods, a breath of fresh air among the stale conventions. If the theme is familiar, the treatment is arresting. The *Bimarcus*, for example, is a strange schizophrenic dialogue 'where Varro, thinking Pirandello-like of two-fold personality, makes the old-fashioned Marcus of the Roman past hold converse with his new self, the other Marcus, belonging to the Roman present'.[12] Elsewhere he points up contemporary decadence by the Rip Van Winkle device of an observer who wakes up after a fifty years' sleep. Treachery, shamelessness, and impiety have taken the place of the old virtues; parricide is a commonplace; the Assembly has become a market, and legal procedure is ruled by bribery.

Varro's references to contemporary events have more feeling as well as more political immediacy than those of Lucilius: he is an apt commentator on the death-throes of the Republic. He mistrusted militarism, like most intelligent soldiers; he deplored the agricultural dislocation and banditry which prolonged civil war produced—fields abandoned and weed-ridden, pirates roving the seas. Robbed of any constructive plan for the future, living only in the glories of the past, he became a pessimist and a determinist, who believed that deterioration set in from the moment of man's creation, a process culminating in the rottenness of his contemporaries, and promising still worse horrors to come. Though he speculated on the nature of freedom and servitude, he remained politically blind enough to be flatly incredulous at the slave rebellions; they offended his sense of the fixed order. He could not perceive that the times had changed; that the exotic Eastern religions he condemned had more to offer Rome now than the barren State creed whose neglect he so often lamented.

Varro's death in 27 B.C. (courted and honoured by that wise propagandist Augustus, who knew the value to be extracted from so venerable a figure) marked the end of an epoch. When Octavian assumed the title of 'the August' even the most diehard Republicans began to realize that the Republic as they had known

[12] J. D. Duff, *Roman Satire* (1937), p. 86. This division of the self is unparalleled in Roman literature, with the doubtful exception of certain passages in Ovid's *Metamorphoses*.

it was doomed. What they could hardly foresee was that the social status and independence of the writer would be profoundly modified under the new *régime*. Ennius, Lucilius, and Varro might have been ineffectual critics, handicapped by the ineradicable reactionary conservatism which they inherited; but they were, on their own terms, *free* critics. Varro felt the first cold blast of authoritarianism, and discreetly retired. Horace, the freedman's son from Apulia who became Maecenas' protégé and Augustus' mouthpiece, is a man between two worlds: the old Republic that was past mending, the new Imperialism that compelled rather than solicited allegiance.

It is very easy to gloss over the implications of Horace's career with a patina of warm, familiar sentimentality. Over-familiarity is perhaps a more insidious hindrance than neglect to the true appreciation of an ancient author; its bias operates unconsciously. The writer slowly acquires what may be described as a posthumous personality, created over the years by all those who have absorbed something of his alien essence into their own civilization. In the process the writer himself is changed. His original text, like some long-suffering palimpsest, is overlaid with the moral, literary, and emotional prejudices of countless generations. He becomes a mirror for their desires. Horace offers us a classic instance of this metamorphosis: he has become, in Mr L. P. Wilkinson's words, 'an international institution, a strand in the literary, social, and even political fabric of European history'. The English in particular, at once sympathetic to his *aurea mediocritas* (with its undertones of gastronomic self-indulgence) and impressed by his patriotic Roman Odes, have almost naturalized him. His British *persona* even survives hostile criticism: 'fat, *beery*, *beefy* Horace' (my italics) was how one moderately puritanical scholar described him.

In recent years the myth has been wearing a little thin, perhaps at least partially through the progressive obsolescence of that self-confident and cultured colonialism which supported it. There is less temptation today to appropriate Horace (as Kipling, for instance, did in 'Regulus') as a mysterious public school totem. The bare truth is that he fought on the wrong side in the Civil

War; returned to Rome a pauper and an Epicurean; attracted attention by his earliest Epodes and Satires; was taken up by Maecenas, given financial security and social position, not to mention Imperial backing; and became, with remarkable ease and speed, a eulogistic Stoic Imperialist. This takes no account, admittedly, of the sheer quality of his poetry, nor of the possibility that his conversion may well have been sincere. But sincere or not, the case of Horace is vitally important as a pointer to changing conditions. It is clear that a patron who controls his protégé's prosperity (and possibly his right to publish) exercises far more influence over his writings than, say, Caesar could over the wealthy Varro. A cynic might regard the Imperial Odes as the price paid for the Sabine Farm. This becomes more applicable as writing grows into a full-time occupation, which it never had been under the Republic. We are approaching the great division in the history of Roman literature. Horace puts the naked truth into the mouth of Trebatius, the lawyer who warns Horace in a well-known dialogue of the dangers now inherent in satire: 'If such a passion for writing carries you away, bravely tell of the feats of Caesar, the unvanquished. You will be well rewarded for your labours.'

Even in the early Horatian satires, with their praise of Lucilius and personal attacks, one perceives the changed climate. There is little in Horace that was not in Varro, and much in Varro which Horace skilfully avoids. His victims are generally unimportant; he gives the unavoidable impression of a pot-valiant *littérateur*, more interested in the business of writing than the actual world he inhabits. Easily, humorously, he knocks off the same old foibles of ambition, greed, and superstition; but with him the traditional passion for country as opposed to urban life has become the city-dwellers' neurotic dream of a golden suburb. The Golden Mean is lapsing insensibly into golden mediocrity.

One very significant aspect of Horace's work in this connexion is its purely 'literary', disengaged nature, which stands in sharp contrast to the Greek models from which he borrowed so much. The point is well brought out by Professor Fraenkel in his recent monumental study. Many modern readers, he observes, 'look on poetry as something clearly separated from any practical activities and from the whole sphere of "real life" '; and while this pronouncement might be regarded as a little *vieux jeu* today, yet it at once provides a highly significant link between the Horatian method and later traditions, setting both (by implication) against the more 'engaged' lyrics of the seventh and sixth centuries B.C., which 'formed an organic element in the life of the society which gave rise to their production'. In a brilliantly stimulating comparison of Horace's 'Descende Caelo' Ode with Pindar's First Pythian, Professor Fraenkel writes:

> The institution of these performances [celebratory hymns, *epinikia*, and the like] was deeply rooted in the very life, religious and civic, of the society: like the whole of that life it came from the gods. That is why Pindar can start from premises of unchallenged validity and, without an effort, make the transition from the *mousikon* that is operative in the present performance to the power of harmony that governs the world. Horace had no such ground to stand upon, and he was fully conscious of it. . . . His poetry, his 'music' was not the joint product of an effort of his individuality and of something that was there before he was born, that existed independently of him and had its roots in a supra-personal sphere. His poetry, though inspired by the Muses, was entirely the work of himself alone. . . . For Horace there exist no singers, no festival ceremonies, no tradition which he can follow. He is alone, left to his experience as an individual and to his personal inspiration. . . . He does not pretend or even wish to be the mouthpiece of a community such as no longer exists; he is determined to remain the man he is, born in a late and distracted age, walking alone.

That is perhaps one of the most fruitful and illuminating analyses of the Horatian dilemma ever made. It explains the poet's passionate yet ambiguous adulation of Augustus, who not only offered him personal security, but seemed to have restored stability to a shattered order; it hints at a human motive behind the formal experimentation, and crystallizes the whole psychological predicament of a sensitive intellectual during the transition from Republic to Empire. It gives a fresh twist to Horace's religious professions. The old Epicurean was no hypocrite; his spiritual yearnings were poured into such vessels as they could find.

Reading the passage quoted above we are at once and forcibly reminded of the contemporary state of European poetry, the agony of the individual sensibility lacking a valid tradition on which to build. Such parallels and associations are inescapable. Horace is suddenly presented in the exact position of T. S. Eliot when the latter was writing *The Waste Land*, and faced, for good measure, with identical difficulties, social, literary, and even linguistic: Horace's predecessor Lucretius, who stood in much the same relationship to him as Mallarmé did to Mr Eliot, was also much concerned (and with good reason) to 'purify the dialect of the tribe'. Horace's novel use of the *bios*, the self-portrait, to illuminate ethical problems by concentrating on the writer's ego, finds a psychological parallel in existential method. His eclectic plundering of Greek models, regardless of period or context, his trick of excerpting one key-phrase and using it as a spring-board from which to launch his own variations, his urban yearning for the heroic—do not all these at once recall Mr Ezra Pound's *Cantos*?

But it is the ubiquitous, half-mythical figure of the Princeps—soon, indeed, to be officially deified—that looms largest in the poetry, lyric and satire alike, of Horace and all his successors. If Nature abhors a vacuum, she surely put Augustus in a position where the morally bankrupt could shift the onus of their guilt on to his broad and dictatorial shoulders. This is what lies behind the gross subservience, the flattery, the paeans and deifications. It was not only a master that was needed, but a god, a supreme moral arbiter: men were tired of making decisions for which they no longer possessed the necessary social or individual assurance of judgment. A century of civil war had exhausted them in every way, and fatally weakened their sense of public responsibility—as Augustus found to his cost. Horace is both the last Republican and first Imperial satirist: we can sense almost the exact moment at which—with what cost to himself we shall never know—his intangible Rubicon of integrity was crossed. In the second part of this essay I shall deal with his successors—the men born under the Imperial *régime*, for whom the Republic was only a memory, whose world was centred, not on the Senate and Roman people, but on one man: benevolent, capricious, just, murderous or insane—Caesar.

II. The Imperial Knife-walkers

Every age, we are told, selects from the past those historical problems most relevant to its own existence. The subtle political and psychological pressures exerted on Roman writers—particularly satirists—from Augustus onwards do not figure very largely in our literary histories. This is hardly surprising. In England, as Orwell forcibly reminded us,[13] the true atmosphere of totalitarianism has never been fully appreciated. We are only beginning, as a result of our own experiences, to discern the skill of the Roman propaganda-machine in Imperial times, or estimate the force of official sanctions that could—then as now—be discreetly exercised against a recalcitrant or indiscreet individualist—particularly against a writer. And not only against a satirist, where the social dangers are obvious: to quote Orwell again, 'there is no such thing as genuinely non-political literature', least of all in a newly-established autocracy. Even a retreat into, say, sterile pastoralism implies a political attitude by abstention.

Now the temper of nineteenth-century classical scholarship was largely on the side of authoritarianism. Imperialism not dissimilar from its Roman prototype was in the air; Caesar and Augustus were seen as benevolently paternal yet firm-handed gods. Macaulay—in a passage attacking Lucan's historical prejudice—could describe Caesar as 'the finest gentleman, the most humane conqueror, and the most popular politician that Rome ever produced'. The revolutionary, the non-conformist, the man against the government—particularly a government with which the Victorian world felt a natural affinity—these were automatically suspect: to be ignored where possible, and denigrated where not. Thus the Augustan *régime* was elevated into an Olympian myth;

---

[13] *Critical Essays* (1946) pp. 149f. The essay itself was written in 1944, and time has done a good deal to remedy the deficiency on which he comments.

and the ugly decades which followed it were written off as mere decadence.

Today we know better than to adopt a superior moral tone when discussing this sick era; nor do we take refuge in the pretence that Tacitus or Juvenal were wildly exaggerating. Informers, Emperor-worship, perversion, torture, luxury—all fade into insignificance beside the monstrous phenomena of Buchenwald or the gas-chambers. Writers have suffered as much as any other class; perhaps more. If the discreet literary trimmers of the Empire do not necessarily excite our admiration, at least they arouse our sympathy and pity. We understand their predicament only too well. Mr Robert Conquest, in 'The Classical Poets,' puts his finger exactly on the subliminal flaw in Augustan and Silver Latin literature:

> They accepted, they valued the lake at its glittering surface;
> Yet their hearts were too deep. Though they ordered all doubts
>   to disperse
> They were poets, and they could not be wholly exempt from
>   its urges
> To open the weirs on their taut or magnificent verse.
>
> With descriptions of reason or nymphs or military glory
> They corrected the impulse. And, for the whole of their lives,
> Like the mermaid on land in the Hans Andersen story,
> Pretending to notice nothing, they walked upon knives.

They walked upon knives indeed; and sometimes they slipped. Seneca, Lucan, and Petronius were forced to commit suicide as an alternative to political execution. Ovid and Juvenal suffered exile. Phaedrus, the Macedonian slave who had been Augustus' freedman, had an unpleasant brush with the redoubtable Sejanus. What other civilization can show such a political casualty rate among writers—till our own times?

For a brief—a very brief—period after the Republic's fall, public sentiment, creative imagination, and Augustus' wishes all worked together in harmony. After a century of internecine bloodshed, Augustus truly appeared to have ushered in a Golden Age: Virgil and Horace responded to the mood of the times with superb poetry. But after the first high summer of enthusiasm,

Rome began to discover the price she must pay for her dictatorship. Political impotence turned the once-powerful Senators and Equites to litigation, literary dilettantism, and further frenzied self-indulgence. Robbed of free speech, they compensated by free living. Augustus was, in a sense, unique: he could temper autocracy with benevolence to a hair's-breadth of good judgment. He knew the value of literary propaganda, and was anxious to preserve at least the façade of the Republican tradition: one is reminded of Communist Poland's recent re-enshrinement of Mickiewicz. But his power was vested in his personality; and his successors, taking over the machinery of government which he had created, showed themselves progressively less enlightened and more wilfully autocratic. The political abuse of laws against *lèse-majesté*—a conveniently ill-defined crime—produced a flock of informers. The *agent provocateur* made his appearance. One Emperor turned megalomaniac, several were paranoid to a greater or lesser degree, another prematurely senile and ruled by a monstrous cabal of Greek freedmen. Tepid flattery could now be interpreted as positive disaffection;[14] and in the moral vacuum which the Republic had left as its legacy, there was no lack of obsequious courtiers to dance the Italian equivalent of the *gopak*.

Under such a *régime* the effect on literature cannot be anything but bad. Opposition, resistance in the modern sense, can do more insidious damage than putting the author in personal danger. When a writer is forced to publish secretly, or not publish at all, a time is sure to come when he feels that it is he who is out of step with the society to which he belongs; when he questions, not only the wisdom but the justice of his attitude. To function in a void; that is the great fear. 'To write poems no one may read', said Ovid, 'is like dancing in the dark.' The effect is to set up a subconscious conflict of deep instinct and social conformity: immediacy is suppressed, the mask is put on. When Orwell analysed the effects of these conditions on modern English prose,[15] he

---

[14] Cf. Czeslaw Milosz's *The Captive Mind* (1953), where a similar trait is noticed as existing in Communist Party circles east of the Iron Curtain.

[15] From 'Politics and the English Language', in *Shooting an Elephant*, p. 97.

might have been writing with the post-Augustan period in mind:

> The inflated style is itself a kind of euphemism. A mass of Latin words falls upon the facts like soft snow, blurring the outlines and covering up all the details. The great enemy of clear language is insincerity. When there is a gap between one's real and one's declared aims, one turns as it were instinctively to long words and exhausted idioms, like a cuttlefish squirting out ink. . . . When the general atmosphere is bad, language must suffer. . . . But if thought corrupts language, language can also corrupt thought. A bad usage can spread by tradition and imitation, even among people who should and do know better.

It is a little difficult for the traditionally educated humanist—perhaps even more so for the professional classical scholar—to appreciate the full force and truth of these words. They have been brought up to accept precisely these vices as virtues; to fill their own Latin verses with stock *clichés* and periphrases; to accept without question—even to imitate—the frightful obsession with a bastard and imported mythology; to denigrate the living speech recorded by Terence, Varro, Petronius, and Apuleius, in favour of the ponderous and artificial literary language, the tropes and figures beloved of the ubiquitous rhetoricians.

Contemporary critics suffered from no such illusions. One symptom of the prevailing authoritarianism is a sharp rise of interest in literature as a detached study, bearing no essential relation to the contemporary life—social, political, or even emotional—that it might have been expected to reflect.

The full-time philosophical or literary *dilettante* is replacing the educated public servant. In an age when, as Phaedrus observed, to be rich was to be in danger, intellectual pursuits—provided the subjects discussed steered clear of anything controversial—offered a soothing diversion. Not unnaturally, under those conditions, the quality of the literature produced deteriorated; and the satirists jumped in to dismember so tempting—and harmless—a victim. Persius, Petronius, Martial, and Juvenal unite to confirm Orwell's diagnosis.

Persius comments acidulously on mechanical antitheses, the

inflated heroic style, self-conscious archaisms, lack of originality: 'Can one call *this* [a specimen quotation] anything but frothy and fluffy, like an old dried-up branch with a huge overgrown bark upon it? . . . Nerveless stuff—it floats in the mouth on the top of the spittle, and comes drivelling out involuntarily.' Both he and Martial attack the unreality of mythological themes. Martial writes: 'You whose reading matter is all Oedipus and dark Thyestes, Colchian warlocks and Scyllas, what do you study but fairy monsters? . . . Why does such trifling literary nonsense appeal to you? Rather read of matters which Life can claim as her own. In my poems you will find no Centaurs or Gorgons or Harpies: my pages smack of man.' Juvenal and Petronius echo these criticisms, and also have some pertinent remarks to make about the unrealities of a rhetorical education, in particular the set historical themes for argument or declamation. 'I believe that college makes complete fools of our young men,' exclaims one of Petronius' characters, 'because they see and hear nothing of ordinary life there. It is pirates standing in chains on the beach, tyrants pen in hand ordering sons to cut off their father's heads . . . honey-balls of phrases. . . . Your tripping, empty tones stimulate certain absurd effects into being, with the result that the substance of your speech languishes and dies.'

It is doubtful how far Imperial satirists were aware of the direct link between this unreal literature and the political conditions of the time. As G. G. Ramsay wrote,[16] 'for the decline of literature there is no more authentic testimony than that of Persius; and yet he seems to be quite unconscious of the true causes of that decline . . . never once does he heave a sigh—even a despairing sigh like that of Lucan—over the loss of public liberty'. Juvenal knows that mythological themes are politically safe; but does not draw the further conclusion that politics are corrupting literature. Instead he paints a pleasant picture of the useless yet enormously detailed mythological knowledge demanded from the grammarian. Nevertheless, we cannot dogmatize on this point. The age demanded concealment of one's true opinions; and every

---

[16] G. G. Ramsay, *Juvenal and Persius* (1918) p. xxviii.

satirist of whom we have record had his own mask. How far we can penetrate it is a matter for conjecture.

Phaedrus, the ex-slave, who lived through Tiberius' and Caligula's reigns, and died early on in that of Claudius, chose the fable or allegory. 'Examine these fables with attention', he openly declares, 'and what useful lessons will you find concealed under them! Things are not always what they seem; first appearances deceive many: few minds understand what skill has hidden in an inmost corner.' Elsewhere he gives a political explanation for the invention of fable: 'Slavery, being subject to another's will, and not daring to speak its desires, couched its sentiments in fabulous form, and by pleasing fictions eluded censure.' Naturally this has set the ingenious combing his pages for obscure historical allu-sions; and several of these, obliquely attacking Tiberius, Caligula, or Sejanus, are fairly certain. More suggestive (in several senses) is the Rabelaisian 'Embassy of the Dogs to Jupiter', a withering satire on the greed, fear, stupidity, and obsequiousness of the Imperial court and the Roman people as a whole. The potentiali-ties of Phaedrus' method are perhaps best brought home in a witty piece describing how the She-Goat (Livia) obtained from Jupiter the favour of a beard, and how offended the he-goats became: Livia was notoriously an *éminence grise* behind the throne.

With Persius, in many ways the subtlest of all the Roman satirists, we move into a different and more familiar world. This valetudinarian young man, who died in the ninth year of Nero's reign at the age of twenty-eight, chose moral generaliza-tion as his mask, and the ivory tower for his habitat. Assured of a large independent income, he spent his short life in a country house some eight miles outside Rome, largely engaged with the highly un-Roman occupation of introspective self-analysis. He displays in his one slim volume of satire a deliberate indiffer-ence to man's political or civic aspects,[17] which reflects his own self-imposed isolation; and he has the intelligent invalid's ner-vous distaste for that robust philistine, the professional soldier.

[17] His notion of a bad political example was Alcibiades; and his concept of freedom completely ignored its political aspects. *Sat.* 4.73ff.

His friends are all literary friends, his Stoicism a comfortable compromise,[18] his experience derived from his well-stocked library. He is perhaps the nearest approach to a Bloomsbury intellectual that Rome ever produced.

The self-examination, the internal reflection which Persius practised were qualities badly needed by such a society at such a time. From Horace's day onwards there appear classic symptoms of *Angst*, hysteria, and mental unbalance[19] in the satirists' accounts of the public temper. The word *phreneticus* passed into common usage, 'much as the terminology of psycho-analysis has been adopted by conversational English'. *Ennui* and *nausée*, those Sartrean *malaises*, find their prototypes in Rome. Wealth was no cure, as Varro said, for the soul's sickness. The State religion had fallen into disrepute despite Augustus' energetic efforts to revive it by propaganda and legislation. The feeling of social impotence is reflected in satirical writing by a strange obsession with castration (actual or metaphorical) and eunuchs, such as the Galli, the priests of the Great Mother. Hysterical women took cures at Sinuessa for the vapours: astrologers and fortune-tellers were all the rage; boredom, inertia, instability, and deep-seated guilt rise from the pages of Martial or Juvenal like a physical miasma. 'Each man makes dreams for himself,' wrote Petronius, 'the wounds of the unhappy endure into the night-season.'

To this atmosphere Persius was obviously very much alive; and unlike his more active or involved contemporaries he made genuine attempts to combat it at a deep level of psychological awareness. He asked questions and touched on themes which Romans normally avoided, seeing clearly that men who were severed from their traditional public functions had to look inwards as individuals if they were to remain whole. He knew that the real canker was to be found, not in external circumstances,

[18] See above, 'The Garden and the Porch', esp. pp. 92ff.
[19] For the wide vocabulary of insanity, and the prevalence of the theme in Rome, *vide* D. M. Paschall, *The Vocabulary of Mental Aberration in Roman Comedy and Petronius* (1939) pp. 75–6, 87.

but in the corrupt self; that tyrants could as easily spring up in a man's diseased heart as be imposed from without. 'What an utter lack there is', he wrote, 'of men willing to venture down into their own souls: all stare at the wallet on the back of the man in front of them. . . . Have you any goal? any mark at which you aim? or are you on a vague wild-goose chase armed with broken pots and mud, not caring where you go, and living by the rule of the moment? . . . Learn what we are, what life we are sent into the world to lead . . . what is your position in the human commonwealth.'

Though Persius resolutely attacks superstitions, his Stoic deism gives power to his religious awareness. You pray to the Gods for grossly material ends, he tells his readers; and—worse —you credit them with the same acquisitive instincts as yourselves. The Gods do not want gold; and for your own part you should ask them to grant you virtue and purity, not profit. It is interesting to compare Persius' attitude with that of the aristocratic and *blasé* Petronius:[20]

'One promises an offering if he may bury his rich neighbour, another if he may dig up a hidden treasure, another if he may make thirty millions in safety. Even the Senate, the teachers of what is right and good, often promise a thousand pounds in gold to the Capitol, and decorate even Jupiter with pelf, that no one need be ashamed of praying for money. So there is nothing surprising in the decadence of painting, when all the gods and men think an ingot of gold more beautiful than anything those poor crazy Greeks, Apelles and Pheidias, ever did.'

Petronius' *Satiricon* is one of the oddest, most tantalizing, and least typical works to have survived from Graeco-Roman antiquity. Because of that great set-piece, the *Cena Trimalchionis,* and the Priapic obscenities scattered at well-placed intervals through the text, the *Satiricon* has always had its devotees. But today all the omens point to Petronius achieving a wider popularity than he has ever done before; and no one would be more surprised than the Arbiter of Elegance to hear himself hailed as the arche-

[20] *Satiricon* 88. The character speaking is Eumolpus; the views are clearly Petronius' own.

typal Daddy of the Beat generation. Yet there is, undoubtedly,
an odd psychological kinship between the *Satiricon* and a novel
like *The Dharma Bums* (or even Mr Nelson Algren's *A Walk on the
Wild Side*): we find the same anarchic bloodymindedness of
behaviour, the same weakness for melodramatic rhetoric in
moments of sexual or emotional crisis, the same headlong
picaresque wandering from scene to scene, with its accompanying
undertones of spiritual instability.

The Priapic religious motif (and, in slightly different terms,
the thematic use of Isis by Apuleius in *The Golden Ass*) makes one
think of the popular Zen Buddhism affected by Mr Jack Kerouac
and his associates: in both cases it may be seen as something of a
literary device rather than an active profession of faith. Indeed,
the contrast between Petronius and every previous satirist lies
in his complete apparent lack of any religious feeling. This is not
only interesting as a side-light on his character, but marks a
definite historical and social development. His irreligion is of the
easy, rational, superior kind that appears at a certain point in any
culture. Phaedrus had heralded the change by noting that blasphemy was becoming fashionable. Varro had attacked Serapis
and Eastern mystery cults in order to defend the national religion:
Petronius is equally contemptuous of both. The first he dismissed
as 'an outlet for wealthy nymphomaniacs'; but he pokes excellent
fun at the second as well—the good old days when 'our great
ladies went up the hill to the Temple of Jupiter in their best
clothes, their feet bare, their hair loose, their thoughts pure, to
pray for rain. And of course down it came at once in buckets—if
that didn't do it, what would?—and everyone went home like
drowned rats.'[21] It is his radical tradesman, Ganymede, who
blames contemporary decadence on the decay of religion;
Petronius himself seems to have shared with Juvenal an amused
and slightly weary disbelief in any kind of eschatology.

We know very little of Petronius apart from what Tacitus

---

[21] Tr. G. Bagnani, *Arbiter of Elegance* (1954) p. 12. He adds: 'Personally I
find it most unfortunate that this passage invariably comes to my mind when
looking at the Ara Pacis.'

tells us, and what we can infer from his surviving work. We do not know exactly when the *Satiricon* was written, though Dr Gilbert Bagnani has argued persuasively for a date round about A.D. 60. We do not even have conclusive proof that its 'onlie begetter' and the Petronius who was Nero's Master of Ceremonies were one and the same person, though we may reasonably assume the identity. A dandy, a connoisseur of the *demi-monde,* an excellent Governor of Bithynia, a man who lived stylishly and died stylishly, he has a distinct appeal for our lower romantic instincts. Yet his book is, in many ways, a bigger mystery than its author.

The text which has survived is only a mutilated series of longer or shorter extracts, which read as though copied from a half-burnt or otherwise partially destroyed archetype. (The *Cena Trimalchionis* itself turned up as late as 1650, in a manuscript discovered at Trau, in Dalmatia: this section, perhaps derived from a different *stemma*, is notably free of *lacunae*.) As a result, our knowledge of what the novel was *about,* its plot and overall thematic structure, remains conjectural in the extreme. Nor—and here we must admit a more baffling loss—can we ever be quite sure of its author's own standpoint. Who is satirizing what? The range is so wide, the tone and target change so often, that the centre of moral gravity tends to get lost.

The central theme has often been taken, with some plausibility, as a parody of the *Odyssey*, anticipating Joyce by two millennia. Encolpius becomes, in more than one sense, an inverted Ulysses, a modern contemptible anti-hero, whose ignominious adventures continually mock by contrast those of his epic prototype. (Juvenal, too, never lost an opportunity to tie a Homeric or Virgilian allusion on to the corrupt men of his own day.) Just as Odysseus was harried by the wrath of Poseidon, so Encolpius suffers from the vengeful attentions of Priapus. In some way, we gather, he has profaned a secret Priapic ceremony, just as he later kills the Priapic goose; but it also seems very likely that Priapus's resentment had a more basic cause. This functional divinity was not—as sometimes tends to be supposed—merely concerned with phallicism as such; he was a garden god, whose emphasis was on fertility. It might be argued, and the whole tenor of the *Satiricon* bears this out, that Priapus afflicted Encolpius with impotence because of his flagrant and incorrigible homosexuality, which could be taken as a species of blasphemy on procreation. Besides, from the novelist's point of view, Encolpius's psychological malaise provides an unparalleled opportunity for repetitive scenes of *risqué* fun. Each consummatory failure is described in lip-licking detail; Petronius has the *voyeur*'s passion for keyholes and chinks in doors. He is, we may note in passing, almost the only ancient author with an observable weakness for scopophilia.

It has generally been agreed that one of Petronius' major targets, at any level, is pretentiousness. *Nihil est hominum inepta persuasione falsius,* he wrote, *nec ficta severitate ineptius*—'nothing is falser than people's preconceptions and readymade opinions; nothing is sillier than their sham morality'. How, then, are we to take the *Cena Trimalchionis*? The simple interpretation has always been that this is a splendid interlude satirizing a jumped-up millionaire *parvenu*; that Trimalchio, the ex-slave turned successful financier, is the spiritual ancestor of Sir Gorgius Midas. He is totally devoid of cultured taste; he makes a vulgar exhibition of his opulence; he produces mythical malapropisms by the score, and cannot tell the difference in literary terms between (as Mr Edmund Wilson has it) a classic and a commercial. 'When Troy was taken', he bawls happily, 'there was this fellow called Hannibal . . . ' and we snicker in superior delight with Encolpius. Then comes Hermeros' angry, dignified reproof: too late we see the trap and wipe the laughter off our faces. Trimalchio and his sort at least, Petronius is saying, have the virtues of honesty, generosity, and simple kindliness. They may be risible, but they have some redeeming features; whereas the twittering intellectual parasites who gorge themselves on Trimalchio's exotic food and sneer at him between mouthfuls have no grounds whatsoever for their complacency. They could never make a penny in business, so they pretend that 'Genius has always had Poverty as his sister'; and their much-vaunted culture, on which they base their claim to moral superiority, is a vapid and artificial sham.

Nevertheless it seems more than possible that Petronius' famous descriptions of *parvenu* vulgarity and cultural yearnings, attractive enough in themselves, had an ulterior purpose. 'People on the other side of the tracks', as Bagnani put it, are shown as 'discussing the same matters that interest the highest and most intellectual society. . . . A highly sophisticated society would enjoy the joke: that the joke was also a very subtle indictment of that society itself would scarcely be apparent.' Was Petronius attacking Neronic society under the guise of Southern Italian low life? If so, he had chosen the subtlest mask of all.

One reason for suspecting this concealed assault on his peers is a unique passage in the *Satiricon* which might have been written by a modern Socialist reformer. 'You go talking about things which are neither in heaven and earth', Ganymede observes deflatingly, 'and none of you care all the time how the price of food pinches. . . . Damn the magistrates, who play "Scratch my back and I'll scratch yours", in league with the bankers. So the little people come off badly; for the jaws of the upper classes are always keeping carnival.' It is a disquieting paradox that sentiments such as these should have been written, not by the struggling hack such as Juvenal (who despised the plebs inordinately) but by an elegant courtier, who yet knew more about the common people and their vernacular than any other Roman writer. Petronius is by no means an unthinking hedonist. His atheism carried with it a sense of transitoriness and illusion: the skeleton grins at the feast, the pleasure of love is momentary and vile. 'Dear, dear', cries Seleucus, recalling a funeral, 'how we bladders of wind strut about. We are meaner than flies; flies have their virtues, we are nothing but bubbles.' It is a far cry from the tradition, public responsibility, and communal sense of the early Republic to this disillusioned, egocentric pessimism. And despite Tacitus' assurance that in the age of the Flavians Rome regained the moral sense she had finally lost with Nero, a glance into the pages of Martial or Juvenal suffices to dispel such optimism.

Martial, a dark-skinned, hairy-legged Spanish hack writer who spent thirty-five years in Rome, is the only Roman satirist who could by any stretch of the imagination be called lovable. Yet he is not at first sight an attractive character. He depended on patronage and the sale of his books of epigrams for a livelihood: thus his flattery is only equalled by his scarifying, almost clinical obscenity. He knew very well what would sell to bored Roman matrons. Having spent many years in gross adulation of the terrible Domitian, he performed a quick *volte-face* on Nerva's accession and flattered the new Emperor for being above flattery. (As that vicious skit *The Pumpkinification of Claudius* showed, today's idol was liable to become tomorrow's scapegoat as death or fortune changed the balance of power.) He continually complained about the life a client led, and wished his parents had brought him up to a trade instead of giving him a useless good education. He abused his wife and cultivated Egyptian boys. His notion of the ideal life was mainly the possession of enough unearned income to permit him to reside outside Rome and entertain his friends. Yet through all his writing we are aware of a quick, caustic, kindly wit, an unexpected tenderness that manifested itself in his love for children, his charming memorial tribute to an old slave, his warm inconsistencies of temperament. Of all the aliens who stayed grumbling in Rome, year after year, he was the only one who in his old age went back to the land of his birth. It is characteristic of the man, we feel, that the Younger Pliny should have paid his fare home.

Martial's twelve books of epigrams remind us that one of the main advantages Roman satire offers us is a picture of contemporary life—the details that conventional literature felt itself above mentioning. Open any standard work on Roman private antiquities—Friedländer, Marquardt, Carcopino—and you will find that Martial, Horace, and Juvenal are cited more often than all other literary sources added together. Martial's mask is the reporter's. Year after year he observed incidents—at the theatre, at banquets, in the bedroom, about town—and made verses out of them. He seldom offered a moral judgment; he did not need to. The facts, piling up into a gigantic, lurid mosaic, spoke for themselves. The pattern was self-created; millionaire actors and flute players who held authority's ear; masqueraders pretending to Equestrian status; the thread-bare guest furtively taking home food in his table-napkin, his head bilious, his feet blistered; the fashionable dandy—depilated, scented, knowledgeable in boudoir-gossip and genealogies; the monstrous banquets; above all, the grim, indefatigable sexual perversions. Nothing in all Roman literature so conveys a sense of flat animal *ennui* as these dreary erotic gymnastics, practised without emotion, almost it seems without desire. The act of love had, like its exponents, lost all context, and existed in a repetitive void.

This cold, calculated, passionless obsession with vice was also noted by Martial's contemporary Juvenal—the last and in ways the most memorable of Roman satirists. (Few poets can have written so many stingingly quotable lines.) Medea and Procne were great sinners, he says, apropos of a woman who has poisoned her children, but they were passionate. 'I cannot endure the woman who calculates, and commits a great crime in her sober senses.' More cynically revealing is his Ninth Satire, seldom translated, which analyses the parody of a client-patron relationship existing between a male prostitute and a wealthy married pathic, for whom, *inter alia,* he sires a child. Unlike Martial, Juvenal has a very lively moral sense—though in him too it was largely conditioned by his personal circumstances. Characteristically, we may note, he also shows an overriding and prurient obsession with the very sexual vices he is castigating—a fairly well-known phenomenon. Not only in the notorious Second, Sixth, and Ninth Satires, but throughout the whole body of his work, the sexual nudge or subtly obscene *double entendre* is never far away. It is impossible not to feel from these two authors that Rome really *was* worse during their lifetime; that the decay, like caries in a tooth, had been eating deeper and spreading wider as the years went by.

'He that hath a satirical vein', wrote Bacon, 'as he maketh others afraid of his wit, so he had need be afraid of others' memory.' It is a prudent rather than a courageous maxim, and might have been composed with Juvenal in mind. For Juvenal (and this is only one of the paradoxes that cluster about that violent shadowy figure), in spite of his *saeva indignatio*, took considerable care to avoid the sword of the executioner. He quotes Lucilius as having said: 'Whom do I not dare name? What does it matter whether Mucius forgive my words or not?'; but though he had all Lucilius' spleen, he tempered it with most un-Lucilian prudence. His waspish epigrams and aphorisms—*panem et circenses, mens sana in corpore sano, quis custodiet ipsos custodes* (this last in a highly and characteristically obscene context)—have passed into the general consciousness of Western Europe. Yet they were overtly directed, not at his contemporaries under Trajan or Hadrian, but at an earlier, bloodier age. He looked back beyond the dark and pathological Domitian to the Year of the Four Emperors: further, before his birth, to Messalina and Caligula and Tiberius. Sejanus and other historical villains are dragged from their graves and butchered anew with fine moral fervour.

In the perspective of time this deliberate anachronism looks less odd; but in fact it is rather as though a contemporary poet were to burst out in impassioned denunciation of Mr Gladstone or the Prince Regent. He is for many readers the archetypal flogger of dead horses; and such may well ascribe the unpopularity of his work during his life and immediately after his death not to resentment but boredom, and the distaste for renewing old and mercifully forgotten horrors.

For such readers, again, this embittered *rentier* is more impressive when less historically specific: castigating homosexual cliques with their hideous mock-marriages, drawing with acidulous Hogarthian strokes the horrors of life in the great metropolis, which (shades of Spengler!) was sucking the country into itself like some vast ulcer; giving thumb-nail sketches of the cheats, liars, contractors, undertakers, or slave-auctioneers who, as one character observes, are the truly successful men in Rome.

This point of view, however, has its limitations. Especially it disregards the immense and lasting popularity of Juvenal after his fourth-century resurrection. From Heiric of Auxerre or Pope Silvester II to Boileau, Dryden, Johnson, and Victor Hugo the line stretches almost unbroken. Some of his apologists might have startled him; particularly those who discovered him to be a fountain of Christian virtues. But a survey of his admirers and imitators reveals the transcendental quality of Juvenal's vision, the applicability of his experience to the needs of all generations who sensed that their world was out of joint. He is classical in the fullest sense. And when we bear this in mind his attitude to his own times becomes more comprehensible. As Professor Highet well observes in his penetrating monograph, *Juvenal the Satirist*, he

> saw the empire as one long continuous process of degeneration. . . .
> He realized (although perhaps his audience did not) that it would be
> trivial to satirize only the men and women of his own time. They were
> end-products of a process which began with the lash of Julius Caesar
> and the wet sword of Augustus, which ran on through the lunatic
> Caligula, through Nero and the civil wars, to the fiendish emperor
> of yesterday and perhaps another monster tomorrow. This realiza-
> tion was one of his chief contributions to satire.

Professor Highet, incidentally, has been the first scholar to give a comprehensive account of Juvenal and his work, in any language. This in itself is significant. Juvenal presents a personality not so much complex as psychologically rare; and a rare puzzle, on the whole, he has proved to the academic world.

He was born into the last years of Nero's turbulent reign: well-to-do, decently schooled, a temporary Army officer as a preliminary to a career in the Imperial service. But time passed; he became a hanger-on at Court, and preferment somehow eluded him. He turned to literature in his idleness; already he was falling into the trap baited for the bourgeois gentleman under the Empire—too proud to work, a property-snob, anxious for the sinecure that he claimed as his natural right. But at the age of thirty he made his first and fatal mistake. A little lampoon about the jobbing of commissions, the influence of actors at Court: it was enough. Exile followed, at the hands of an Emperor from whom exile was a light punishment, to the frontiers of Egypt, probably at Assuan.

There can be little doubt that this event, involving not only Juvenal's disgrace but the confiscation of his patrimony, marked

178

the turning-point in his life. After Domitian's death he returned to Rome, indeed; but as an impoverished ex-gentleman with a blot on his record, a literary hanger-on at the mercy of arrogant patrons. The pattern is a familiar one: we remember Swift's impotent resentment and fear of Sir William Temple, Johnson's ignominious ejection by Chesterfield's servants.

Nil habet infelix paupertas durius in se
quam quod ridiculos homines facit.

It needed a peculiarly hierarchical society to produce conditions where such a man would starve rather than turn his hand to business; and both first-century Rome and eighteenth-century England supplied it. Juvenal is supremely and typically unaware of Roman economics;[22] for him commerce consists of cheap crooks and speculators, fantastic luxuries, vulgar sewage-contracts, grain for the mob. It is typical of the man and his milieu that though he admires Lucretius, he is completely uninterested in his scientific theories; that he objected to gladiatorial shows not because they were cruel but because they were common; that he used philosophy (of which he was largely ignorant) mainly as a stick with which to beat the Stoics for their personal habits— though in later life he did drift into a mild Epicureanism; and that his criticisms of society are always directly conditioned by his own status in it.

There are one or two further deductions that can be made about him. He had a tender spot for children (so, curiously, did Martial); he almost certainly married a lady of society, who treated him abominably. (In all likelihood she divorced him when he went into exile, if the violence of the Sixth Satire, which matches the lazar-house imagery of *Lear* or *Timon*, is an accurate guide to his own wounded feelings.) Connected with this are the strong hints, again confirmed by Martial, that in late middle-age he may have become an active paederast. It is pleasant to believe (as Professor Highet does) that in his advancing years he at last received recognition from Hadrian in the form of a sinecure at the Athenaeum; that after the bitterness and terror and rage he died in his modest

22 Cf. above. pp. 148–9.

rentier's paradise, free from his nagging obsessions with the wealth he could never achieve, the aristocracy to which he never belonged, the contractors and subtle Greeks whose ways he could not understand and whom, like Cato, he hated in his baffled mistrust.

Just when the banked-up fires of his envy and bile finally found public utterance, in that sustained piece of invective the First Satire, is uncertain: probably early in Trajan's reign. Its venom and violence and variety of theme are extraordinary, and the more concentrated for having been suppressed so long. Bogus tragedians, millionaire forgers, married eunuchs, female big-game-hunters, murderers, perverts, crooked politicians: they crowd thickly through the streets, elbowing honest folk to the wall. It is all so vivid that we may not notice the single driving theme behind the motley, the obsessional equation of *wealth* with crime, vice, and corruption. *Quidquid agunt homines*: the world was to be Juvenal's oyster. Yet, in the very next line, he characteristically narrows his field.

> et quando uberior *vitiorum* copia ?—

'and when was there a richer crop of *vices*?' Never, surely, if the Satires are a fair picture. The first five attack the twin targets of aristocracy and wealth from every angle. The nobles of Domitian's court are exposed as swindlers, homosexuals, corrupt and money-grubbing toadies. Such a catalogue might easily become a bore; but it is redeemed by the vigour of the verse, the cruel and vivid accuracy of Juvenal's observation. Here are Domitian's Cabinet, cringing and trembling, offering advice on how to cook a monster turbot. Here, worse still, is the wretched client at his patron's dinner: openly snubbed, served from filthy cracked pottery by a negro slave, chewing at mouldy bread; while at the high table the host stuffs himself with crayfish and swills his Falernian, and his carver gesticulates like a ballet-dancer at the loaded sideboard.

This capacity for packed observation reaches its climax in the Third Satire, on the horrors of life in Rome, which Samuel

Johnson imitated in his *London*. The theme of the power and wickedness of the Big City forms yet one more link between Juvenal and European satire from the eighteenth century to the present day: De Quincey, Cobbett with his Great Wen, Balzac, they all fulminated against what Spengler called the Megalopolis. Yet Juvenal, like Johnson, could not bring himself to turn countryman: the urban poison had gone too deep. He stays, a complaining Jeremiah, among the rumbling drays, the chamber-pots emptied out of windows, the garrets under the tiles, the fires and heat and dust and flies, the nocturnal drunks and Mohocks. Like the Irishman, he will beat his nurse; but he cannot do without her.

Above all, dominating the gabble of the Forum, the jerry-built flats, the stink and intrigue and bustle, are the women, who are anatomized savagely and at length in that great scabrous centre-piece the Sixth Satire. Here a most curious fact strikes us. If the nobles and bourgeois of the Empire were weak, degenerate and dilettante in their ambitions, their wives and sisters most certainly were not. To quote Professor Highet again:

> all the women are strong characters, stronger than their husbands, possessed by furies of ambition, wilfulness and lust, utterly selfish, boldly irresponsible, courageous, ruthless, remorseless. Evidently the profound spiritual maladjustment from which Rome suffered in Juvenal's day had sucked away the strength of her men and intensified the passions of her women.

Perhaps it was because their oblique, unofficial power had never been challenged, because their role remained unaltered, that they thus gained in strength. Dictators, emperors, reigns of terror might come and go, free speech be lost, democracy made a mockery, the fabric of society be turned upside-down, but women still possessed their own adjustment, could still use their sex as a weapon to disarm the most cruel or insatiable male adversary. In the end it was they who had the last word.

As he grew older, and his circumstances eased, Juvenal mellowed correspondingly. In his later satires the blazing fire gradually fades to embers—though it could flare up again for an acidulous attack on the barbarous Egyptian *fellaheen* among whom he had spent his exile. He is still preoccupied with money; but now he has some of his own. He has, too, in accordance with his newly acquired Epicureanism, gathered a few friends about him; the savage isolation of his middle age is gone. Pessimistic, but peaceful and resigned, he turns from the particular to the general, to a sombre analysis of man's restless ambitions. We know the Tenth Satire better under the title of Johnson's adaptation: *The Vanity of Human Wishes*. 'The infinite variety of lives', Byron wrote in his Journal, 'conduct but to death, and the infinity of wishes lead but to disappointment.' The noble expression of this theme was Juvenal's last great achievement.

When we consider Juvenal's influence on subsequent European literature, it at once becomes clear that his popularity is conditioned not so much by his sheer qualities of literature (though a basic minimum of epigrams, those bitter drops of wisdom wrung from his life's experience, are perennial) as by some similarity of social conditions to those in which he himself lived. Hence his frequent adaptation rather than translation. The Augustan Age contained just such impoverished but intelligent writers as did its Roman prototype, and an almost identical system of patronage; though it lacked the physical cruelty, the tremendous class struggles which Juvenal knew, and which our own times have re-enacted. Each took from him what they needed; yet the man who wrote of 'an age of absolute monarchy, vast wealth unevenly divided, fat cities swelling like tumours . . . rich perfumes mingling with the smell of decay', could not but reach his zenith of popularity in the seventeenth and eighteenth century world of Venice or London or Madrid. Their writers approved his morals but deplored his vulgarisms: as Boileau charmingly put it:

> Le latin dans les mots brave l'honnêteté,
> Mais le lecteur français veut être respecté.

The Middle Ages had not been so nice; it was nothing rare for a questionable Pope to be dubbed *inter Socraticos notissima fossa cinaedos*.

Dryden, who began by preferring Horace, changed horses (to use his own type of metaphor) in mid-stream: 'Horace', he observed, 'is always on the amble, Juvenal on the gallop.' And indeed, as the Age of Reason plunged towards revolution, Juvenal was carried like a banner in the van of the attack. Rousseau and Marat quoted him on the title-pages of their pamphlets (what fitter prophet for a bourgeois revolution?); Burke in the House of Commons when recommending compromise with the American colonists. Hugo admired him as a political rebel, Flaubert fell in love with his style. Byron, in *English Bards and Scotch Reviewers,* devoured him whole:

> Still must I hear?—shall hoarse Fitzgerald bawl
> His creaking couplets in a tavern hall,
> And I not sing?

But as the right of free speech spread, with the growth in England of the legalized Opposition's power, the satirist began to slip into the background, his venom to dissipate itself in newspapers, and, later, the radio or cinema. Pamphleteering, as Flaubert remarked in the *Dictionnaire des Idées Reçues,* was no longer done. There have been few notable verse satirists in the late nineteenth century, still fewer in our own. Perhaps the most remarkable was G. G. Belli, who died in 1863, the author of numerous brilliant satirical sonnets in the Trastevere dialect, which attacked wealth and privilege (mostly ecclesiastical) with all Juvenal's ancient vigour and obscenity. In recent times Roy Campbell stands almost alone—though in prose we have a Huxley, a Koestler, or an Orwell to set beside him.

Was Juvenal a poet? The question has been asked often, and is largely meaningless. That he was a great artist is beyond dispute. In structure (like Faulkner or Wolfe) he was often erratic but always striking. His trick of quoting or parodying epic tags from Homer and Virgil in a new, mundane context (which criticized contemporary *mores* by the implied contrast with heroic times) has found an echo in *The Waste Land* and Mr Ezra Pound's *Cantos.* His themes were not particularly new, but he made them into something unique: a coherent social criticism of institutions. Lucilius had been on the edge of this; Horace had quietly dropped it. That peevish mother's boy Persius lacked the experience to handle it, though he tried; it was left to Juvenal to bring it to full fruition and bequeath it to posterity.

Yes: Juvenal is a writer for this age. He has (in spite of his personal preoccupations) the universal eye for unchanging human corruption; he would be perfectly at home in a New York dive or a rigged political conference, ready to pillory the tycoons or degenerates who were elbowing him out of an easy job in some international organization. Bureaucrats have taken over from aristocrats, but his cry still goes up; and if we finally weary of its savage brilliance, it is simply because the thought underlying it is so utterly negative, and, in the last resort, so ignoble in its purpose. The writer must compel our respect; but the man can never command our affections. Nevertheless, Juvenal is an historical no less than a literary landmark. He crystallizes for us all the faults and weaknesses we have watched gaining strength at Rome through the centuries: when his minatory voice dies away there is nothing left but to sit in silence, and listen to Gibbon's great rhetorical epitaph on a nation that sold its soul to win the fruits of the known world.

9

Some Versions of Aeschylus

A STUDY OF TRADITION AND METHOD IN
TRANSLATING CLASSICAL POETRY

I

Nearly every discussion of translation begins, or tries to begin, with a general definition. There is the word; the word implies a concept; the concept must be definable. Classical scholars in particular, nurtured at a tender age on Plato's Theory of Ideas, persist in imagining that somehow, somewhere, there is to be found the Perfect Translation, of which all their laborious versions partake in some degree. To such an optimist the history of translation—especially verse translation—in his own field cannot but present a depressing spectacle. The theorists, like Gibbon's Byzantine heretics, contradict each other at every turn; and what is worse, they show the most lamentable discrepancies between theory and practice. As Dryden acidly observed, 'many a fair precept in poetry is, like a seeming demonstration in the mathematics, very specious in the diagram, but failing in the mechanic operation'. In the circumstances it is little wonder that the one point over which everyone seems agreed is that the Perfect Translation is an unattainable will-o'-the-wisp. Nothing, it has been suggested, improves by translation except a bishop.

Translation is not, at any level, an ideal art; it is a crutch for human infirmity, a technique to improve various sorts of communication. Any artistic merit it may have in its own right is purely secondary. Furthermore, we cannot cover it with a single blanket definition. It may be used to interpret at an International Court, to disseminate a scientific treatise, to enable Finnish poetry or Chinese philosophy to spread beyond their immediate linguistic frontiers. Mr Theodore H. Savory, in his useful little book

The Art of Translation, suggests that there are four clearly differentiated types of translation, roughly corresponding to four separate categories of reader. There is the purely informative translation, which carries no associative or aesthetic undertones; the 'adequate' translation of prose literature, where subject-matter is far more important than style; the 'literary' translation as generally understood; and the translation of scholarly works, particularly those with a scientific or technological bias, in which accurate interpretation of subject-matter is the prime requirement. As he makes clear, much of the perennial argument about how translation should be conducted can be done away with, and many contradictions resolved, by the realization that a translation intended for any one of these categories may have little relevance to readers outside it. This essential multiplicity of object at once makes senseless any overall or absolute 'theory of translation'. One version may be aesthetic in intention, another purely utilitarian; yet both will be justified on their own terms, and both require an equally exacting, though far from identical, discipline in the translator.

It is generally agreed that the whole concept of what translation means, and the laws or principles governing its practice, have undergone a radical change during the last few years. Just what has brought this metamorphosis about is not so clear. In this essay I propose to deal, more or less exclusively, with the *Agamemnon* of Aeschylus. On this thread it may be possible to hang one or two more widely-framed conclusions about the problems of translating poetry in general, and classical poetry in particular. By working out just what the various translators of the *Agamemnon* were at, we may also come to understand the revolution in method which is apparent when we examine some of the most recent versions.

There are over fifty English translations of the *Agamemnon*. This fact is not, I think, an entirely disinterested tribute to Aeschylus' poetic genius. By far the greater number of these versions seem to have served as a prop on which the scholarly poet *manqué* could peg up his own threadbare Muse. Such an

186

ungenerous conclusion is supported by the unfailing way in which each version reflects the borrowed light, not so much of Aeschylus, as of whatever poet was in fashion at the time of writing. In the eighteenth century the great choruses of the *Agamemnon* speak with Dryden's voice; they seem begging to be set to music by Purcell. In the nineteenth, the Romantic Revival is faithfully reflected: Scott, Tennyson, and Shelley usurp their original. Towards the *fin de siècle* we recognize the accents of Swinburne, Patmore, Francis Thompson, even Austin Dobson. The conclusion one is tempted to draw is that the history of Aeschylean translation—indeed, of classical translation generally—has been a subtle process of self-flattery, modifying itself according to changing fashions from one generation to the next. But this would, perhaps, be an over-simplification.

II

Poetry, of whatever kind, makes more complex and multiple demands on the translator than any other medium. To translate even the most highly wrought prose is easy by comparison. As Mr L. W. Tancock observed recently:

> The poet uses words differently from the prose-writer; words for him are colours, units in mosaic of sound, noises intended to startle a slumbering memory into resurrection of things thought to be dead and forgotten. This sort of thing can only be dealt with on its own terms, and a *similar* pattern or song may be produced which may have a similar effect, but it will not be a translation, any more than a passage written for oboe will be the same when played on a harpsichord, though the notes may be the same.

In other words, the physical shape and texture of word-pattern used by the poet, the associative or emotive qualities inherent in his imagery—these, no less than mere denotative 'meaning', have to be dealt with and, somehow, reproduced. Clearly the translator faced with a task of this delicacy and magnitude is bound to betray his own formative influences more obviously than anyone dealing in the relatively neutral and viable medium of prose.

Since Greek and Latin poetry are woven into the very fabric of our literary tradition, we may well have a blind spot for this danger when translating the classics. Arthur Waley somewhere quotes a well-meaning Victorian clergyman who rendered a Chinese poem as follows:

> Oh fair maiden so shy and retiring
> At the corner I'm waiting for you
> And I'm scratching my head and inquiring
> What on earth it were best I should do.

In this Chinese example, where we have no tradition of pastiche to distract our judgment, the incongruity is at once apparent. But the same incongruity in the classics has, till very recently, tended to escape us. Greek and Latin have become domesticized in this country through the centuries: our forefathers referred familiarly to Cicero as Tully, as though he were a creation of George Eliot's. When English translations first acquired any vogue—that is, in the sixteenth century—most readers were acquainted with their Latin or Greek originals. The purpose of a translation then, and for as long as a classical education remained the rule rather than the exception, was the tasteful embellishment of the original according to contemporary poetic fashion: ingenious variations on a well-known theme. Chapman, for instance, when describing the buffeting of Odysseus' raft, writes of the winds' 'horrid tennis'. Pope shackles Homer's loose-flowing hexameters in the Augustan elegiac couplet; and I have often wondered if the unwary reader exists who, after reading J. W. Mackail's translation of the *Odyssey*, went around under the pleasant delusion that Homer was a spiritual ancestor of Omar Khayyam.

The Greek dramatists were comparatively late in being translated; they did not make their appearance till the early part of the eighteenth century. That first Renaissance enthusiasm which dealt with Homer, Virgil, and Ovid—not to mention prose writers so diverse as Hippocrates and Lucian—totally neglected

Aeschylus and Sophocles. There was, indeed, one solitary version of Euripides' *Phoenician Women*, published in 1566 by George Gascoigne and Francis Kinwelmersh; but as it was a translation of an Italian adaptation from a Latin version of the original, it is a moot point whether it can fairly count as a translation at all. It is interesting to note, though, that it established the practice of using blank verse to represent the Greek iambic line, and rhymed stanzas for the Greek choral strophes: a convention which was followed by the overwhelming majority of translators, almost till the present day.

Now this in itself implies a very clear attitude to what a translator's duties are. The nearest prosodic equivalent to a Greek iambic is not the blank verse line, but the Alexandrine, with its extra foot. A Greek chorus never in any circumstances rhymes; rhyme was virtually unknown to both Greek and Roman poets. One would never guess, from the thumping quatrains beloved of most translators, at the subtle rhythmic variations of the original—unless, perhaps, one was acquainted with the original already. And here, I think, lies one key to much that puzzles us in early versions of the *Agamemnon*. They were, like all translations, made for a specific purpose; but the purpose was not that which we have brought before us today, when our main aim is to bring ancient literature within the reach of intelligent readers who could not otherwise appreciate it. In the eighteenth and nineteenth centuries, as we have seen, most readers of such versions would have an educational background which enabled them to compare translation with original. This applies more particularly to the Greek dramatists than to, say, Homer or Virgil, whose appeal was much wider. If Aeschylus remained untranslated till the eighteenth century, it was because his complex imagery and apparent obscurity had no attraction for the general lettered public. His audience remained restricted, on the whole, to the circle of scholars who knew his text—and at this time, we should remember, Greek studies still lagged far behind Latin.

This assumption of a bi-lingual public persisted long after the facts continued to warrant it. In the late Victorian period, and even in the present century, there is still the feeling that a verse translation is an exercise in literary virtuosity. Such a notion was given some sanction by Dryden, who excused his own embroidery of original texts in the following manner:

> And where I have enlarged them, I desire the false critics would not always think, that those thoughts are wholly mine, but that either they are secretly in the poet, or may be fairly deduced from him; or at least, if both these considerations should fail, that my own is of a piece with his, and that if he were living, and an Englishman, they are such as he would probably have written.

Within the last few years this proposition was given a fresh airing—appropriately enough—by the Public Orator at Cambridge, Mr L. P. Wilkinson, in his book *Ovid Recalled*; and his complaint that there was no easy way of reproducing the Alcaic stanza in English called down a stinging rebuke on his head from Mr J. B. Leishman:

> There certainly is not, for it was by no easy way that Horace produced it; nevertheless, I am convinced that no translator can hope to achieve even moderate success unless he attempts to reproduce it as closely as his language will permit, and refuses to deceive himself and others with vain notions of being able to invent 'some stanza that recalls the movement of the original'. For his business is not to 'recall' its movement to those who already know the original, and do not require to have it recalled, but to communicate it to those who cannot read the original for themselves. . . . And I will insist that the syllabic pattern of the lines . . . can be reproduced exactly, and the movement of them . . . very much more closely than has commonly (and, perhaps I may add, lazily) been supposed.

This recalls another endemic fallacy cherished by the majority of translators. 'Everybody', Mr Savory writes, 'believes that it must be easy, that he could do it if necessary, and that he is qualified to criticize the efforts of those who practise it.' Perhaps to counter this suggestion, translators themselves have always been liable to indulge in Flaubertian grumbles about the difficulties, even the absolute impossibilities, of their task. This amateurish attitude means that there are comparatively few works available on the principles of translation (though in recent years some excellent studies have been published) and those that are available tend to contradict one another flatly and subjectively over their most basic assumptions.

It is easy enough for us today to see that Dryden's apologia is little more than a transparent device to let the translator enlarge his own ego to his heart's content. As one famous practitioner, the late Professor Gilbert Murray, somewhat ingenuously observed: 'A translator cannot help seeing his own work through the medium of the greater thing which he loves.' What is interesting is why the device was so generally accepted. Obviously if one's audience already had access to one's original model, fidelity was not the moral necessity it has today become; one was writing for readers who not only tolerated, but demanded, elegant pastiche, and lacked our modern passion for historical objectivity. But the logical sanction, I suspect, was largely derived from a practice characteristic of the English classical curriculum: I mean Greek and Latin verse composition. This curious discipline required—and still requires—that a student should turn an English poem, ballad-stanza, lyric, sonnet, blank verse, what you will, into Virgilian hexameters, Ovidian elegiacs, or Horatian alcaics. It was inculcated at school, at an impressionable age, and reinforced with the cane whenever one made a false quantity. What more natural than to assume that a converse process was equally inevitable; that Greek iambics should be turned into blank verse, and Greek choruses into fashionable rhyming lyrics? Now, with this in mind, let us turn back to the *Agamemnon*.

III

The first translator of Aeschylus, Robert Potter, is an intriguing figure; partly because he *was* the first, and also because his version held the field undisputed for fifty years and more. It appeared in 1777, and ran into countless editions; it was still being reprinted in 1892, when there were twenty-five rivals jostling for the lead. Potter, like many translators, was a divine and a schoolmaster. His Aeschylus was followed by versions of Sophocles and Euripides, all of which he sedulously dispatched to Lord Thurlow, the

Lord Chancellor. His reward was 'the second canonical stall in Norwich Cathedral, which he held till his death. . . . Thurlow, in giving the stall, observed, "I did not like to promote him earlier for fear of making him indolent".'

Despite the great popularity of his translations, Dr Johnson stoutly dismissed them *en bloc* as 'verbiage', a verdict with which the modern reader may be tempted to concur. Here, for the first but by no means the last time, we find that flaccid, colourless blank verse, without character or distinction, beneath which Aeschylus' superb iambics have so often been buried. The Chorus addresses Clytemnestra:

> With manly sentiment thy wisdom, lady,
> Speaks well. Confiding in thy suasive signs,
> Prepare we to address the gods; our strains
> Shall not without their meed of honour rise . . .

A prolonged diet of such stuff put me in mind of the final lines of Calverley's inimitable Browning parody, 'The Cock and the Bull':

> Excuse me, sir, I think I'm going mad.
> You see the trick on't though, and can yourself
> Continue the discourse *ad libitum*.
> It takes up about eighty thousand lines,
> A thing imagination boggles at:
> And might, odds-bobs, sir! in judicious hands,
> Extend from here to Mesopotamy.

When we turn to the Choruses, we see that Gray and Dryden have been there before us. Here is Potter's version of the *kyrios eimi*, that magnificent opening choral strophe:

> It swells upon my soul; I feel the pow'r
> To hail the auspicious hour,
> When, their brave hosts marching in firm array,
> The heroes led the way.
> The fire of youth glows in each vein
> And heav'n-born confidence inspires the strain. . . .

This stupefying bromide, as I have said, held the field for half-a-century. On its own terms it obviously satisfied the customers: a consideration as corrupting here as in the field of popular television, but equally valid for its immediate ends. The first protest

was raised in 1829 by James Kennedy, who wrote, in the preface
to his own translation:

> The expression of the ancient has either been marred by diffuse-
> ness, or his meaning obscured by dullness, or his spirit evaporated
> amidst the display of overwrought diction. Too often has the unity
> ... been sacrificed to a passion for ornament and variety; thoughts
> not his own are incorporated into the body of his composition;
> a species of intellectual ingraftment, which produces the direct
> opposite effect to that of the gardener's art, infecting the parent stem
> without deriving from it vigour and nutriment.

Unfortunately Kennedy neutralized the sting of the rhetoric by
producing a version as permeated with dullness, overwrought
diction, evaporation of spirit, and intellectual ingraftment as his
predecessor: but he did print, above his own translation, the
German rendering by J. H. Voss. This latter is a remarkable
achievement in that at one stroke it achieves both modernity and
equivalence: Voss turns iambics into Alexandrines, and his choral
passages catch the exact rhythms of their original. Here are the
first two lines of the play, the Watchman's appeal for relief from
his vigil, as Voss rendered them:

> *Gebt, Götter, fleh'ich, dieser Mühn Erledigung,*
> *Der Hut, ein Jahr an Länge, da gelagert ich, &c.*

That is the rhythm and accent of Aeschylus; and Voss also has the
honour of seeing that the first line of the *kyrios eimi* Chorus is,
and can be rendered as nothing other than, a hexameter:

> *Macht ist mir zu erhöhn* † *bahnglückliche Stärke der Männer . . .*

In Germany, if not in England, a point had been reached by the
eighteen-twenties where the original—not translator, public, or
contemporary fashion—was the most important thing. The point
was raised over here during the next few years, and argued
at length in scholarly periodicals. One translation embodying
Voss's principles appeared in 1839, and was a failure. In 1848 the
famous scholar John Conington produced an *Agamemnon* which
put the clock back to Potter; but he did have one pertinent
observation to make in his preface—which, as so often, contained
much more of value than his text:

> There are some measures now tolerably congenial to our language [he wrote] which our fathers would have regarded as unnatural and affected; and the breaking up of conventional forms of phraseology, which has been for some time past going on under the influence of such writers as Mr Carlyle, will allow us to hazard many expressions which could not have been used twenty years ago.

Substitute T. S. Eliot or Dylan Thomas for Thomas Carlyle, and the same verdict, word for word, could be applied to translations of Aeschylus today. This, partially, is what Mr Day Lewis meant when he said, apropos his version of Virgil's *Georgics*, that if a classic is worth translating at all, it must be translated afresh every fifty years. Translation is a substitute, an inadequate substitute at the best, for original literature: the requirements of each generation from a version will be bound to differ.

But Conington's words implied something more. Fashion, we have seen, changes from age to age: yet the text of Aeschylus (*pace* our more enthusiastic textual critics) does not. Every translator is conditioned by his own assumptions and dogmas, the literary conventions of his time, what he sees as the restrictions of the medium in which he is working. Therefore there are elements in Aeschylus—not always the same elements—which successive generations of translators will be bound to ignore, or transmute into something else. As long as the translator believes that Aeschylus must be turned into English poetry or English drama, with all the associations that such terms imply, this is inevitable. One generation will be unable to digest his startling metaphors and polysyllabic compound adjectives; another may jib at the apparent obscurity of his thought and imagery. Rhyme is in the very fibre of English verse, and Aeschylus is rhymeless: something has to give way, and it is not usually the translator's patriotism. Aeschylus, we are told, must be presented to the English reader in a recognizable English dress, on the grounds—or so it is still sometimes alleged—that the first business of a translator is to catch readers. It might be argued that this savours of the confidence trick: the hungry sheep look up, and are fed with spurious matter. Like the proverbial mean farmer, the translator equips his sheep with green-tinted spectacles, and proceeds to offer them straw.

At first, as I have suggested, this did not matter; the audience was an informed audience, and never supposed that Aeschylus was a spiritual ancestor of the English Augustans. But as the nineteenth century advanced, and the reading public increased, there was a growing demand for enlightenment and interpretation over the great classical authors. It is interesting to speculate what notion the Greekless layman must have formed of Aeschylus from the versions offered him: I have recently perused every single English translation of the *Agamemnon*, and, with honourable exceptions, a more depressing experience could hardly be conceived by the mind of man.

The overall impression gained must have been that Aeschylus was a limp, third-rate hack versifier, the very worst kind of Poet Laureate, who had somehow managed to stumble on a really powerful theme. This theme he then proceeded to obliterate with every stultifying *cliché*, verbal or prosodic, known to the English language. It is hard to explain the proliferation of these versions; during the latter half of the Victorian period a new one appeared almost every year, virtually indistinguishable from its predecessors.

It might be argued that this was due to most translation being done, not by poets but by scholars, yet when we turn up the two nineteenth-century poets who did have a shot at the *Agamemnon*, we find that they are, if anything, worse than the rest. Edward Fitzgerald achieved, certainly, what no one else has done before or since: he made Aeschylus *coy*:

> Not beside thee in the chamber,
> Menelaus, any more;
> But with him she fled with, pillow'd
> On the summer softly-billow'd
> Ocean, into dimple wreathing
>   Underneath a breeze of amber
> Air that, as from Eros breathing,
>   Fill'd the sail, and flew before . . .

As for the famous, or notorious, 'Browning version', it went, in theory, to the other extreme: Browning announced his intention of being 'literal at every cost save that of absolute violence to our language'. Unhappily, he took the word 'literal'—as many a schoolboy has done before or since—to mean a word-by-word construe. This notion, which outrages every law of linguistics, has played havoc with otherwise well-intentioned translators.

It was in 1878, a year after the Browning Version, that one isolated translator took a leaf out of Voss's German book and produced what is, to all intents and purposes, the first English rendering of the *Agamemnon* which is recognizably Aeschylean. He was not a poet by calling, but the author of that abominable Latin Primer still inflicted on schoolboys learning the rudiments of grammar: Benjamin Kennedy. Open his version at the first page, and the Watchman begins to speak in accent and rhythm about as near to Aeschylus as any translator had hitherto come:

> Still have I asked the Gods deliverance from these toils
> throughout my long year's watch, whereto I lay me down
> upon the Atreidae's roof, arm-rested, like a dog,
> and know by heart the congress of the nightly stars,
> with those which bring to men winter and summer-tide . . . &c.

That is the last time we see the Alexandrine in an English translation of Aeschylus till Mr Louis MacNeice introduces it, somewhat sparingly, into his 1936 version. Though heavy in vocabulary, clumsy in versification, and baffled by the complexities of the Aeschylean chorus, Kennedy still contrived to get nearer the heart of the matter than Potter and his imitators. But Kennedy's reward was the indifference of scholars and public alike, who would not be ready for nearly fifty years to digest the innovations (paradoxical that they should be so) which Kennedy had adopted.

Meanwhile poetic fashions were changing in England, and Aeschylus, as usual, moved with the times. By the turn of the century Swinburne and the Nineties had brought their roses and raptures to the long-suffering choruses; and England's discovery of the virtues inherent in French drama shackled swift-moving iambic speeches in the elegant straitjacket of the heroic couplet

—a perversion hitherto largely confined to such authors as Homer or Ovid. In 1829 James Kennedy had referred in passing to 'the rhyming couplets of the French School, a style of versification so abhorrent to Tragic expression, and over which even the genius of a Dryden failed of achieving a triumph'. Both practices obtain in the version by W. R. Paton, published in 1907. Here is the close of the Watchman's speech:

> The rest I speak not; on my tongue a weight
> Lieth; but could these walls articulate
> They'd tell it best. Gladly if one but wot
> I speak; if not, gladly remember not.

And here the truly Swinburnian Chorus addresses Clytemnestra:

> Tell all that thou durst, for the hearts of thy servants are fain
> To be healed, that are sick with the mist of despond, till again
> From the fires of the altars doth gleam sweet hope, and represses
> Thought that thirsts for the corsive [*sic*] of love's caresses.

From here, of course, it is only a step—less than a step, perhaps —to the scholar-translator who has more profoundly influenced the popular conception of Greek Drama than anyone else in this century: the late Professor Gilbert Murray. Now if Professor Murray had lived a hundred, or even perhaps fifty years before he did, no great harm would have been done by his work. His audience would have appreciated exactly what he was at, and applauded his ingenious virtuosity: it is not everybody who can convert a chorus-ending from Euripides into the very accents of 'The Garden of Proserpine'. But since his charming period-pieces were mostly composed after the First World War, they had a highly unlooked-for effect. Up and down England there were thousands of innocents who very likely went to their graves imagining that this was the way Aeschylus or Euripides actually wrote. They gave the credit for Professor Murray's poetic sensibility to the Greek dramatists on whom he modelled himself; and since Aeschylus was dead, and Professor Murray, with scholarly modesty, refused to take any of the credit, error crept in and persisted. Mr T. S. Eliot saw the dangers of all this as early as 1920: in a splendidly trenchant article[1] he wrote:

> Greek poetry will never have the slightest vitalising effect upon English poetry if it can only appear as a vulgar debasement of the eminently personal idiom of Swinburne. . . . That the most conspicuous Greek propagandist of the day should almost habitually use two words where the Greek language requires one, and where the English language will provide him with one; . . . that he should stretch the Greek brevity to fit the loose frame of William Morris, and blur the Greek lyric to the fluid haze of Swinburne; these are not faults of infinitesimal significance.

Let us take two typical examples from Professor Murray's *Agamemnon*. Late in the play he makes Clytemnestra address the Chorus as follows:

> Woulds't fright me, like a witless woman? Lo,
> This bosom shakes not. And, though well ye know,
> I tell you . . . Curse me as ye will, or bless,
> 'Tis all one. . . . This is Agamemnon; this,
> My husband dead by my right hand, a blow
> Struck by a righteous craftsman. Aye, 'tis so.

So much for the iambics: now for the lyrics. A few lines later the Chorus are made to riposte as follows:

> Thy thought, it is very proud;
> Thy breath is the scorner's breath;
> Is not the madness loud
>   In thy heart, being drunk with death?
> Yea, and above thine eye
>   A star of the wet blood burneth!
> Oh doom shall have yet her day,
>   The last friend cast away,
> When lie doth answer lie,
>   And a stab for a stab returneth.

It requires, so far as I am concerned, a very great effort of imagination to put oneself in the place of the scholar who offers this kind of thing to posterity. Human nature is frail, and the possibility that my own favourites may suffer a similar fate fifty

[1] 'Euripides and Professor Murray', reprinted in *Selected Essays* (3rd ed. 1951) pp. 59–64. This piece deserves to be read by all students of translation.

years hence does nothing to alter my prejudice. Perhaps, when I am too old to object, we shall have Homer served up in *terza rima*, or Catullus converted into Empsonian ballades, just as Mr Ezra Pound has turned out a version of Sophocles' *Trachiniae* in what might be termed Hill-billy Esperanto. Here is the beginning of one of his Messenger speeches: 'All started when he had a letch for the girl, and when her pre-eh-Genitor 'Rytus wouldn't let him put her to bed on the Q.T. . . . . ' It is not mere prim academicism to object to such catchpenny stuff; Mr Pound's ephemeral Americanisms are no less artificial and unreal than the Wardour Street versions he so despises. The same objection applies in all cases: these versions are essentially misleading. At their best they convey some of the denotative sense of their original; yet often even this is so thickly coated with modern associations as to be virtually unrecognizable. As A. E. Housman said in another context, we turn to such works for many things, but not for help in trouble.

At the same time we must face the fact that this convention was almost universally accepted, in one form or another, till very recent times. It was not only the scholars, normally conservative in aesthetic matters, who fell into the habit: eminent poets, as we have seen, were no less ready to lend a hand. And when we find a translator—Housman himself—in whom the two qualities blended to an eminent degree, and see that he too is tarred with the same brush, we simply have to accept the phenomenon, with the reflection that times have changed, and that yesterday's orthodoxes are always liable to become tomorrow's heresies.

There is, then, a radical split between the old and new ideas of what a poetic translation of Greek drama should aim at and achieve. For our ancestors it was adaptation or pastiche; for us it is imitation, *mimesis* in the fullest sense of the term. These two attitudes, incidentally, reflect a much wider and more general change in ethical attitudes. Earlier generations were interested in incorporating an ancient poet as a kind of guest member in the Athenaeum of English literature. We are more concerned with hearing him talk about his own tradition—through an interpreter, of course, but one who does his best neither to soften the words he hears, nor to overlay them with false associations. For forty years and more now there has been an increasing number of people who wanted to know—not knowing in any way—what Aeschylus actually said, as near as could be, and the texture of his poetic imagery; people who looked to a translator to use his Golden Bough, his double tongue, to pass them into the ancient world.

Now this, whatever its other merits, the old kind of translation did not: though as an exercise in English parody or pastiche it had undoubted value. Its virtues were those of the prize composition; and this was nowhere more apparent than in its synthetic, conventional archaisms. The principle followed was the same as that in the worst kind of historical novel. This is an archaic work, therefore it must be given a flavour of antiquity. The historical provenance of that antiquity is unimportant. Malory for Herodotus? Shakespeare or William Morris for Sophocles? Ingenious, and very tasteful. It did not occur to these translators—indeed, why should it, in their day and age?—that a translator's real business, almost his moral duty, is what Mr J. B. Leishman pointed out in his essay on Horace: not to 'recall' an original, by some vague semi-parallel, to those who knew it already, but to reproduce something utterly unknown for those who have no notion of it at all.

IV

This was the situation after the First World War; and it was in fact then that the modernist movement in translation began. Coincidence, I suspect, played a large part in the revolution: the coincidence that at this precise moment new trends in English poetry came closer to the form and spirit of Greek drama than ever before. Ezra Pound, T. S. Eliot, Wyndham Lewis, the Imagists—all these swept away the lingering prejudice against so-called *vers libre* and the absence of rhyme. The toughest bastion was thus stormed almost by accident. It is significant that the first type of classical poetry to receive adequate translation—formally,

aesthetically, and rhythmically—was the Greek choral strophe.
H.D.'s versions from the *Iphigeneia in Aulis* and the *Hippolytus*
actually appeared a year before Professor Murray's *Agamemnon*,
but at a time when forward-looking English poets were bursting
out into free verse, and the dissemination of Hopkins' methods
made experiment with choral rhythms, compound adjectives, and
Aeschylean metaphor highly attractive. Then in 1928 Sir Maurice
Bowra and Professor Wade-Gery produced a felicitous version
of Pindar's Pythian Odes on similar lines; and there followed a
succession of complete tragedies—Aldington's *Alcestis* in 1930,
MacNeice's *Agamemnon* in 1936, Fitzgerald's *Oedipus Coloneus* in
1941, and so through to the contemporary works by Rex Warner
and Professor Richmond Lattimore.

But not all forms came as easily as the choral lyric; it was not
till 1944, for example, that Mr Warner took the step (which looks
simple in retrospect) of turning to a variable English Alexandrine
instead of traditional blank verse to represent the Greek iambic
trimeter. Since the Alexandrine is an exact stress-equivalent, it
seems fair to assume that Mr Warner's predecessors were still
working empirically rather than from any *a priori* principles.
Some, like Yeats and Mr Aldington, avoided the problem
altogether by using prose; others, such as Mr MacNeice, varied
their blank verse line in a way which suggests the influence of
Murder in the Cathedral or *The Family Reunion*. Nor was it till 1940
that Mr Cecil Day Lewis found a way of dealing with that most
intractable of verse-forms, the hexameter. Here as nowhere else
the difficulty of transposing a line governed by accentual metre
into one dependent on stress rhythm seemed almost insurmount-
able. Robert Bridges' attempts at an *accentual* equivalent merely
did unnatural violence to English: only Calverley, in his fragment
of Book I of the *Iliad,* came anywhere near to making even a
regular stress-hexameter sound like a natural growth. The
inevitable effect, despite such desperate devices as almost line-by-
line *enjambement,* was one of flat and unrelieved monotony, as any
reader of H. B. Cotteril's *Odyssey* will testify.

Nevertheless, the problem could not be abandoned to the

doubtful mercies of blank verse or the heroic couplet. The hexameter, as Matthew Arnold pointed out, is a precipitate, *falling* line: whereas in the iambic line so often and so dubiously used as an equivalent the reader painfully plods uphill with Sisyphus. Mr Day Lewis employed 'a rhythm based on the hexameter, containing six beats in each line, but allowing much variation of pace and interspersed with occasional short lines of three stresses'. This at once provides the rushing dactylic movement so essential for the free flow of the hexameter, and avoids the deadly monotony of a regular English line of this type. In 1952 Mr Day Lewis followed up his *Georgics* with a more ambitious version of the *Aeneid*, and the same year saw the appearance of Professor Lattimore's *Iliad* in the same style and rhythm.

So far, so good: but attributes, as Socrates pointed out, are not the same as definitions. What is the theory behind the method? One can fairly easily isolate certain translators—Mr MacNeice, Mr Warner, Mr Day Lewis, Mr Leishman, perhaps above all Professor Lattimore—who might, perhaps, be said to form a 'modern' school; yet it is almost impossible to find an exposition of the basic principles—conceptual, emotive, linguistic, prosodic, semantic—on which they have worked. A good deal has, indeed, been written on translating Greek and Latin poetry; but little of it by successful translators (Mr Leishman honourably excepted) who, I suspect, most often arrive at the right method by instinct, without consciously formulating any principles at all. On the other hand, much of the scholarly criticism available is useless where not downright misleading; it fails either through initial errors of principle, or (when the principle itself is sound) by illogical application in practice, and arbitrary concentration on one or two aspects of what is essentially a multiple problem.

One of the few enlightening statements of guiding principle published by a practising modern translator is perhaps the article Mr MacNeice wrote in connexion with his version of Goethe's *Faust*. His ideal hypothetical verse translation, he declared, would have to satisfy the following conditions: a balancing of masses, a broad pattern equivalent to the original; conceptual accuracy—all 'prose' meanings to be brought out without addition or subtraction; connotative faithfulness—all poetic colour and suggestiveness to reappear in identical shades without loss of lustre; an equivalent line-for-line rendering; the order of words to correspond in general, and the imagery in particulars; the original rhythm-patterns and rhyme-patterns to be preserved; the phonetic texture to remain unaltered. It is of course, as Mr MacNeice admitted, impossible to satisfy all these conditions completely. But that is no reason why critics should condemn the method *in toto* for only achieving partial success. There is no such thing as a perfect verse translation; the translator's practical aim may be expressed by the formula $T = O$ minus x, where T stands for translation, O for original, and x for the irreducible minimum error incurred by translator and working medium in combination.

The concepts governing this methodology—the first comprehensive and logical attempt to come to grips with real rather than ideal problems in translation—had already been touched on by Miss D. C. Woodworth and Sir Harold Idris Bell. The former made a clear distinction between conceptual sense, affective symbolism, and formal significance, stressing the importance of considering all three in any translation; the latter, echoing this argument in slightly different terms, and adding some shrewd comments on the semantic difficulties incurred by a translator attempting exact conceptual equivalents of such words as *Geist* or *numen*[2], concluded with the round declaration that 'in all true poetry meaning and expression, content and form, are an indivisible whole, neither having any substantive existence apart from the other.' If these conclusions are valid, the effect will be to

---

[2] Every language carries social and metaphysical implications far beyond a mere lexicographer's reach. What is the French for 'home', or the English for *menu*, or the Spanish for 'jungle'? How are we to translate such an idiosyncratic phrase as *l'esprit d'escalier*? What are the subtle distinctions between 'culture', *culture*, and *Kultur*—or even 'mother', *mère*, and *Mutter*, which Mr Savory (for example) treats as interchangeable? We are, it is clear, sequestered behind more than physical frontiers; there is an Iron Curtain of speech as well as politics.

condemn, either wholly or partially, the bulk of existing translations from the classical poets—or at least to relegate them to the status of paraphrase or meta-poem.

Confirmation appeared in 1953 from Mr John MacFarlane, whose article 'Modes of Translation' deserved a wider circulation than that afforded by the *Durham University Journal*. Mr MacFarlane, I suspect, is a linguist; at any rate, he deals very shortly with woolly-minded translators who 'play semantic parlour-games' or define their aims metaphorically, with talk of body and soul, paintings and engravings, or the pouring out and evaporation of spirit. (This habit is not entirely dead even today: M. Georges Mounin has defined a translation as 'a pane of glass through which we look at the work of art. This glass may be clear, or distorted, or coloured'—an image more useful than most of its kind.) Mr MacFarlane explodes the fallacious concept of the so-called 'literal' translation, in which many who rightly aimed at interpretative fidelity (such as Browning) bogged down hopelessly. A word, as he points out, acquires meaning only in a concrete linguistic and situational context. He further demolishes the notion of 'pure conceptualism'—that is, words as information alone: there is always an apparatus of referential symbolism present. All language, as Russell observed, is vague; no precise equivalent between precise symbols can ever be reached. Mr MacFarlane confirms Bell and Miss Woodworth, in greater detail, to maintain that sound and sense are structurally united and essentially indivisible.

This trend towards multiple representationalism is bound to have been affected by the new public for which classical translations cater today, and which is hinted at by the phenomenal success of the Penguin Classics. Discussing Mr Day Lewis's *Aeneid* (to which he came, he admits, 'with all the prejudice of my classical convention') Professor R. G. Austin writes:

> Mr Day Lewis's audience, and his readers, differ from any public that any other translator has written for, a public in general less familiar with the original than any other has been. . . . He was bound to ignore all the accreted influence of four-and-a-half centuries

of translators, and start afresh. Mock-Tudor or mock-Georgian or mock-anything was unthinkable . . . *there had to be nothing intermediate between Mr Day Lewis and Virgil.* [Italics mine.]

The translator today has, as he never had before, a moral responsibility towards his readers. They rely on him absolutely: they have no valid check on his activities. He can no longer, if he is honest, indulge in poetic dilettantism, urning his original into some fashionable form of English verse. He can no longer make specious excuses about the letter killing the spirit, or the essence of a translation being lost by over-fidelity. The old jeer that his work is bound to be either a bad translation or bad poetry has lost its point.

Perhaps the most immediately effective factor in modernist theory is its concept of translation as a practical science rather than an idealistic art. It establishes recognized criteria from all the fields involved, against which any translation can be tested. This is an enormous step forward. It also means that it is better for a version to succeed partially along the right lines than to achieve a perfection irrelevant to translation properly considered. Compare, for instance, Housman's version of Horace, *Odes* 4.7 with that by Mr Leishman:

Housman: But oh, whate'er the sky-led seasons mar,
          Moon upon moon rebuilds it with her beams:
          Come *we* where Tullus and where Ancus are,
          And good Aeneas, we are dust and dreams.

Leishman: While, though, waning moons can mend their celestial
             losses,
          we, when we've fallen to where
          pious Aeneas and richest Tullus and Ancus have fallen
          linger as shadow and dust.

Traditionalists may say that Housman's version is fine poetry, while Leishman's is not, and that is all that matters. But Leishman's version has its poetic quality, and it is more essentially Horatian than Housman's. Leishman preserves the First Archilochian metre in a stress-equivalent: it is no argument at all to say that this metre is unfamiliar to English readers. Texture, rhythm, and verbal usage are all far closer to their original. Housman's rhymed quatrain sets up emotive responses in the reader's mind which have nothing to do with Horace at all: it suggests an English, not a Roman tradition. Similarly, a Greekless reader studying Mr F. L. Lucas's version of an Aeschylean chorus—

> This murder's absolution—
> What witness grants it thee?
> Who dare? (Though his sire's pollution
> Could add its curse, maybe.)

would be very far from appreciating Aeschylus: the jaunty rhythm and rhymes at once bring Charles Wesley to mind. This, I imagine, was not Mr Lucas's intention. But the damage is not merely that of translation *per se*: to think of Charles Wesley, however subconsciously, means equating Aeschylus' *mentality* with his also; and thus at once an impassable barrier is erected between the lay reader and the Greek original without his knowing it.

Today, to introduce inappropriately modern notions or diction into one's interpretation of ancient literature has become a cardinal crime. Nothing can be taken on trust. And even today we can learn more of the spirit of Greek tragedy from seeing such a film as Michael Cacoyannis's *The Girl in Black* than from reading any number of scholarly books on the subject by well-meaning Englishmen. The translator today is, literally, the last link binding modern readers to the ancient world. It is his duty to refrain from interposing himself, insofar as is humanly possible, between us and the great dramatists who lived in that other, remote world. As Louis MacNeice wrote:

> And how one can imagine oneself among them
>   I do not know;
> It was all so unimaginably different
>   And all so long ago.

V

Then there are the permanent, inherent difficulties which confront any translator of Aeschylus. Let us assume our translator to be in accord with modern representational theory: how, without being either unintelligible or plain ludicrous, is he fully to convey the sense, rhythm, and texture of his original? Aeschylus presents special problems. He indulges, as I have already remarked, in violent metaphors and compound adjectives which provoked unkind attention even in Aristophanes' day. The pattern of his plays is stiff and ritualistic; it has as much meaning as, but little more movement than, the pattern on a Bokhara carpet—which it also resembles in texture. Over and above these idiosyncrasies are the problems common to all Greek drama—the use of language which strikes an English ear as mere padding or tautological repetition (though we accept it in Isaiah or the Psalms); the curious, almost to us comic understatement; the forced antitheses; the solemn enunciation of the obvious.

All this was brilliantly brought out by Housman in one of the subtlest parodies in the English language. He called it, simply, *Fragment of a Greek Tragedy*; and it is aimed as much at the pedants who attempt an over-literal 'construe' as at Aeschylus himself. Those who are interested may identify the quotations he has worked into the text; taken literally, the parody is hardly a parody at all. The Chorus begin by questioning Alcmaeon:

> O suitably-attired-in-leather-boots
> Head of a traveller, wherefore seeking whom
> Whence by what way how purposed art thou come
> To this well-nightingaled vicinity?

After a brisk exchange of dialogue the Chorus then soliloquises, in choral strophes:

> In speculation
> I would not willingly acquire a name
> For ill-digested thought;
> But after pondering much
> To this conclusion I at last have come:
> *Life is uncertain.*
> This truth I have written deep
> In my reflective midriff
> On tablets not of wax,

> Nor with a pen did I inscribe it there
> For many reasons: Life, I say, is not
> A stranger to uncertainty.

After a good deal more of this, the unlucky Eriphyla, inside the house, utters a cry which any reader of the *Agamemnon* will at once recognize; and indeed the closing lines of the parody all have a horrid familiarity:

Er: Ah, I am smitten with a hatchet's jaw,
And that in deed and not in word alone.

Ch: I thought I heard a sound within the house
Unlike the voice of one that jumps for joy.

Er: He splits my skull, not in a friendly way
Once more: he purposes to kill me dead.

Ch: I would not be reputed rash, but yet
I doubt if all be gay within the house.

Er: O, O, another stroke! that makes the third!
He stabs me to the heart against my wish.

Ch: If that be so, thy state of health is poor;
But thine arithmetic is quite correct.

Now this type of idiom presents a formidable obstacle to the translator. He cannot draw on familiar English patterns to re-assure his audience, because that would be to give them a false impression; on the other hand, if he indulges in pseudo-literalism, he is liable to produce unintentionally ludicrous effects. Even Greek-based derivative words are liable to shift their meaning perilously in the course of the centuries, as the late Francis Cornford pointed out in his preface to Plato's *Republic*—of which he made a superlatively good translation:

> Many key-words, such as 'music', 'gymnastic', 'virtue', 'philo-sophy', have shifted their meaning or acquired false associations for English ears. One who opened Jowett's version at random and lighted on the statement that the best guardian for a man's 'virtue' is 'philosophy tempered with music', might run away with the idea that, in order to avoid irregular relations with women, he had better play the violin in the intervals of studying metaphysics. There may be some truth in this; but only after reading widely in other parts

of the book would he discover that it was not quite what Plato meant.[3]

This business of the 'meaning' of the words assumes a twofold difficulty when we are dealing with a poet—especially a poet so complex and allusive as Aeschylus. For many years those scholars who interpreted his text—and also were largely responsible for translating him—worked on the dogged assumption that everything he wrote had one single, finally ascertainable meaning, without overtones, ambiguities, or referential symbolism. They treated him, in fact, as if he were an historian, scientist, or grammarian; they credited him, as critics and scholars will, with their own habits of thought and unspoken assumptions. Thus when they wanted to elucidate his meaning, which they supposed could be separated off from the texture of his poetry as cream is separated from milk, they translated him into prose—a practice which led to much unnecessary puzzlement. Bold metaphors and pregnant symbolism were obelized as corrupt, or emended into comforting, comprehensible common sense; and much time and ink were wasted in arguing whether Aeschylus meant A or B, when he probably implied both—with C, D, and E thrown in associatively.

These prose translations of the *Agamemnon* are among the comic curiosities of literature. They veer between the incomprehensible and the bureaucratic: in 1823 H. S. Boyd made the Chorus ask Clytemnestra: 'What intelligence having received, induced by what annunciation, in divers places hast thou scattered fragrance?' In 1950 Professor Fraenkel, in his titanic three-volume edition, is still at it: 'Like base bronze, when rubbed and battered, so he becomes indelibly black when brought to justice; for a boy runs in chase of a flying bird after bringing an intolerable affliction upon his people.' When we read this, we realize (if we did not do so before) that to translate a poet into prose is a completely meaningless act, which implies a gross conceptual fallacy in

[3] Nevertheless Cornford himself was capable on occasion of blurring Plato's meaning in order to achieve linguistic clarity: in philosophical translation some quaintness of phrase may have to be retained. See the sensible remarks of Mr D. J. Furley, *Aspects of Translation* (1958) esp. pp. 57ff.

the translator's mind as to the very nature of poetic expression and poetic logic. At the best a good half of the poetry's significance is lost; at the worst we are led straight into Jabberwocky Land.

The only tolerable prose version known to me (which, it might be argued, was not really prose at all, certainly not in the choruses) was that made in 1911 by Arthur Platt, Housman's friend and colleague at University College, London. He translated the *Agamemnon* into the English of the Authorized Version, and made the lyric passages sound surprisingly like Jeremiah at Babylon:

> In the home also of every man is mourning;
> Their hearts are melted as water,
> Much anguish pierces them to the soul.
> For those whom they sent forth they know,
> But there returns to them no more a living man,
> But dust and ashes in a little urn . . .
> My spirit broods over these things in the darkness,
> Awaiting to hear that which shall come.
> For the gods are not regardless of the man of blood,
> But the grim Fury finds him after many days.

Such a method has its advantages. It catches something of the original's ritual and lyric intensity. It avoids rhyme. Above all, it presents Aeschylus's antiphonies and repetitions in a guise which the English ear, through long familiarity, is prepared to accept. Nevertheless, combined with pseudo-theological interpretation, it has done Aeschylus more harm than good. The associations it carried virtually identified the Greek dramatist with the Hebrew prophets in moral purpose; and Professor Hugh Lloyd-Jones has shown us just how misleading *that* notion can be.

Translating ancient poetry, then, is neither impossible, nor, *per contra*, the soft option so many people once believed it to be. It bears very little relation to turning out a set of elegiacs for a college prize, and demands several talents very seldom united in one person. Ancient poetry is proportionately harder to translate than modern; the language is more stubborn, the allusions less familiar, the forms totally alien. A much greater co-operative effort is also required of the reader, even supposing the translator to perform his task adequately. But the reader, acclimatized by tradition to Greek poetry which apparently resembles English, may shy away from the effort of adapting himself to the unfamiliar; therefore he must be helped—yet not misdirected in the process. To cap it all, drama is notoriously the hardest branch of Greek poetry in which to succeed, and Aeschylus the most intractable dramatic poet. Throughout much of his work scholars still argue as to what his corrupt text says, and when that is decided, the interpretation still frequently eludes them. A classical scholar who is also a creative poet, yet with enough sense of Delphic self-abnegation to let another poet use him as a mouthpiece—where is such a paragon to be found? Certainly they are rare; but there can be no doubt that Louis MacNeice, Rex Warner, C. Day Lewis, and Professor Lattimore are to be numbered among them.

A favourite climate had, of course, already been established when Mr MacNeice came to write his version of the *Agamemnon* in 1936. Two poets—both of them, be it noted, deeply soaked in the classical tradition—had made it possible for Aeschylus to come straight through to an intelligent public: Gerard Manley Hopkins and Mr T. S. Eliot. Hopkins' sprung rhythm and compound adjectives, his massy richness and roughness of line, his pregnant complexity and multiplicity of symbolism, his cosmic, hierarchic religious sense—all these have Aeschylean affinities. They attune our ears to the great thorny, striding choruses, with their breath-taking metaphors—so queerly modern today, so outlandish to our grandfathers—which form the backbone of the *Agamemnon*.[4] As for Mr Eliot, he thoroughly domesticated the entire structure of Greek tragedy, so to speak, by borrowing its trappings wholesale for his two early plays, *Murder In The Cathedral* and *The Family Reunion*. Anyone who has assimilated these plays, formally and thematically, should not have the slightest difficulty in appreciating Aeschylus.

Half the trouble in the past has been the *unfamiliarity* of the

[4] There is another much-loved poet who springs to my mind when I read Aeschylus: if only Dylan Thomas could have translated the *Oresteia* or the *Prometheus*—or, best of all, Euripides' *The Bacchae*!

Greek pattern—the convention of the Chorus, half in the play, half out of it, declaiming what to us, with our less ritual tradition, may seem ponderous truisms; the blatantly stylized set speeches; the faintly ludicrous exchange of single-line dialogue, or *stichomythia*, which Housman parodied with such relish. The English stage tradition is one of conventional realism, just as the English poetical tradition—at least as the general public conceived it till very recently—is one of romantic rhymed lyrics. It requires an effort of the imagination to move out and meet a new concept half-way, to accept its conventions at their own value. Here is where the more cautious traditionalists make their basic mistake.

They remind us, in the first place, that the *Agamemnon* was a play, written for performance before an audience: and this point we may readily concede. It is, indeed, something more than a play; though it is misleading to compare Greek drama to oratorio, nevertheless the music, dancing, and recitative were integral to the playwright's total effect, since he himself was responsible for them. Any translation must aim, ultimately, at being *performed,* before a live audience. But, say the traditionalists, you cannot expect an audience to digest these thorny unfamiliarities: they must be given something they can both understand and recognize. This is both to insult the modern audience and do a disservice to Aeschylus. After all, an Athenian audience was not daunted by his notorious difficulties: why should their modern counterparts be spoon-fed? Secondly, the conservative translator is depressingly anxious to find a good excuse for dodging hard work. 'The rhymeless metres of Greek', Mr F. L. Lucas declares, 'are too remote from English for successful imitation.' This today is simply untrue.

Let us turn back for a moment to Professor Fraenkel's conundrum of base bronze and flying birds. Mr MacNeice's version makes no concessions to popular intelligibility or prosaic glossing; but by matching his original image for image, he produces an effect which is strange, indeed, but very far from ludicrous—and which remains, most important consideration, *poetry*:

> But the mischief shines forth with a deadly light
> And like bad coinage
> By rubbings and frictions
> He stands discoloured and black
> Under the test—a boy
> Who chases a winged bird
> He has branded his city for ever.

That is an almost literal translation; it catches the exact cadence of the original; and it could never have been written by an English poet. Yet it is immediately striking to an English reader. The same firm mastery of Aeschylean rhythm and metaphor is apparent in the very first lines of the play, with the surging Alexandrines catching Aeschylus' iambics as never before:

> The gods it is I ask to release me from this watch
> A year's length now, spending my nights like a dog,
> Watching on my elbow on the roof of the sons of Atreus
> So that I have come to know the assembly of the nightly stars
> Those which bring storm and those which bring summer to
> men,
> The shining Masters riveted in the sky—
> I know the decline and rising of those stars.
> And now I am waiting for the sign of the beacon,
> The flame of fire that will carry the report from Troy . . .

This century has seized on Aeschylean themes with peculiar avidity, as a perusal of French literature no less than English at once reveals. *The Family Reunion*, indeed, with its pursuing Furies and obsession over blood-guiltiness, is simply the old Orestes-myth retold in a modern romantic setting. (In the production I saw the Furies popped up, rather incongruously, behind the French windows, all swathed in butter-muslin.) In *Murder in the Cathedral*—which is Mr Eliot's *Agamemnon*, just as *The Family Reunion* is his *Eumenides*—the Chorus catch just that note of agonized involvement which we note in Aeschylus:

> A rain of blood has blinded my eyes . . .
> How how can I ever return, to the soft, quiet seasons ?
> Night stay with us, stop sun, hold season, let the day not
> come, let the spring not come.

> Can I look again at the day and its common things, and
>   see them all smeared with blood, through a curtain of
>   falling blood?
> We did not wish anything to happen.
> We understand the private catastrophe,
> The personal loss, the general misery,
> Living and partly living . . .

Those were the women of Canterbury; and here are the old men of Argos, after Agamemnon's death. The translation, again, is Mr MacNeice's:

> I am at a loss for thought, I lack
> All nimble counsel as to where
> To turn when the house is falling.
> I fear the house-collapsing crashing
> Blizzard of blood—of which these drops are earnest.
> Now is Destiny sharpening her justice
> On other whetstones for a new affliction.
>   O earth, earth, if only you had received me
>   Before I saw this man lie here as if in bed
>   In a bath lined with silver.

Despite the similarity of tone and texture between these two passages, the second could not be anything but Greek in origin, and the first, despite its obvious borrowings and allusions, is quintessentially English. The value of their correlation—the general aid which Mr Eliot's plays bring to our appreciation of Aeschylus—is in the main the dispersal of this unfamiliarity I have mentioned. Modern lyrics, modern verse dramas have no *real* identity with ancient tragedy; but through them the modern reader and playgoer has a stepping-stone back to the past. The transition is made that degree easier. And of course the translator is helped too: he no longer has to fight against the sheer grain of contemporary taste. He has an audience which is prepared to accept a version of Aeschylus much nearer in form, feeling, and imagery to the original than was possible half a century ago.

Yet I do not believe that the position now reached is entirely the result of a fortunate but fortuitous literary coincidence. This is an age of self-criticism. We are no longer sublimely convinced that what is right for us—whether in politics, morals, literary taste, or anything else—is necessarily right for everyone. Whereas the Augustans and Victorians assumed unhesitatingly that the proper way to deal with an ancient author was to stamp him into modern dress, we are more likely, as a first reaction, to say: 'How can we bring out the foreignness, the *otherness,* of this author?' We are no longer, on the whole, interested in the irrelevant business of producing something to flatter the translator's creative personality. His personality is at a discount; he now aims, or should aim, at being a kind of transparent communicating vessel for his original. The result may be odd by traditional English standards; but that is not its proper criterion. If it evokes something of the rhythm and usage of that alien, unknown poet — not a comfortably familiar adaptation transposed into contemporary terms — then the bounds of knowledge have been truly extended, the frontiers of darkness pushed back.

Index

15*—E.I.A.   217

INDEX

Wesley, Charles: 206
Whitman, Cedric H.: 27ff.
Wilamowitz-Moellendorff, U. von: 27
Wilkinson, L. P.: 110, 112, 115, 125, 159, 190
Wilson, Edmund: 173
Witkiewicz, S.: 94n.
Wolf, F. A.: 28–9, 37
Wolfe, T.: 183
Women in antiquity: 89, 156, 181
Wood, Robert: 29
Woodworth, D. C.: 203

Works and Days, The: 38, 39–40, 41, 123

Xenophanes: 78

Yeats, W. B.: quoted, 10–11, 49, 201
Yugoslavia: 29

Zen Buddhism: 171
Zeno of Citium: 86–90
Zeus: 40, 41
Zoëga, G.: 29